The First
Lady Diana

The First Lady Diana

The Life of Lady Diana Spencer, 1710–1735

VICTORIA MASSEY

a&b

To Jodie

This edition published in Great Britain in 2000 by
Allison & Busby Limited
Suite 111, Bon Marché Centre
241–251 Ferndale Road
London SW9 8BJ

Copyright © 1999 by Victoria Massey

The right of Victoria Massey to be identified as author of
this work has been asserted by her in accordance with the
Copyright, Designs and Patents Act, 1988

A catalogue record for this book is available
from the British Library

ISBN 0 7490 0491 6

Printed and bound in Spain by
Líberduplex, s.l. Barcelona.

Contents

CONTENTS

Acknowledgments

Ishould like to thank The British Library Board, and the County
Archivist of Devon Record Office, for allowing me to make use of
manuscripts in their ownership and custody. The quotations from the
letters of Diana as Lady Russell and Duchess of Bedford appear by kind
permission of the Marquess of Tavistock and the Trustees of the Bedford
Estates, those from Sarah Duchess of Marlborough and her family by kind
permission of His Grace the Duke of Marlborough, and the Seymour letters
by kind permission of The Duke of Somerset. I should like to thank Earl
Spencer for personally searching the family bibles for me at Althorp, and
approving the use of quotations from the 18th century letters of his family.
My thanks to members of the staff at Blenheim Palace, Woburn, and
Althorp, for assistance in securing pictures to illustrate the book, and the
photographers who photographed them. I should like to thank the assis-
tants at Dunstable Library for tracking down so many obscure books for me
over the years, the Minet Library for access to information on the Russell
Manor House at Streatham, the Totteridge library for information on 18th
century Totteridge, Hugh Cave and the Norwich Library for information on
Thorney, the library at Cheam for details of Cheam manor house, and Ken
Dickson on the muniments of Little Gaddesden church. I should especially
like to thank Dr Frances Harris, Curator of the Manuscript Collections at
the British Library, for her whole-hearted encouragement and specialised
assistance over the years. My thanks also to Vanessa Holt for her belief in
my book, and for finding me the wonderfully enthusiastic team of Allison
and Busby's new London House to publish it.

I have been on the receiving end of so much encouragement from children, granddaughter, extended family, and friends, it would be impossible
to name each one individually here, but my warmest thanks for every scrap
of interest shown. Not least, my loving thanks to my husband for listening
to me thrash out my thoughts over so many breakfasts over so many years.

Spencer-Churchill
Family Tree

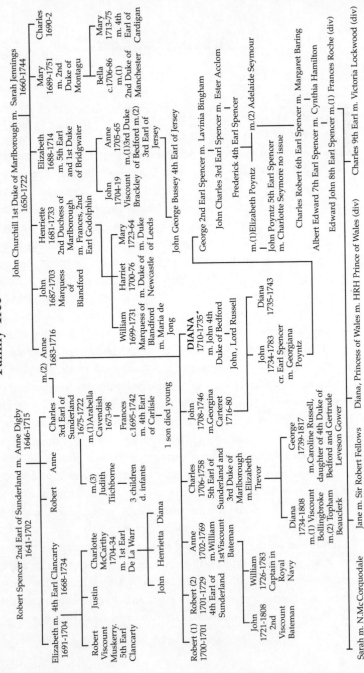

Introduction

I first became interested in the eighteenth-century Lady Diana Spencer when the present day Lady Diana Spencer's engagement to the Prince of Wales was announced. Along with the rest of the world I was excited by the hopes and speculations that such a 'fairy-tale' romance must always bring in its wake. At the same time I happened to be looking into a story concerning the eighteenth-century Charles Spencer, the 3rd Earl of Sunderland, who lived at Althorp and had a daughter named Lady Diana Spencer. Further research showed me that the Sunderland title had become absorbed in the Spencer-Churchill line when the first Lady Diana's brother became not only 5th Earl of Sunderland but also third Duke of Marlborough; and like the present-day Diana's brother, he was named Charles. One of the conditions of Charles inheriting Blenheim Palace was that he should alienate Althorp to his younger brother John, whose own son John was later created the 1st Earl Spencer. It is from this family that the present 9th Earl and his sisters Sarah, Jane and the late Diana, Princess of Wales, directly descend.

Yet what happened to the first Lady Diana? Women in history tend to marry and become absorbed into other dynasties, and unless they make a very big noise indeed are often lost to posterity. But by now my curiosity was raised, and as the media fed me with the daily happenings of the present-day princess, I found I needed more and more to learn about her ancestor.

Research into the lives of true historical characters is always deeply rewarding for the writer, the journey into dusty archives not a chore but an exhilarating adventure; and for me there was the added magic of returning to the present day to find my character's descendant flashed at me daily from TV, newspapers and magazines. I found that the lives of the two Dianas were following a similar course, both having lived at Althorp as children, rubbed shoulders with royalty, and moved in rich and aristocratic circles. Both had suffered sadness when parted from their mothers at six years old, one through death, the other through divorce, and both were proposed as a bride for a Prince of Wales. As it turned out, both would die tragically young. They were tall, fair and slender, known for their beauty, and concerned for the happiness of others. Indeed the more I came to know one Diana, the more I felt I understood the other, so that at times they seemed one and the same person. The big difference was that they lived in very different times.

My chief source of information concerning the past Lady Diana was found in Gladys Scott Thomson's *Letters of a Grandmother*, published during the Second World War. This book contained a fascinating collection of letters to Diana from her grandmother, the Duchess of Marlborough, covering the time from her marriage until her early death, and provided a useful outline of Diana's life and background. What it did not contain, however, were letters from Diana herself. Her grandmother stated in one letter how she had read through her granddaughter's letters a second time, and burned them. So it was, when I came to look through catalogues for manuscripts under Diana's name, my expectations were low. There appeared to be nothing under her maiden name, nor under her married title, the Duchess of Bedford, so I concentrated on the letters of family and friends, hoping to build up some kind of picture of her.

I recognised at once how much Diana was loved, finding many mentions of 'dear little Di', and learned that the British Library Manuscript room where I read was on the site of her aunt the Duchess of Montagu's house, later home to the British Museum until the present building was put up on the spot. I also learned that Diana's town house after her marriage was Bedford House which had stood right next door in Bloomsbury Square. This and the hushed room in which I worked, and the leather-topped mahogany tables all helped me feel close to my subject. For weeks I absorbed myself in the letters of mother, father, sister, brothers, aunts, cousins, and felt closer to Diana every day, though sadly I had not yet heard Diana's voice. It was like one of those puzzle pictures for children, the background perfectly drawn and coloured, with only a white shape where the main subject should be. Why had the Duchess of Marlborough burned her favourite grand-daughter's letters when so many of her other grandchildren's letters were kept? Was it because these were too painful to behold?

To help me fill in my 'white space' I visited the several grand houses in which the eighteenth-century Diana had lived, studying the portraits of her and her family, and reading all I could about her times. The present-day

Diana's wedding to the Prince of Wales had meanwhile taken place, and soon after the honeymoon I visited Althorp, where I knew both Dianas had spent parts of their childhood. Here I saw the painting, attributed to Charles Jervas, of the eighteenth-century Diana as a three-year-old infant with her mother, the picture hanging over a door above the grand staircase, and wondered if this had inspired the future princess's parents to name their child after her? The princess's father chose to be interviewed standing before this picture for a television interview, and told how he had tobogganed on a tray down this staircase as a boy, and as a man spent hours in the muniments room getting to know the 'ladies' of the house, so it seemed very likely. Just as the eighteenth-century Spencers had brought their children to visit their grandparents at Althorp, so had the modern-day Spencers; and the story that the first Lady Diana had almost married the Prince of Wales of her day would certainly have been told. It was a story that would charm any little girl, not least a child sharing the same name as the little girl in the picture. Did the present-day Diana think, 'When I grow up I *shall* marry the Prince of Wales'? As I moved on into the next room I noticed the guide smiling dreamily out through a window; following her gaze I spied a tall, slender girl striding across the lawns below, and my heart missed a beat. Surely this was the princess. As I left the grounds, police with their dogs were inspecting the surrounding ditches, and later I learned that an impromptu visit had indeed been made by the newly wed princess, escaping her homesick loneliness at Highgrove. To me it was as if I had not only seen the princess, but the ghost of the first Lady Diana, slipping silently through the grounds.

Aware that the eighteenth-century Diana and the present-day princess were becoming altogether too fused in my mind, I disciplined myself, as I worked, into detaching my desires from the real facts. By now I had built up a satisfying story around the eighteenth-century Diana, with only her words and thoughts missing. The day came when I knew I had read enough of her background, and as Thomson had said that not a scrap of Diana's writing remained at Woburn, I made a last-ditch effort to find her in the British Library Index. I would learn later that the manuscript collection into which I delved so freely had only recently been acquired from Blenheim Palace, the Index still in process of being carefully compiled. By now I was also aware that for a short period in her marriage, the first Diana was addressed as Lady Russell. I decided to look for her under that – and there she was! My hand trembled as I made out my application slip, posting it through the familiar slit in the wall, then waited tensely at my table. Suppose this was not my Diana but another Lady Russell? The letters when they came were unbound, delivered in lead-lined boxes, and in each box was a hard linen folder tied up with tapes, as they must have been when kept at the Palace. Even Gladys Scott Thomson, a vigilant researcher, would have had difficulty penetrating the Blenheim archives during the Second World War. If there had been just one letter from Diana in those boxes I should have felt my prayers were answered. Instead there were many. Some of Diana's letters might have been burned – as her grandmother implied – but only a few. As I turned the first yellowed page I felt I was about to meet Diana herself. The letters were immaculately collated in date order (in time they would be bound, and joined with an excellent crossed index). By now I knew so much about Diana that I was perfectly able to imagine where she was and how she looked when she wrote them, and was familiar with the people she talked about. Here were letters to her grand-mother from the age of seven years old until just weeks before her death, and letters to governess and friends. They were written in a clear and legible hand, and her words seemed to call out to me from the page. I read and read, copying them down in pencil with a blind hand while turning with the other, letting out the customary sighs and occasional laugh of all deeply absorbed researchers, often stopping tears that would otherwise have ruined the manuscript.

The weather grew from dull and rainy to stiflingly hot, as it had been in Diana's own last summer at Woburn, and at lunchtime I would stagger out of the museum's cooling system into the glare of hot Bloomsbury to pace the pavements, working out just where the old Bedford House had stood – the house where Diana lived in town, and where she died. Then I was back at my leather-topped table, reading and scribbling for all I was worth. I once entered the building to find a red carpet leading up the stone steps to the porticoed entrance; the Prince of Wales was on a visit to observe the remains of a primeval 'bog' man found near my own Cheshire birthplace, and I should have enjoyed meeting him and telling him that while he was looking at my possible ancestor, I was researching that of his wife.

As I continued reading through Diana's letters I became aware that she was pregnant and suffering a 'terrible sickness'; the Princess of Wales was pregnant, and sick as well. The 250-year-old manuscripts exuded a sickly sweetness that caused me to feel groggy, especially when I saw what looked to me like faded bloodstains on Diana's letters. As one Diana grew lean, so did the other, and I even feared for the princess. Yet despite the eighteenth-century Diana's sickness, her letters were as exuberant and cheerful as the present Diana's smiles were sunny and joyous, both women voicing their belief in the future, and their concern for others. Diana's last letters were so unbearably poignant I had to fight back tears as I handed back the boxes for the last time, and fled from the building. Once through the portico pillars, and down the steps into the front court, I passed through the wrought iron gates, and turned left towards where Bedford House once stood. I should not have turned a hair to see sedan chairs and horse-drawn coaches pass me by. From Bloomsbury Square, I veered left into Bedford Place. Here I believed was once the passage leading to Diana's sickroom, where her grandmother, bathed in tears, sat in the outer rooms. The street was clear so I let my own tears fall, brushing them away when I reached Russell Square. As I walked to the tube, the pavements were stacked with racks of brightly coloured postcards of the smiling princess, her lips glossy, her eyes shining under blue eye-shadow, her diamond tiara sparkling, happy with her little boys.

The fact that my story had so 'downbeat' an ending worried me then. Would readers who enjoyed the romance and glamour of the princess want to read of so tragic a death? Might it even affect the princess herself? Only as time went on did it become clear that the royal couple was unhappy. Even so, death was more final than divorce. I wept silently when my eighteenth-century Diana died, and would weep profoundly and unbelievingly on the day the death of the princess was announced. Just as I had rejoiced with the world at her wedding, so I cried with the world at her death, and to me it was a double loss. My first professional thoughts were that no one would want to know about the eighteenth-century Lady Diana Spencer now – that the name Diana would fade into insignificance. Only as that terrible week went on, and that great crowd released its joint sorrow, I saw that I was wrong, and that Diana, Princess of Wales, would never be forgotten. That the Palladian stable block at Althorp, built by Morris for the eighteenth-century Diana's brother Charles, was to be made into a museum in the princess's memory by *her* brother Charles, was especially significant. More and more I felt that the story of the First Lady Diana must be told.

CHAPTER ONE

Sunderland House

'the House in Pickadilly . . .'

Lady Diana Spencer, or 'dear little Di', as her family liked to call her, was born in London on 31 July 1710, when most members of the aristocracy had left for their country houses or for Bath, or gone to Windsor with the queen. But Diana's mother, the Countess of Sunderland, was very fond of children, and a baby born out of season was neither here nor there. As she had written to her own mother only nine months before: 'If I had 20 Children I am sure I should be so fond of every wone that it would be impossible for me to part with any out of the house but to my dear mama if you desired it.'[1]

The countess's mother was the redoubtable Sarah Churchill, Duchess of Marlborough, chief lady-in-waiting to Queen Anne, whose husband John Churchill, the first Duke of Marlborough, was currently leading the British army against France in the Wars of the Spanish Succession. Whereas, under ordinary circumstances, the countess disliked letting her children out of her sight, she was willing to part with them at such a time, since she suspected her mother was lonely. As she said in the letter, 'It would be very unjust in me . . . to denigh you the pleasure of 'em while they are little when I have left 'em all to you when I dye, believing you are so kind to me you would take 'em.' She hoped her dear mama would soon see 'dear papa' home from his campaigns for the winter, begging her to say 'nothing in a letter about what I say of the children nor to anybody ever . . . for may bee Lord Sunderland might not take it well of me, tho he would do anything I desired.'[2]

The countess's name was Anne (née Churchill) and her husband Charles Spencer, the 3rd Earl of Sunderland, was a radical Whig and Secretary of State. He had fathered five children by Anne (as well as a little girl, Frances, from a former marriage) the eldest son Robert having died at nine months old, and the eldest surviving child also being named Robert, Lord Spencer. This second Robert was fourteen months old when his sister Anne joined him in the nursery, and when Lady Anne was four years old, their brother, the Honourable Charles, was born. Charles was eighteen months old when brother Johnny joined them, and he six months old when Diana was conceived. It was a very lively and noisy family, therefore, which awaited the arrival of the unborn child.

The Countess of Sunderland was the second of the four beautiful Churchill daughters and, like her three sisters, was lady-of-the-bedchamber to Queen Anne. At the time Diana was conceived, the countess and her family were living in St Albans House, a grand residence in St James's Square, the first to have been built here. As Norfolk House, it was later destined to become the birthplace of George III. As well as 'three large rooms forward and two little ones backwards', it boasted an enormous ball-room two stories high, decorated with magnificent murals by Thornhill.

Not only was the house magnificent, it was domestically convenient, having New River water piped to it through hollowed-out tree trunks, and 'chimneys that did not smoke'. With so many children crowding the nursery, the earl had decided the house was 'too small' for him, and put it up for sale, although the prospective purchaser, Lady Wentworth, declared it 'soe strong it would last forever'. But Sunderland had his eye on a larger property, the family spending time in a house in the queen's privy garden while work on it was carried out. The house in Piccadilly would be called Sunderland House.[3]

The decision to move to Piccadilly had taken seed as early as 1707, Anne writing to her mother that she would 'do no more in the House in Pickadilly till you come to town, but I went to see it . . . and like it mightily for it stands mighty well, and is well turned and a great deal of room, but should not be dear until he will do something to it'. Like many of the great houses around St James's Palace, it was built at the time of Charles II's Restoration, and stood on the site of present-day Albany. The previous owner, Sir Thomas Clarges, had recently died, and the grandson who inherited it was keen to sell. The countess found the house 'Extreamly old both within and without, quite gone to rewing', but knew her mother would like nothing better than to help her make 'a place pretty', to sew curtains and covers for it, and help choose the décor. By the following year it was described as a 'stately new building'.[4]

Sunderland House, as Clarges' House was renamed, stood on the north side of the Piccadilly high street (then named Portugal Street in honour of Charles II's queen), almost opposite Wren's fashionable St James's Church, and Mr Fortnum's newly established grocery store. With its balustraded platform roof, its park-like garden to the rear, it was a virtual palace, and to the west of it stood the Earl of Burlington's palatial Burlington House.

Sunderland had already set the queen's gardener Henry Wise to plant one hundred and thirty-seven lime trees in the garden, and 'jessamines and honeysuckles' to sweeten the air. Like the house of the earl's mother, the dowager Countess of Sunderland, next door to the east, it stood 'discreetly within a courtyard with green-grown trees before the Gate'. Both buildings boasted a porter's lodge, a coach house and stables (Sunderland's to be demolished to make room for a library), and were sheltered from the street by a high brick wall. Sunderland took possession of the house in January 1710, just seven months before Diana's birth, at a cost of £4600, an enormous sum of money at the time; but as it would remain in the family for thirty-five years, it would prove well worth the outlay.[5]

Despite the many inns and coffee-houses that proliferated in the area (the Three Cornish Daws 'over against my Lord Sunderland's house', and 'Naked Boy's Alley' close by), the house was considered pleasantly situated. Several other grand Restoration palaces lined the street, older residents remembering the site as 'Ten Acre Field'. There were open fields to the north, the Hampstead and Highgate hills clearly visible from the Sunderland House windows. Fresh country air blew in from north and west, and ass's milk was fetched daily from St James's Park for the children. The Countess of Sunderland set out fortnightly for the queen's palaces in her sedan chair, leaving her housekeeper to take care of the house.[6]

Mrs Dale, the housekeeper, bustled busily through the vast newly furnished rooms, her keys jangling at her waist, opening the chests of tea, coffee and spices, sent up from Mr Bull the merchant. She distributed 'salts of lavender' and 'spirits of harts horne' to fainting ladies and to gentlemen, too, for Sunderland kept 'lavender and harts horn' in two 'little christal bottles'. Mrs Brewer, the washerwoman, scrubbed the household linen, spreading it in the fields to dry, while 'Harry the helper', 'Nan the housemaid', the 'dairy maid', 'Judith the nursemaid' and 'Mary the Cook' contributed to the general running of the house. The servants were referred to as 'the family', while tradesmen dropped in with their wares. Peter Flournoys, as well as being Lord Spencer's governor (both tutor and guide to the child), acted as steward for the countess, noting each household purchase in his notebook, including corn from the corn-chandler, coal from Mr Perkins the 'coleman', oil from the 'oyleman', and 'flambos' to light up the street after dark. When the servants' pewter was to be mended, a Mr Hancock saw to it. There was the butcher, the baker, the fishmonger, the confectioner and 'My Lady's chairmen' to be paid, while shoes for the earl cost five and sixpence a pair. These latter were worn through so quickly they were eventually ordered by the dozen, and a guinea was paid for the footman's boots.[7]

Queen Anne had been kindness itself to the Marlborough daughters, giving each £5000 at their weddings, and accepting all four as her ladies-of-the-bedchamber. Her own seventeen children were now dead, and her consort had died recently, leaving the court less than the most scintillating of places. Jonathan Swift observed how at one of her assemblies the queen stood with her fan in her mouth talking only to those nearest her (ignoring himself), and rushing away when it was time for dinner. On another occasion he observed how Diana's mother sat whispering behind her fan to her neighbour and fellow lady-in-waiting, the Countess of Burlington, assuming that he himself was the subject of her remarks. If charmed by Lady Sunderland's looks, he was piqued by her presumed malice, sending a message through Lord Rochester saying that he believed her 'not as much in love with me as I am with her'. The countess had doubtless read his pamphlet *The Conduct of the Allies* (to prove 'one of the most effective political pamphlets ever published'), which seriously discredited her family. Though written anonymously, the countess appears to have suspected Swift to be the author.[8]

Diana's birth heralded the arrival in London of the twenty-five-year-old George Frederick Handel, who captivated the English court with his brilliant setting for trumpets, a Russian diplomat reporting that his 'writing for trumpets made a sensation'. Four months later he was delighting a diamond-studded audience with his Italian opera *Rinaldo* at the Queen's Theatre in the Haymarket, Nicolini in the title role. The production was so sensational (live sparrows were set free to fly among the audience) that it ensured a continuing popularity for Italian opera in England. Diana was just two years old when the composer moved in next door as a guest at Burlington House. Her mother's friend Lady Burlington (to whom she had whispered so earnestly behind her fan) was mother to the seventeen-year-old Earl of Burlington, already a patron of the arts, under her guardianship and tutelage.* As friends and neighbours, Diana's parents were almost certainly invited to their musical entertainments, and as these were held out

---

* As a minor peer, Burlington would be appointed a guardian by a body of parliamentary delegates, in this case his mother, under whose guardianship he remained until he came of age.

of doors in warm weather, Handel's music would drift over the garden wall to filter into the next door nursery. Not surprisingly perhaps, Diana developed a life-long love of opera.[9]

Diana's mother was famous for her cloud of fine golden hair inherited from her own mother. With her tiny but perfectly shaped form, her lovely face and sweet nature, she was considered the most beautiful of the four Churchill sisters. Yet they, too, had each inherited different combinations of their parents' famous good looks. Together with their handsome dowries, this had led to them marrying men of great wealth and title, each boasting a splendid house in town and country. The youngest sister Mary had married the Duke of Montagu, living her winter seasons at Montagu House in Bloomsbury. Set in seven acres of land, boasting magnificent gardens, it would later accommodate the British Museum. As a young girl, Mary had flocks of male admirers, shocking her mother by 'sitting at an assembly with many fine ladys as if it were a market for sail'. She was only thirteen when proposed as a bride for the future Montagu, the two marrying when they were both fifteen. Frivolous and fond of clothes, her letters to her mother were full of 'white satin', 'black lace' and 'furbelows', but when the babies began to arrive in quick succession, her letters became entirely devoted to baby-care talk. In six years she bore her husband three boys and two girls, once writing: 'I have sent the child to see my dear Mama to day being the first time of his going out since his illness, though I fear he stinks mightily of his plaister that is not yet come off.' In another she wrote, 'The great worke of the poore childs being weaned was begun today', the mother 'afraid to leave him with servants'. Yet despite her tender care, none of the boys, and only one little girl, survived infancy. This was Isabella, named 'Bella' by her family; and when she was six she was joined by a sister Mary. Diana was then three years old.[10]

The second youngest Churchill daughter was Elizabeth who married Scroop Egerton, the 4th Earl of Bridgwater. Scroop had hotly pursued Elizabeth as a girl, and despite his mother-in-law thinking him a 'fool', their marriage was idyllically happy. Their son John had the title Lord Brackley, and his sister was Lady Anne Egerton. John was six when their cousin Diana was born, his sister five. Their mother Elizabeth was described as 'agreeably tall' and spoke without 'saying too much or to little'. When in town the family lodged 'over against St James's stables', which the Duchess of Marlborough described as 'big as most houses', and in fact the whole house belonged to Bridgwater, who had inherited it from his father. It overlooked Green Park, and a pretty house known as Bridgwater House still stands on the spot.[11]

The eldest of the four Churchill sisters was Henrietta, heiress to the Marlborough dukedom in her own right. Pert and flirtatious, she married Francis, the son of the Lord High Treasurer (a post soon to be known as Prime Minister), Earl Sidney Godolphin. Godolphin had married John Evelyn's 'soul mate' Margaret Blagge, who died of a fever following her son's birth. As Godolphin was not tempted to remarry, his daughter-in-law Henrietta played hostess for him at Godolphin House. This stood immediately to the west of St James's Palace. Henrietta and Francis had two surviving children, William (nicknamed 'Willigo') and Harriet. When Willigo was born prematurely, Henrietta sent word to the father through a servant, saying, 'Go tell the fool I've got him an heir!' Francis had proved a dull if kindly husband for Henrietta, since his interests lay chiefly with horse breeding (he bred the famous Godolphin Arabian), while Henrietta preferred country dancing and entertaining poets and playwrights at Godolphin House. Willigo (to be known as Lord Blandford) was eleven when his cousin Diana was born, his sister Lady Harriet aged nine.

Diana's paternal grandmother, the dowager Countess of Sunderland, lived next door to Sunderland House, their gardens interconnecting. The dowager busied herself rearing several grandchildren by her daughter Elizabeth, Countess of Clancarty, who had died in exile in Frankfurt, her widower the Earl of Clancarty being a proscribed Jacobite. The earl had asked for his children to be reared in England, his eldest daughter, Lady Charlotte McCarthy, being the same age as her cousin Lord Spencer.[12]

Sarah, Duchess of Marlborough, had long enjoyed splendid apartments at Kensington and St James's Palaces, where several of her grandchildren were born, and although she owned two fine homes in the country, she felt an urgent need for a house in town. At the time of Diana's conception, her relationship with Queen Anne had begun to deteriorate badly, and she was weary of the court. After the death of her only remaining son Lord Blandford, she had become more and more remote, the queen being deeply hurt at her neglect. Gradually the queen had turned her affections to Abigail Hill, a poor cousin of Sarah's whom she had 'raised from the dust', placing her as the queen's bedchamber-woman. Returning to court after a long absence, Sarah found Abigail sweeping into the royal presence without so much as a tap on the door or a curtsey, and discovered she was talking politics with the queen. Abigail (a cousin of Lord Harley who subsequently became Lord Treasurer) had then married Samuel Masham (later to be dubbed knight) in the presence of the queen, and without informing Sarah.

Realising just how completely she had been usurped in the queen's favour when Abigail was installed in her Kensington apartment, Sarah was forced to consider alternative accommodation. Remembering that the queen, in their happy days together, had given her a piece of land right next to St James's Palace, she embarked on building herself a house there and commissioned Sir Christopher Wren to design it. His splendid St Paul's Cathedral had been completed at last, but 'suspecting the poor old man was put upon by his workmen', Sarah finally sacked him. Instead she hired workmen of her own, and had finished the building when her granddaughter Diana was one year old. This was Marlborough House.

Diana's mother, as Lady Anne Churchill, was fourteen when proposed as a bride for the then Lord Spencer, heir to the 2nd Earl of Sunderland. His first wife Arabella Cavendish had died of smallpox after only three years of marriage, and their little girl Frances had been left to the care of her aunt, the Duchess of Newcastle. Anne's father, the Duke of Marlborough, strongly disapproved of the match between Spencer and his daughter, fearing the newly bereaved lord would not cherish her enough. But with her 'charming new cloaths' and a 'fan' Anne was duly sent to Althorp to meet him. With her travelled her future mother-in-law, the Countess of Sunderland. On their way to Althorp the two travellers stopped off at Dunstable to buy presents of straw boxes made by Huguenot refugees to send home to Anne's sisters.[13]

Lady Anne was already on familiar terms with the countess, whose husband, the 2nd Earl of Sunderland, was then still alive. Together with the queen, she had stood godmother to Anne. As babies, both Anne and her sister Henrietta had been cared for by the countess when their mother was obliged to follow after the court, nursing them through the 'heats' and 'fevers' of infancy, and had witnessed the arrival of Anne's first 'great teeth'. She appeared to be a fussy and motherly person, expressing huge delight when Henrietta was 'so kind as to leave her dinner and sit in my lap today'. Anne, however, was ten years younger than the countess's son, her proposed husband, and he was not altogether the most attractive of men. A doctrinaire Whig, Queen Anne thought him 'a brazen free thinker' and 'a Republican', while Swift remembered how he hoped to 'piss on the House of Lords'. He would 'often refuse the title of Lord, swore he would never be called otherwise than Charles Spencer, and hoped to see the day when there would not be a peer in England!' When the Marlboroughs voiced their objections to him, his mother wrote anxiously in his defence, saying she was 'sorry if Lord Spencer has any faults', and assured them he 'never will have any to a wife'. He was 'very good natured and strictly honest', she insisted, and:

> those heats that he shows – though I don't pretend to excuse them, proceed from an honest heart that has had the misfortune to fall into the acquaintance of a Party that are of a crucifying temper.

As to the 'mistakes such company made him run into', they would be 'broke loose from with a little experience'.[14]

Far from 'loosening' himself from the Whigs, Spencer converted Sarah from moderate Tory to Whig, and she in turn converted her duke. The young people were married in 1700, and Anne, with her long golden tresses and minute figure, became toast of the Kit-Kat Club. When Vanbrugh came to lay the foundations of the King's Theatre in the Haymarket (to be built with money raised by the Whigs) it was Anne who laid the first stone. On it was inscribed the affectionate nickname given to her by the club: 'The Little Whig'. A wine glass for the Kit-Kat Club was engraved:

> All nature's charms in Sunderland appear,
> Bright as her eyes, and as her reason clear . . .[15]

Two years later, when Robert, the 2nd Earl of Sunderland died, Lord Spencer submitted willingly enough to becoming 3rd Earl, and the tearful Queen Anne was bullied into accepting him as Secretary of State. Four years later Sunderland moved into his splendid house in Piccadilly, his beautiful wife at his side, a male heir and two spares in the nursery, a slender flaxen-haired daughter to delight his eye, and a new baby on the way. He had every reason to feel pleased with himself, as had his young countess, delighted with her house, and setting out to the queen's palaces in her chair, tapping the roof with her fan, attended by maid and footboy.

In his youth Sunderland was considered a man of 'extraordinary hopes, and very learned for his age'. He was educated at the University of Utrecht and at nineteen began collecting rare books, becoming one of England's most notable bibliophiles. Queen Anne's brother-in-law, the King of Denmark, had offered him £30,000 for his 'incomparable library', but Sunderland refused to sell. To accommodate his fine collection he had two rooms knocked into one in his Piccadilly house, later demolishing his stables in order to extend it into the garden. He rented land from his mother to quarter his horses. The Duchess of Marlborough had come to admire him greatly at the time of his marriage to her daughter, describing him as 'a man of the most open zeal for the interest of his country', though it was not to last.

The newly decorated 'Crimson Damask bedchamber' at Sunderland House was a reflection of the earl's passionate nature (he also wore a crimson nightgown), but with 'blue' in his own dressing-room, and 'yellow' in Lady Sunderland's dressing-room'. The 'Green' drawing-room was hung with fine tapestries and furnished with carved mahogany furniture, and set about with japanned cabinets, Indian tea tables and China jars. As the painter Antonio Verio had once lived here, cherubs and nymphs may have sported on his ceilings. Although bookish (his library included first editions of Homer and Virgil), the earl lacked musical ability, answering 'no' when asked whether he could play an instrument, but that he could make a 'large country out of a small one'. When Lady Sunderland was asked if she would have musicians at Althorp, she had said 'yes', but only if she did not have to 'eat with 'em!' This was doubtless a thrust at the Burlingtons next door, where Handel and fellow artistes were very comfortably ensconced, and on intimate terms with their master. The Sunderlands' musical instruments consisted of a spinet and a harpsichord consigned to a bedchamber, with an 'organ compleat' in the chaplain's dining-room.[16]

Diana's father was a generous, if extravagant, host, sweetmeats and fruits piled high on his prized marble side-tables, and dishes of every variety covering his mahogany dining-table. His wife presided over the ladies, having the 'happiness to oblige and charm by her inimitable and most engaging affability, everybody who sate there'. Indeed life would have been idyllic had it not been for a very unpleasant episode that occurred in the previous year, which would colour the remainder of Sunderland's life. It was 5 November 1709, around the time Diana was conceived, a day generally devoted to marking the discovery of Guy Fawkes's gunpowder plot, and this year also commemorating the twenty-first anniversary of the landing of William of Orange at Torbay. Since that event had led to the expulsion of the Roman Catholic James II from his kingdom, and to the Protestant William and Mary becoming king and queen, it was deemed just cause for celebration. Churches throughout the kingdom held services of remembrance, and a parson named Dr Henry Sacheverell was invited to preach at St Paul's Cathedral. Sacheverell was a high-church Tory, already known for his ranting and raving against toleration and dissent; but when with a 'fiery red overspreading his face', and a 'goggling wildness' in his eyes, he proceeded to attack from the pulpit the queen's Whig ministers, the response was one of shock. The parson fulminated against the 'crafty insidiousness of pretended friends in high places', referring to Godolphin and Sunderland as 'Wily Volpones'. He appealed to the congregation to close ranks against such men, in the hope they would 'quit the Church, of which they were no true members'.[17]

Sunderland was listening to a more gentlemanly sermon preached in the St James's palace chapel, but when the parson's diatribe appeared in print, becoming an overnight best-seller, its content very soon reached him. The Dissenting author Daniel Defoe advised his readers to laugh at the parson, and leave him to 'vent his gall', but instead the mob cheered Sacheverell as he passed by in his coach, and the churches where he preached were packed to overflowing. As this could seriously affect the results of the coming parliamentary elections, Sunderland and Godolphin were nervous for their futures, and together with other Whig members of the Cabinet, persuaded parliament to have the parson impeached.[18]

Sacheverell's trial took place in the great Westminster Hall, on 27 March 1710, just two months after the Sunderlands had taken possession of their Piccadilly house. The queen decided to attend the trial herself, and on the first day, wearing a 'thin hood' over her face, and purple to match the lining of her chair, was carried across St James's Park to the hall. On her way she found herself surrounded by an assortment of her subjects crying 'God save your Majesty and the church', and expressing the hope she was 'for Sacheverell'. The doctor himself, driven in his coach from Temple Bar to the great hall, was likewise surrounded, the mob hanging from his coach 'like a swarm of bees'. One bystander who failed to cheer him received a gash in the head. Outside the Westminster Hall another kind of crowd queued from seven in the morning till nine, dressed in their best clothes and carrying picnic baskets. When the doors were opened, they burst in, scrambling for the seats ranged in tiers around the hall. They were to wait another three hours while the dignitaries robed themselves before the trial began, the occasion being treated as a holiday.[19]

Wren had designed the seating, a throne placed in the centre as a symbol of the queen's presence, but she did not use this. The architect had also designed for her a special box with curtains, where she could sit unobserved by the crowd with her ladies-in-waiting. To the right of this box was another for the maids-of-honour, and before the throne was the woolsack, just as in the House of Lords. Flanked on either side of the woolsack were eighty-foot benches, those to the left for members of the Commons, those to the right for the minor peers, peeresses, and 'ladies and gentlemen'. Then there was the 'bar' before which the prisoner stood. The senior 'peers in their robes' were the first to enter the hall, seating themselves solemnly behind the woolsack; and behind them sat the Lord Chamberlain's 'special company'. The 'peers minor' entered two by two, among them Diana's brother Robert, the ten-year-old Lord Spencer. Although the eleven-year-old Willigo was not just now possessed of a title, he too was present, and when the trial ended wrote to his famous grandfather, the Duke of Marlborough, at the Hague: 'I have been at Doctor Sacheverell's trial every day and am against him!' [20]

Diana attended the trial as a four- to five-months' embryo, curled up in her mother's womb, the countess sitting among the peeresses when not on duty in the queen's box. The great hall echoed under the hammer-beam roof, the gilded wings of twenty-six carved angels catching the light from blazing torches below. In pride of place were hung the French standards captured at Blenheim by the Duke of Marlborough, and under the massive oak-beamed roof sat the 'ordinary' spectators. The ladies' gowns 'filled the hall with brilliant colour', and as the queen was yet to arrive, her chief lady-in-waiting sat alone in the royal box.

The Duchess of Marlborough would be fifty years old in a few weeks' time, and being short-sighted, when the proceedings began she decided to leave the box and make her way to the Commons' benches where she could more easily observe the prisoner at the bar. Sarah had thought the parson's sermon 'a heap of bombast', and would be surprised to find him suitably dressed, with clean gloves and a 'well managed handkerchief'. Large and handsome in a florid way, he caused many women at the trial to fall in love with him, some even to faint away. When the queen arrived at four o'clock in the afternoon Sarah was obliged to join her in her box, and as the trial looked likely to go on for several days, asked the queen if her ladies might sit. The queen said she was perfectly willing.

On the following day (the queen again late) Sarah once more made for the Commons' benches, this time taking several ladies with her. But when the Sergeant of Arms appeared in front of them brandishing a scroll with an order of the House of Commons to have them removed, the crowd murmured with delight. When the queen arrived, Sarah was demurely awaiting her in the royal box, she and her fellow ladies-in-waiting seated. Two ladies-in-waiting arrived late, however, the Duchess of Somerset and Lady Hyde, who both remained standing. Sarah was convinced they did this only to humiliate her, and that they had ambitions to take over her offices. As Groom of the Stole, Keeper of the Privy Purse and Mistress of the Robes, Sarah had hoped on her retirement to transfer these appointments to her daughters. Resolved to speak to the queen on the subject of whether the ladies should sit or stand, Sarah called on her at the palace next morning. The queen was preparing for a very busy day, and had pressing appointments, 'snapping' Sarah up. Had she not said that her ladies should sit, she asked, adding that she hoped she had heard the last of it.

Sarah was deeply shocked at what she described as the queen's 'brutality' towards her, though in fact her own behaviour to the queen had been far from polite of late. Swift had observed her handing the queen her gloves as if there was a 'smell under her nose'; and once, when Sarah and the queen were climbing the steps of St Paul's Cathedral to take part in a Thanksgiving Service marking one of Marlborough's many victories, when the queen attempted to explain why she was not wearing the jewels Sarah had carefully laid out for her, Sarah had hissed at her to be quiet!

Sacheverell's trial continued for more than three weeks, the Countess of Sunderland and her sister Henrietta being deeply concerned for the outcome of the case. The Whigs and the Tories had used the occasion to expound their arguments of principle rather than question the rights and wrongs of the preacher, Sacheverell complaining that 'tho' I am the person impeached, my condemnation is not the thing principally aimed at'. He was just 'an insignificant tool of a party, not worth regarding'. Allowed to make a speech in his own defence (toned down, if not written, by Swift and Atterbury), his delivery brought tears to the eyes of the spectators, some women sobbing out loud. The Countess of Sunderland was counted among the latter, but insisted it was because 'the name of God was taken in vain'. The mother-to-be had every reason to weep for the future of her family, for when the parson was voted guilty by only sixty-nine votes to fifty-two, and merely suspended from preaching for three years (his sermon burned before the New Exchange), the Tories conceived the outcome as a victory. Sacheverell was carried shoulder-high in a chair on poles, making a triumphal progress into the country.[21]

The trial had meanwhile caused riots in the city, mobs plundering the low-church meeting houses, tearing down the gallery rails and burning a pulpit on a bonfire. Six meeting houses were attacked in all, vandals removing tiles from the rooftops and doors from their hinges, and terrifying the people inside. Men in 'gentlemen's habit' were seen hovering in the background, presumed to be Tories egging on the plunderers. As most of his days were taken up by the trial, Sunderland worked deep into the night, two of his fellow Cabinet ministers calling on him in fear for the safety of their houses. When told that the mob was on its way to plunder the Bank of England (a Whig establishment), Sunderland took chair for St James's Palace. Here he found the queen shaken and pale, and as many of her troops were away serving with Marlborough in France, she offered to put her own horse and guards at his service. Asked about her own safety, the queen replied bravely, 'God will be my guard!' Her personal bodyguard refused to leave her side, however, unless ordered to do so in writing. Sunderland assured him he should have it next day. Meanwhile he whispered to the guard to 'send a party to the Bank', and only to resort to violence 'if absolutely necessary'. By this time thousands of rioters were milling around Lincoln's Inn Fields, the soldiers making a circuitous approach in order to avoid a head-on collision. One hundred and five people were committed to gaol that night, but although there were casualties from sword and sabre cuts, not a single shot was fired.[22]

With the trial and the riots over, and Easter approaching, the Duchess of Marlborough was determined to reach a better understanding with the queen. Their relationship was at such a low ebb that it was becoming embarrassing not only to herself but also to her husband, affecting his standing with his allies in the war. Quite convinced that the queen was entirely in the wrong, Sarah begged to be granted an interview.

The friendship between Sarah and Her Majesty had been so strong in the past that the queen had suggested Sarah should call her 'Mrs Morely', while she addressed Sarah as 'Mrs Freeman', so that no difference should be felt between them. Whenever they were apart, the queen had sent daily letters to Sarah, and though most were on trivial matters, all proclaimed her undying affection for her friend. Sarah had kept them all, while insisting that her own letters to the queen be burned. It was because the queen now feared Sarah might publish her letters to her that she reluctantly granted her an interview – on condition she should not mention the name of Abigail. She also insisted that she, the queen, need answer nothing Sarah said.

It was dusk when the Duchess of Marlborough arrived at Kensington Palace, where she was kept waiting by the queen's page. At last she was admitted into a dimly lit closet where the queen was on the point of writing to her. As soon as Sarah began to speak, the queen interrupted her, declaring that if she had anything to say she should put it in writing. Sarah replied that she was shocked, having never previously known the queen refuse to hear a person speak. She went on to say that she had heard rumours to suggest she had spoken disrespectfully about the queen, something she was no more capable of doing than 'killing my own children'. The queen agreed, if ironically, that 'many lies were told'. When Sarah asked exactly what she was accused of saying, the queen reminded her that she had agreed to see Sarah on condition she did not need to answer anything. When the duchess asked how she could possibly clear herself if she did not know the particulars of the charge, the queen turned her face away and appeared to blush. Now, every time Sarah attempted to speak to her, the queen repeated the same phrase over and over: 'You desired no answer and you shall have none.'[23]

Sarah had certainly spoken disrespectfully about the queen, encouraging her secretary Maynwaring to compose ballads concerning a lesbian love affair between the queen and her bedchamber-woman. Sarah sang these ballads at her own musical assemblies, and even sent copies of them to the queen. Naturally Anne was too embarrassed to discuss the subject, and Sarah, who for so many years had exercised so much influence with the queen, was now deeply frustrated. When the queen rose to walk to the door, Sarah followed after her in an attempt to prevent her leaving, finally crying out 'the most disrespectful thing I ever spoke to the queen in my life', and left the room in tears.[24]

The duchess sat alone in the long gallery, wiping away her tears. When calm she returned to scratch on the queen's closet door, which surprisingly was opened to her. Sarah asked the queen if it would be better for her not to wait on her at Windsor Castle as usual that Easter, since people might think it odd if they did not speak to each other. The queen merely reminded Sarah that she never refused to speak to any person, that Sarah was welcome to come to the castle whenever she wished, and that she herself would not be uneasy about it.

In their earlier, happier days together the queen had granted Sarah a house in Windsor Park, together with the appointment for life of Ranger of the Great Park. The house, named Windsor Lodge, was set on high ground at the end of a splendid avenue of elms, two miles from the castle. Previously enjoyed by another royal favourite, William III's Earl of Portland, it was very large and comfortable, and surrounded by beautiful gardens. There were fountains, sundials and trim box hedges, and Sarah was especially delighted with the 'pretty deer' that grazed close up to her gates. Her duke had built a splendid block of stables to house the fine horses he sent her from Flanders, and when he was home they rode out together in the park. This Easter Sarah holed herself up here to be away from the court, and when her daughter Sunderland heard of it she wrote to say she thought it 'very wrong for my dear Mama to stay in the Country', assuring her 'it will do me no harm whenever you care to be troubled with us to come to Windsor for a day or two'.[25]

The Duke of Marlborough, having heard of his wife's quarrel with the queen, advised mother and daughters to go into the country, the court being a country of 'tygers and wolves'. In response to Swift's *Conduct of the Allies*, Sarah was determined to write a full vindication of her life and work with the queen, and spent some time at her house at St Albans. Here she seethed with annoyance on hearing that the queen no longer intended to bestow her high offices on her daughters, believing she, Sarah, had not 'behaved herself suitably to it'. The queen's promise, made 'in the heat of affection', was now null. As to the daughters, Queen Anne thought one was 'cunning and dangerous', another 'Silly and Imprudent' and the third 'just like her Mother'![26]

At the beginning of June Sarah overheard another rumour, this time that the Earl of Sunderland was to be dismissed from office. Anxious for her pregnant daughter, his wife, and for the effect this would have on the standing of the Duke of Marlborough with the allies, Sarah took coach for London. From her lodgings in St James's Palace (which she still had) she wrote a letter to the queen begging 'upon her knees' to defer Sunderland's dismissal till (at least) the end of Marlborough's campaign. On the same day the queen received this letter, Sunderland was dismissed. The queen kindly offered him a pension of £3000 per annum, but the earl refused it, saying: 'If I cannot have the honour of serving my country, I shall not plunder it.'

The queen's ladies-in-waiting generally left the court some weeks before the time of their 'lying in', to take to their beds in one of the town palaces. As the Countess of Sunderland was in the eighth month of her pregnancy, she may have returned to town with her mother. The birth and christening of her son Charles three years earlier had cost £70.5s.6d, including several yards of 'holland' purchased from Mr Bull the merchant, together with the cost of nurse, midwife and cakes. There was also 'the care of Lord Spencer and Lady Anne at Kensington'. By the time Diana was born, the Kensington apartment was firmly in the hands of Abigail, but Sarah may well have looked after her Spencer grandchildren at St James's Palace. Ten shillings and ninepence had been paid to the sexton at St James's church for 'the Registering of Mr Charles in ye parish books', and the birth and christening of his sister Diana were registered in much the same way.[27]

The Duke of Marlborough, writing on 10/21 August 1710 from Villers-Brulin in France, where he was busy laying siege to Béthune, said: 'I am very glad Lady Sunderland is safely delivered', and begged his wife to give his 'compliments to her'. Diana had been born on 31 July, and would be christened eleven days later (presumably at Sunderland House), the events recorded in the St James's church register as: 'Diana Spencer of Charles & Ann Earl & Countess of Sunderland'. Such a tiny baby would not be carried across the dusty Piccadilly high street, not even into the cool of Wren's St James's church with Grinling Gibbons's exquisite marble font, for disease was rampant at that time of year, and babies of the aristocracy were generally baptised at home. Charles Trimnell, Bishop of Norwich, who was Sunderland's private chaplain (and till recently the Rector of St James's church), was well placed to carry out the ceremony, cakes and sweetmeats being served to family, friends and godparents. Many toasts would be drunk, and as the infant was the first of the Spencer children to be named 'Diana', clearly some careful thinking had taken place.[28]

The Duchess of Marlborough had recorded her children's birth dates in her family Bible, including the names of godparents, and it is likely that the Sunderland family, too, kept a similar record. Bibles containing records of the Spencer children's births were preserved at Althorp before and after this period, but this vital one is missing. The only clue we have to Diana's godparents, therefore, is contained in the letter written by the Duke of Marlborough congratulating his daughter on her child's birth. The duke ended his letter with a request to know the name and age of the Duchess of St Albans's son, adding, 'for whenever it is in my power I should be glad to do what she desires'. From this it would appear that the Duchess of St Albans (her name Diana) was invited to the child's christening, and as it was usual to name the child after the same-sex godparent, she may have agreed to be Diana's godmother, Marlborough responding by promising an army place for her son. The name Diana was anyway a happy choice, embracing the names of both the baby's mother and sister, and that of her Spencer grandmother, without actual duplication. Another good reason for the name to be given was that hunting was Queen Anne's favourite sport – one she was currently enjoying at Windsor – and of course Diana was Goddess of the Hunt.[29]

Eight days after Diana's birth, and just three days before her christening, her great-uncle, the Lord High Treasurer Godolphin, received notice to quit. This was especially shocking to the Whigs since the queen had promised (after dismissing Sunderland) to 'make no more changes'. It was also a great insult to Marlborough. How could he hold up his head at the head of his army while his family was discredited at home? At the time of Diana's conception, her family was practically ruling the country with Queen Anne, and by the time of her christening they had fallen from grace. No longer was her father Secretary of State, no longer was her great-uncle Lord High Treasurer, and the Whig government was soon to be dissolved. The elections were begun soon after Diana's christening, the Countess of Sunderland climbing out of child-bed to comb her golden hair before her dressing-room mirror, ready to entertain 'men whose votes she wished to influence'. Her efforts, however, would prove in vain, for the majority of voters had grown weary of the wars and tired of the taxes necessary to pay for them. Swift's biting comments in his *Conduct of the Allies*, together with the Sacheverell victory, were the last straw. There was a landslide victory in favour of the Tories, and any shortage of Tory peers in the House of Lords was overcome by the queen's expedient of creating more.[30]

Diana was five months old when her famous grandfather returned from his campaigns for the winter, having never once lost a battle. But he was a changed man as a result of the queen's usage of his family, sick at heart and much 'fallen away'. Sarah's town house was not yet finished, she and her duke taking up residence with their daughter, the Duchess of Montagu. When the duke went to pay his duty to the queen, there were tears in his eyes. With him he brought a letter of submission from his duchess. The queen was unmoved by it, coldly asking Marlborough to order her to return her gold key of office within three weeks. When the duke begged for more time, the queen responded by demanding it be returned within three days. A day later, when Marlborough complained of army places being sold over his head, the queen declared she was unable to discuss the matter until his duchess returned her key. It was now wanted on the next day. When Sarah received this message she threw her golden key into the centre of the room, begging her duke to return it at once. She later remarked that this was 'the more ridiculous because this was a day or two before the time which she herself had fixed for it'.[31]

The Duke of Marlborough departed sadly for France, his friends advising him to continue in the wars despite the insult to his family. Although deeply humiliated by the dismissals of his wife, his son-in-law and his friend Godolphin, he declared he must put the safety of the country first. Another summer of battle passed, and after his brilliant capture of Bouchain, he returned, only to receive notice from the queen to quit office. He threw the royal letter of dismissal into the fire. Even Swift, who 'loved him not', disliked his 'being out'. The one person to delight in his dismissal was the queen's enemy Louis XIV, who chuckled: 'The affair of displacing the Duke of Marlborough will do all for us that we desire!'[32]

Diana's mother and aunts, the queen's ladies-of-the-bedchamber, promptly resigned.

Chapter Two

Althorp

'like a Princes Court of brick and stone very fine . . .'

The Countess of Sunderland, 'with nothing in ye world to vex me but my housekeeping', was free now to enjoy her children to the full. But suffering from the 'collick' two months after Diana's birth, she visited Bath to take the waters. She left her mother to negotiate the pay still owed her as lady-of-the-bedchamber, saying, 'I give my dear mama many thanks for your kind letter of ye 4th and your goodness in taking any trouble about my pretensions of the salary as Lady of the Bedchamber', and 'Whatever you think right for me to do, I shall be sertain is so.' She added, with a touch of irony, 'I believe one may depend on their not paying me to-much'![1]

The town supplied a variety of entertainment, and while their mother took the waters the older children could sample 'cakes and fruit sillabubs and other sumer liquours' in the King's Mead, and take walks in the Orange Grove; and while their parents were absorbed at cards in the Assembly Rooms, might saunter by the river watching the gentlemen play bowls. Mr Flournoys may well have gone with them, being like a second father to the children. Once, when their mother was obliged to travel with the court to Tunbridge Wells without them, he wrote telling her how he took 'the sweet children' to visit their Sunderland grandmother in the coach, and not wishing to trouble her with 'too many at once', had left baby Charles behind. The dowager countess had been cruelly disappointed by this omission, and swore mock 'revenge', insisting that Charles should visit her later.[2]

Flournoys kept a strict eye on Lord Spencer's expenses, totting up the cost of his schoolbooks and clothes. In the bitter winter of 1709 (when ink froze in the inkwells) the young lord's gloves had cost twelve old shillings and sixpence, a new 'hatt' four shillings and sixpence, and no amount of money was considered too much for his schoolbooks, with Montaigne's *Essays* and a 'hudibrass' costing ten shillings, French books and maps fourteen shillings, and the 'Copernican Sphere', from which to study the stars, five pounds seven shillings and sixpence. He was enrolled with a drawing master for five shillings, receiving drawing lessons at one guinea a month, and supplied with penknife, pencils, crayons and 'colours'. As the grandson of the great Captain General who never lost a battle, he was sent to view the 'fortifications in Russell Street'. He was also taught to fence, supplied with a 'pair of files and a pike'.

There are no records of Lady Anne's education, but she almost certainly joined her brother for French. As one of the many thousands of Huguenots who fled the persecutions following the revocation of the Edict of Nantes in 1685, Flournoys would speak the language fluently. When old enough the children attended church every Sabbath, Robert provided with two shillings and sixpence to tip the pew keeper at St James's. During the week he went to the play. He saw Congreve's *Love for Love*, and *Macbeth* for eleven shillings, including 'ye hire of ye hackney coach'. One birthday he had his hair cut 'once in all' for seven shillings and sixpence, and was given ten shillings to take his cousin Lord Brackley, and his sister, etc., to the play.[3]

With his mother's blue eyes, her golden hair and her sweet nature, it was natural that the Sunderland heir should be so indulged. He cantered on horse-back through Hyde Park, tipping the gatekeeper at Christmas (not forgetting the sweeper), sporting splendid new riding gloves. He saw the 'moving pictures and the monsters' of which Jonathan Swift said later, he never saw anything 'so pretty'. There was 'a sea ten miles wide, . . . ships sailing in the sea . . . discharging their Canon', and a 'great sky with moon & stars'.[4]

But the healthiest place for the children was in the country. In the summer they were piled into a coach to be driven to their splendid country seat in Northamptonshire. Althorp had been in the family for 200 years, John Evelyn, the diarist, visiting it when Diana's father was an infant. He described it as standing in 'stately woods and groves in a park with a canal', and 'most nobly furnished'. The original Elizabethan house had been destroyed by fire, and rebuilt in classical style, the moat drained and turfed with a 'sweet carpet'. The intrepid traveller Celia Fiennes passed by when Diana was in her second year, describing the house as 'like a Princes Court of brick and stone very fine', surrounded by a 'large park wall'd in of a good extent'. Evelyn had found the park 'full of fowle, and especially hernes'. Lord Spencer, and later his brothers, would learn to hunt, shoot and fish here, essential skills at times when fresh meat was not readily available. Diana would spend much of her time in the nursery (together with Charles and Johnny), brought down and shown off to guests when tea was served. The rooms would open up about them like a picture book, the children absorbing the history of their ancestors from their portraits on the walls.

The early Spencers had made their great fortune from sheep, the first Baron Spencer owning as many as 19,000. Wool, as well as the meat, was the essential commodity of his time, the baron growing so wealthy from his product that he was able to entertain James I's queen, Anne of Denmark, at Althorp when she travelled down from Scotland to join her husband in his new kingdom. With her she brought her elder son Prince Henry, the two being lavishly entertained with a masque. On the following day they went hunting in a wood especially planted for the occasion, and a new hawking stand had been set up for the occasion.[*]

The 1st Baron Spencer's son William established a race-course at Althorp, and married Penelope Wriothesley, daughter of Shakespeare's patron, the 3rd Earl of Southampton. It was to this earl that Shakespeare dedicated his *Venus and Adonis* and *The Rape of Lucrece*, and is believed by some to be the person to whom he addressed his sonnets. William Spencer named his own first son Henry after this celebrated grandfather, the boy growing up to be exceptionally handsome and brilliant. Less complicated in his love life than his grandfather, he wooed the much sought-after Lady Dorothy Sidney, the beautiful 'Sacharissa' of Edmund Waller's poem 'Go, lovely Rose'. The two married, and for his service to the Royalist cause in the Civil War, Henry was created first Earl of Sunderland. His portrait at Althorp shows him dressed in armour as he was when slain at the battle of Newbury by a 'canon bullet', aged twenty-three. His grieving wife was left to rear three children alone, Robert, the Sunderland heir, being two years old when he became 2nd Earl of Sunderland. His two sisters 'Doll' and 'Pen' were not much older than he, and a boy Henry, born after his father's death, died as an infant.[5]

Diana's great-grandmother Dorothy busied herself roofing over the old Althorp courtyard after her husband's death, creating the magnificent hall that is there today, as well as the grand staircase. Young Robert was brought up and educated with Henry Sidney, who, although his uncle, was born at the same time as himself: mother and daughter gave birth in the same year. Robert spent time with him on the traditional 'Grand Tour' of Europe before coming of age, when he was betrothed to Lady Anne Digby, daughter of the Earl and Countess of Bristol. Although she was plump, pink and pretty, with round golden ringlets, marshmallow pink cheeks, and enormous blue eyes,

---

[*] The hawking stand is still at Althorp. The present 9th Earl Spencer used it as his bachelor quarters.

the diarist Samuel Pepys reported how, with 'the wedding things made and everything agreed upon the wedding', the prospective bridegroom absconded, 'nobody yet knows whither', and sent a letter next morning begging 'a release from his right and claim to her'. He left her family with the 'liberty to say and think what they will of him so that they do not demand the reason for his leaving her, being resolved not to have her'.[6]

Robert's reason for turning so suddenly against the marriage was not revealed – perhaps, with so little to do, Anne had piled on weight during his absence – her portrait at Althorp showing her to be decidedly rounded – or he had left a lover overseas. After another year spent abroad, where he had his portrait painted leaning on a monument showing *Time* overthrown by *Cupid*, Robert returned to do his duty by his betrothed. The marriage took place in 1665, the seventeen-year-old girl having suffered much from being ditched. Anne was a complicated person, gushing and motherly on the one hand, yet deeply devious on the other. Evelyn described her as a 'woman of great soul' and a 'wise and noble person', yet Queen Anne thought her not only a 'cheat and a hypocrite', but the 'greatest jade that ever lived'.[7]

There were reasons for this ambiguity. Diana's paternal grandfather, a brilliant politician, was, like his wife, highly devious and enigmatic. He was known as the 'Trimmer' for the way he altered his religion and politics to suit the needs of successive rulers, having served both Charles II and James II as Secretary of State. When James came to the throne, Robert showed every sign of embracing the Roman Catholic faith, but when the Catholic king was forced to flee to France he dropped all pretence and made for Holland. His uncle Henry had already preceded him there, taking a copy of the official invitation inviting the Protestant William of Orange to accept the English throne. As a known supporter of James, Sunderland was imprisoned on arrival, but was soon released, his countess and children joining him in Holland. He was now seen walking to the Calvinist church on Sundays, preceded by his servant carrying an enormous Bible.

During this 'Great Rebellion' the Countess of Sunderland kept up a regular correspondence with her husband's uncle, Henry Sidney. Known as Beau Henry on account of his extraordinary good looks, he had seduced, among other women, James II's first wife Anne Hyde, Duchess of York and mother of the future Queen Anne; and as the countess's letters were written in cipher, rumours arose of an incestuous relationship between herself and her husband's uncle. In fact the letters were sisterly in tone, containing political information passed to Henry in the guise of family and social gossip, and had more to do with espionage than incest. One of her husband's sayings was: 'What matters it *who* serves His Majesty, so long as His Majesty is served?'[8]

The Countess of Sunderland had long been a friend of Princess Mary (Queen Anne's sister), now married to William, Prince of Orange. The countess's brother, the Earl of Bristol, gave shelter to the prince on his arrival in England at the head of 15,000 men. The Digbys' Sherborne Castle in Dorset was used to print leaflets proclaiming William as king, the prince negotiating the change of monarchy with the future Duke of Marlborough here. As a result of all this, the prince's invasion of England was 'rapid and bloodless', he and Queen Mary soon seated safely on the English throne.[9]

Diana's father received an excellent education while in Holland, but once William and Mary were settled on the throne, he returned with his parents and sisters to England. Despite his former deviance, the 2nd Earl of Sunderland was to serve as President of the Council, Lord Chamberlain and Lord of Regency under William and Mary's rule. When he died in 1702, 'safe in the arms of the Church of England', he was interred at the church in Brington above Althorp. His uncle Henry (who had become Earl of Romney) never married, but was beleaguered by numerous illegitimate offspring, and died from smallpox two years after his nephew. He had lived close to the Countess of Sunderland in St James's Square.[10]

For all his faults and double dealings, Robert the Earl of Sunderland had worked hard to make Althorp splendid. He employed Le Nôtre (who laid out the gardens at Versailles) to design the Althorp gardens, and had an Italian architect remodel the house. After he died, his countess was left less well off than she had hoped, and despite her affection for Diana's mother, took her son to law over the ownership of two houses in the country. One was at Upper Boddington in Bedfordshire, the other at Wicken near Wormleighton. It was settled that she should have the Bedfordshire house, Charles the house at Wormleighton, which is still part of the Spencer estate. The dowager may also have pressed claims over the St James's Square house, which had been given her by her mother, the Countess of Bristol, and this might have been the reason why it was sold. The Duke of Marlborough thought the dowager 'malicious', and on hearing she was ill and in a 'dangerous condition', remarked that he hoped she would 'leave the world with that tenderness I think she owes her son'.[11]

When Diana was almost two years old, her grandfather the Duke of Marl-borough gave a feast at his house in St Albans to celebrate the anniversary of his most famous victory at Blenheim. The house was named Holywell House, there being a 'holy' well in the garden which once belonged to the abbey, and here Diana's mother and aunts and their brother Jack had grown up. On the bowling green the duke now erected his campaigning tent, a magnificent affair with scrolls and clusters of grapes woven into the fine arras work, and brass fittings that would glitter in the sun. The tent had been sent to England at his wife's request, Marlborough writing from the Hague: 'I have but one tent which was made in Turkey that is fit to be brought over, and that you may be sure I shall do.' With its cool interior and quaint furni-ture, it would delight the children, Marlborough charging visitors sixpence a head for admission. The gentry and townsfolk mingled on the lawns, while military music was played. Afterwards the Spencers moved on to Woodstock in Oxfordshire, where the Earl of Sunderland, Maynwaring and Vanbrugh were busy inspecting the works of Blenheim Palace.[12]

The palace in process of being built at Woodstock stood in the grounds of a former ancient palace, and was a gift from the nation in recognition of Marlborough's victories over the French. Since the building was not yet habitable, the family and guests stayed at High Lodge on the hillside, made comfortable by Sarah for that purpose. The present party was finishing dinner here when the ex-Lord Treasurer Godolphin joined them, calling on his way to Holywell House. He declined dinner, having eaten on the way, but commented favourably on the dessert of figs, nectarines, peaches and plums, picked freshly from the palace gardens. When he reached St Albans Godolphin fell suddenly ill, the Marlboroughs becoming alarmed when it became clear he was dying. As well as being father-in-law of their eldest daughter Henrietta, Godolphin had been Marlborough's friend since they were pages at court together, and Sarah also valued him highly. Among those who called in to see him was Robert Walpole, who had been Secretary of War and Treasurer of the Navy under the Whig administration, and lately incarcerated in the Tower when the Tories came to power. Sarah had visited him in prison, leaving with him her account of her life with Queen Anne. Walpole strongly advised her not to publish, but as Sarah found any kind of suppression or criticism difficult to accept, she doubtless had words with him. Before he died, the ailing Godolphin turned to her and said: 'If you ever forsake that young man, and if souls are permitted to return from the grave to the earth, I will appear to you and reproach you for your conduct!' It was advice Sarah would not take.

On Godolphin's death Sarah wrote in her Bible: '. . . at two in the morning the Earl of Godolphin died at the Duke of Marlboroughs house in St Albans, who was the best man that ever lived'. Years of striding across Europe at the head of a great army, countered by diplomatic visits to great foreign courts, had meanwhile left Marlborough unsuited for his enforced retirement in a small country town. With his friend Godolphin no longer there to console him, when the Tories accused him of raking off a percentage of his soldier's 'bread money' for his personal use, and of deliberately leading his officers to their deaths in order to sell their commissions, he felt it was high time to leave the country. The government had meanwhile stopped financing the work on his palace and, as Sarah said, it would be 'ridiculous if he should have to pay for his own present'. She promised to join her husband abroad later, and as her town house in the Mall was complete, she retired there to pack.

Sarah left her pet bird with her Sunderland daughter's neighbour Lady Burlington, and made a 'lottery' of her jewels and other fine things for her children and grandchildren to 'raffle for'. Her eldest grandchild Willigo (who now boasted his father's previous title of Lord Rialton now he had become Earl Godolphin) and his sister Lady Harriet were duly invited to tea. It was a simple matter for them to trot along from Godolphin House, passing St James's Palace on their way, and to enter the gates of the new Marlborough House. Sarah said later how she 'sent for my Lord Rialton and his sister my Lady Harriot to take leave of them, and gave him a pair of brilliant diamond buckles, and Lady Harriot a little diamond necklace'. Enjoying her role of indulgent grandmother, she called for tea and milk 'to please the children', then offered them a second cup. When the children told her that 'Mama had said they should drink but one cup', Sarah made it half milk, saying they might drink it, and took it on herself 'it should do them no hurt'.[13]

Next day, 'melting in tears at the thought of parting from her children to go in a packet boat to Flanders', Sarah received a terse note from the children's mother, Henrietta:

Dear mama you have bid mee allways when I took any thing ille to tell you, and I can not help for severall reasons beeing concerned that after the children said I had told em not to drink two cups of tea, that you made em, and since this could be of no use to their health, and may make em venture to do other things that I forbid, I hope you will grant this from your most Dutiful Daughter . . .

Relations between Sarah and Diana's aunt Henrietta had been strained ever since 'having a great mind to be thought a wit', she began keeping 'the worst company a young lady can keep'. But Henrietta was of a 'careless nature', and wrote to her mother, after she had left for the continent, to ask if it was true she would like to have Lady Harriet 'come to you and be like your child, and always live with you'. The child was now thirteen, and spoke French, which would be of 'great use' to her; and 'any room for such a child would be good enough', or at least 'as good as she has here'. Sarah said that Henrietta thanked her before Harriet arrived, 'which was the only thanks I ever had'.[14]

We do not know what presents, if any, the Spencer children were given by their grandmother. The children of Mary, Duchess of Montagu, received nothing, Sarah remarking that their mother had 'enough diamonds at her wedding to cover a table'. Indeed Mary, like her sister Henrietta, was often in Sarah's bad books, Diana's mother often called on to smooth things over between her mother and her sisters, once writing despairingly to her:

> I am so sensible of my own misfortunes, that I must say all I can for my sisters, which is that I never saw what you think [wrong] in either of 'em.[15]

The Spencer children had many uncles and aunts to visit while their grandparents were abroad, the nearest of them at Althorp being the Montagus, whose house, Boughton, was in Northamptonshire. Owned in addition to Beaulieu in Hampshire, it had beautiful gardens designed by the same Versailles gardener who had laid out those at Althorp. The Duke of Montagu was a fun-loving uncle, and a great prankster, putting spiders into people's beds, and squirts in the garden. He had his serious side, however, enquiring into the worlds of medicine, masonry and archaeology, and was said to please his friends with entertaining conversation.

Diana's Bridgwater aunt and uncle owned Ashridge in Hertfordshire, once a monastery, and set in a forest with two kinds of deer, and squirrels dancing from tree to tree. As the hunting lodge of Henry VIII, his three royal children, Elizabeth, Mary and Edward, had spent their summers here. The Bridgwater family had purchased it from the crown in 1605. Diana's Bridgwater aunt enjoyed the domestic round here, collecting eggs from her speckled hens, and taking pride in her October brewing. She sent casks of the ale to her parents abroad. Quietly reticent, when it was time to deliver her son to Eton, she would fight back her tears, hurrying afterwards to her sisters in the country.

Francis and Henrietta, the new Earl and Countess Godolphin, in addition to owning Godolphin Hall in Cornwall, possessed 'Gogmagog' near Newmarket. Francis was among the first to improve the English racehorse here, importing Barb and Arab sires into England, and from his famous Godolphin Arabian all modern English thoroughbreds descend through the male line. If Henrietta found little to amuse her in the country, the races would bring all kinds of people to Newmarket, and she might therefore enjoy the company.

Diana's father favoured town life to months in the country, visiting Althorp only for the elections. He was said to have a taste for 'low women' and gambling and this would keep him in town; later he added homosexuality to what were considered to be his vices. His passion for his wife, nevertheless, appears to have been intense, if evident chiefly through her continual pregnancies. Just now she was having miniature portraits painted of her family, to be set round with diamonds, writing to her mother overseas:

> The man who did my sister Montagus of the Duke is run away, but my Lady Harvey had one done by an other man who shall do these; if you please, the diamonds shall be of the bigness ye had some set round your picture, which cost forty shillings apiece but they are now something dearer.[16]

As well as these miniatures, full-scale portraits were being painted of family individuals. One was of the countess with her three-year-old daughter Diana, the painting attributed to Charles Jervas who collected pictures for Marlborough while studying the old masters in Rome. He painted Swift, among others, later becoming court painter. He was a good colourist with 'a sense of style', and although his portraits of women are sometimes thought weak, this painting of Diana with her mother is charming. Dressed in white, the little girl sits on a rock, thistles springing up at her feet, and she smiles eagerly at a bird about to alight on her mother's finger. The child's pale blonde hair is combed back from her face, her eyes a keen blue-grey. The bird has a bright scarlet breast with a dark head and tail. Sarah badly wanted paintings of her grandchildren for a house she was furnishing abroad, fearing she might never see them again.[17]

Meanwhile, the dreadful conditions of the roads and jolts from unsprung coaches failed to prevent the countess from sending her children to and from the country as the seasons demanded. A coachman was paid £4.16.3d for 'going to Althorp to fetch the children, and back', suggesting that the countess did not always go with them. On 2 March, after a long winter in town, she wrote to her mother: 'My children are all thank god very well but I intend with your leave to send 'em after this month to St Albans which air agrees I think with everybody.' The children were still at St Albans on 19 October, their mother writing to their grandmother: 'My family is very well but only Lord Spencer in town. I send for the other children next week . . .'[18]

So it was that the children grew accustomed to long journeys in unsprung coaches, the carriage slung on straps between the wheels, heated with no more than a vessel of burning charcoal, rattling along roads no better than cart tracks. Having breathed the sweet air of St Albans, they were ready to face winter in town. The Whigs were planning an anti-Tory demonstration in November, having collected a thousand pounds in the previous year to make grotesque models of the Pope, the devil and Dr Sacheverell, which would be paraded at a 'mighty procession' at midnight. The last time this demonstration had taken place the militia had been raised, the wax figures being seized by members of Harley's cabinet and locked up in Whitehall. Lady Sunderland was game to try again, however, writing to her mother: 'The Hanover Club intends to burn a pope today (if it is not taken in Custody again) being queen Eliz: birthday. . .'[19]*

But by the spring of 1714 the countess was far from well, writing to her mother that 'my feavor is gone, but I am so excessive sick that I can hardly sit up enough to write these few lynes'. She believed herself pregnant again, and, though she had never been 'so bad in this condition', knew it was 'what I must bear for a great many months'. Having recovered a little in May, she wrote again saying:

> Tho' I have not heard from my dear Mama since I was ill I believe you will not dislike to hear that I am better. I think out of danger of

---

* The 17 November 1558 was Elizabeth I's official birthday, 'when the bells rang out to symbolize a new reign . . . even after her death'. Elizabeth would represent the Protestant succession . . . Neville Williams *Elizabeth I*, p.37

miscarrying, but yr Doc: Hambleton will have me stay at home this fortnight or three weeks till the time is over that miscarried last time, and I am easily persuaded to it, being so sick and week that I am never so easy as on a Couch . . .[20]

This last letter was edged with black. On 22 March 1713 Anne's beloved sister Elizabeth had died of smallpox, her two young children Lord Brackley and Lady Anne Egerton being taken into the care of their Bridgwater grandmother. Anne had been especially close to 'Betty' (as her sister was named as a girl), who was her close companion during the early years of her marriage. When Sarah had asked Anne to challenge Elizabeth over some imagined misdemeanour, Anne had firmly refused to do so, saying, 'I am unwilling to tell Lady B your message, because it will add to the trouble of not hearing from you to give reason; so I hope you will write . . .' Feeling so unwell herself, Anne feared for her own small children should she die, rewriting her will in the form of a letter to her husband, writing on the cover: 'Not to be opened till after I am dead'. Grief at her sister's death had contributed to Anne's sickness, and her whole family was in shock. The Duke of Marlborough, hearing of his daughter's death, fainted, hitting his head on a marble mantelpiece.[21]

Queen Anne was also ill that winter, fear for the consequences of her death hanging over the court like a shroud. Her cousin Sophia of Hanover was officially next in line for the throne, but many would have preferred James II's son, the 'Pretender', as king. Marlborough had taken the precaution of seeking his pardon, sending a gift of £1000, while simultaneously offering loyal service to Hanover! The queen was said to keep a sealed paper on a string about her neck, believed to contain her true wishes for the succession.

The Electress Sophia, full of high spirits despite her eighty years, surprised everyone when she died suddenly in June 1714, her ambition to have 'Queen of England' written on her tomb unfulfilled. Her son George was now heir to the throne, a man of whom Queen Anne strongly disapproved. On 31 July, when Diana was celebrating her fourth birthday, the queen lay in a coma at Kensington Palace. She died the following morning, on the same day that the Duke and Duchess of Marlborough landed at Dover. A cannon gun salute was fired as the couple disembarked, and they made their way to London in a glass coach through cheering crowds, the road strewn with flowers. The Hanover reign had begun.

CHAPTER THREE

Holywell House
'poor little Dear Dye'

W hen Diana celebrated her fourth birthday at Althorp, the house-keeper, Mrs Dixon, was taking care of them. The children had arrived on 18 July 1714, remaining here till the beginning of October, and when news broke that the queen was dead, their mother joined them from Bath. There was fear of an outbreak of Civil War, and questions were asked as to whether the Pretender or the Elector George of Hanover should be proclaimed king; but when George finally set foot on English soil, 'not a mouse had stirred against him'.[1]

Althorp was no longer the great sheep-rearing centre it had been in the first Baron Spencer's day; only twenty-six sheep, twenty lambs, four oxen, a cow and its calf were kept at Althorp now, but this was enough to feed family and servants. When here, the children enjoyed a mixed diet of beef, veal and mutton, with the occasional rabbit, and a variety of fresh vegetables from the garden. Flournoys acted as head of the house in the absence of the earl, some-times having special company to dine with him; and when news came that George I had landed at Greenwich, a hod of strong beer was sent up to the village of Brington 'to drink ye King's health', and there was merry-making at Althorp. Now it was time for the family to return to London.[2]

Three pounds and ten shillings was paid for 'ye harness for ye left of horses when my Lady went to London', and a further fifteen shillings for a 'place for a maid in ye carage', with 'Glass for ye coach and frame'; and a fresh supply of charcoal was purchased to keep the family warm on the long journey to London. The atmosphere in the coach must have been one of simmering excitement, the chief topic of conversation being of the new clothes and new liveries to be purchased for the coronation.[3]

The first official document that George I signed as king of Great Britain was the one reinstating Diana's grandfather as Captain General of the British Forces. George had commanded the Rhine armies during the wars, with Marlborough over him as Commander in Chief of the Grand Alliance; and although George resented his comparatively inferior position at the time, he admired the duke's gifts of strategy both on the battlefield and as ambassador for his country. The duke and duchess were among the first to greet the king when he landed at Greenwich on 18 September, torches hissing in the damp mist as he said to the kneeling Marlborough in French: 'I hope your troubles are all now over.'[4]

The king was essentially a shy man who disliked pomp and ceremony, settling into St James's Palace where he required the use of only two rooms, one in which to dine, the other in which to sleep. He would be pleased to have his Captain General and the Duchess of Marlborough living next door to him, and when it was time for him to appoint his new Ministers of State they were close at hand to promote the interests of their sons-in-law. It was decided to let the position of Lord High Treasurer lie dormant for a while, since it had tended to give too much power to the possessor, the king needing time to familiarise himself with his new court. Diana's uncle, the Duke of Montagu, became his lord-of-the-bedchamber, and her aunt the Duchess of Montagu was appointed lady-of-the-bedchamber to the Princess of Wales. Sarah found the widowed Earl of Bridgwater 'such a manifest fool' that she could get him nothing better than Chamberlain to the Prince of Wales, and Diana's father, Lord Sunderland, stood with bated breath as the names of the two Secretaries of State were announced. He turned pale when Stanhope and Townshend were named, and his cheeks blanched further when it was announced he should be Lord Lieutenant of Ireland.[5]

Although a prominent position, a private yacht being provided for journeys to and from Ireland, and the bearer of the post becoming master of the court there, it held small attraction for someone with Sunderland's ambitions. The appointment tended to be given to ministers suffering some kind of disgrace, and he would be separated from the seat of government by the Irish Sea. The Countess of Sunderland was devastated by the news, the thought of uprooting herself and her family to go to a strange country filling her with dread, as also did the prospect of becoming centre of a court. Still far from well and mourning her sister Betty, she wrote to her sister, the Duchess of Montagu:

> My dear sister M. knows by this time how miserable I am in Lord Sunderland's having a place that will hurt his circumstances and give me the fatigue of being mistress of a Court when my heart is too heavy.

She felt 'not fit to be a spectator' in a court, let alone mistress of one. Another reason for her distress was that it 'will take me from the only friend

I have, your dear self'. Since sister Elizabeth's death Anne had grown closer to Mary, confiding her worries for young Lord Spencer. His latest tutor, a 'man in Hemstead', had been taken into the office of Townshend, the new Secretary of State, and now that she was 'to go into another country' she had 'nowhere to trust him'. Her parents had promised, meanwhile, to use all their power to persuade the king to provide their son-in-law with a more personally congenial post, and with the coronation imminent, Sunderland might be able to put off his departure for a time.[6]

The coronation took place on 20 October, and since the procession to Westminster would pass through St James's Park, one of the best views of it could be had from the Marlborough House windows. Where better for the Spencer children and their several cousins to gather? The children's grandparents, parents, aunts and uncles were to be among the nobles in the procession, wearing crimson robes trimmed with ermine, and gold coronets upon their heads. The gentlemen on horseback wore richly embroidered satins, the king a crimson velvet robe trimmed with ermine and gold lace, his coach drawn by six white horses. On his head was a circle of gold and diamonds, to be replaced by the St Edward's crown. The park was thronged with gilded coaches, the royal foot guards walking before and behind the king, muskets rested on their shoulders.[7]

After the religious service a great banquet was given in Westminster Hall, the ladies in the gallery letting down baskets on strings to the tables below, the gentlemen there placing portions of chicken and bottles of wine in them to be drawn up. The Duchess of Marlborough and her daughters were seated in places of honour, ladies facing their lords, reflecting sadly on the one daughter who was missing. At Marlborough House the children would be served cold meats, salads, cakes, jellies and fruits, and when the adults returned there would be dancing and junketing into the night. Now aged four, Diana was quite old enough to appreciate a sky lit up with great bursts of fireworks, but the composer Handel was keeping a low profile during this coronation, saving his *Fireworks Music* for the next one, the English composer William Croft chosen to compose the coronation anthem.[8]

As Ireland was just then enjoying a period of calm, and the Tory Parliament in England was about to be dissolved (meaning that the elections must be fought again, the king looking for a Whig majority) the Earl of Sunderland had further excuse to prolong his absence from the Emerald Isle. The king had his wish and a Whig Parliament was to meet in the following spring. Some former Tory ministers were threatened with impeachment, Harley, the ex-Lord High Treasurer, imprisoned in the Tower, while Bolingbroke, the former Secretary of State, and Ormonde (who had replaced Marlborough as Captain General), escaped to France.

The elections may have brought the children and their mother to Althorp in February 1715, where 'my lady' and her company were served a gargantuan meal of '4 gurmitszuors [?], lambs heads, two lobsters, and asparagras and ham', and the older children served with 'two chickens between them'. 'Lady Dy' (the baby of the family) was fed mutton, together with her usual addition of 'puddin'. Sadly, their grandmother, the dowager Countess of Sunderland, was to die in April, being almost seventy years old. She had lived through the reigns of Charles II, James II and William and Mary, and if reviled by Queen Anne, had outlived her to see the first Hanoverian monarch on the throne. Her body was carried to the church at Brington and laid beside that of the 2nd Earl.[9]

The dowager's death left her grandchildren by Elizabeth Clancarty without a guardian, and her lease on the house in Piccadilly had to be sold. The younger McCarthy brothers and sisters appear to have been distributed among various McCarthy relatives, while Diana's cousin Lady Charlotte expressed a wish to live at Sunderland House with her Spencer uncle and aunt. This did not meet with the wishes of the earl and countess, however, since Charlotte had been lavished with favours by her grandmother when she lived, giving rise to jealousy within the Spencer family. Diana's mother had complained to Sarah that though 'I had always thought La[dy] Sun[derland] would give extravagantly to Lady Charlotte out of vanity, to provide for her [and] I think she ought to think herself oblig[e]d to, but not to have a son quite out of her thoughts that she has made by her own faults in so bad a condition'. Diana's father felt, 'considering her temper', that it would 'not be right' for the fourteen-year-old to live with them, especially as she had a lady's companion now, which would put her on a 'thousand priorities, that are neither right for her age, & circumstance, nor convenient for any body else'. His wife, he said, was of the same mind, having spent 'many uneasy hours in thinking how to present it in the softest manner to Lady Charlotte, but was allways determind not to agree to it, upon no account whatever'. In the event the girl was sent to Canterbury, but this was by no means the last the Spencers would see of her.[10]

On the last day of August, Diana's father, having managed in his position as Lord Lieutenant of Ireland never to set foot on Irish soil, was released from that post, becoming Lord Privy Seal. Lady Sunderland was greatly relieved, sending her heartfelt thanks to her mother, saying: 'My dear mama never misses any opertunity to be kind to my Ld Sunder[land] and me, and has so often had it in her power that all I can say of my thanks will be but repetition; in this I am happier then words can express . . .' But if all was well for the Spencers, it was not well for the country as a whole. On 6 September the Jacobite rebels raised their standard in Scotland, and Great Britain was plunged into civil war. Perth fell to the rebels, and a further rising was expected in the south. The king, working closely with his Captain General, sent troops to Devon to abort any attempts at a landing by Ormonde, and the situation was grave. In Scotland only the stronghold of Edinburgh remained in Protestant hands, and though the Lowland rebels were soundly beaten when they crossed into England, on 22 December James Francis Edward Stuart, the 'Pretender', landed in Scotland. Without arms or troops of his own, he was put at the head of the rebel army, marching it into Dundee.[11]

Christmas came and went, the Spencers having revelled in roast suckling pigs and spiced Christmas pies; and on 'Twelfth Day' a bean cake would be purchased and served to the children. The child to find a bean in his or her slice would be 'king' for the day. Meanwhile, in the real world, the two rival kings for Great Britain fought for supremacy. Marlborough in his sixty-sixth year was suffering headaches and dizziness, so was unable any longer to take horse into battle, but when the Thames froze over he was observed venturing onto the ice with the Prince of Wales. Did his grandchildren follow, to delight in the 'Frost Fair' with its 'flying coaches' and games of skittles? Gaming tables and a goldsmith's shop were erected on the thick ice, a milliner's stall sold 'famous Tunbridge Ware', and two printing presses provided news of the rebellion. The Pretender had marched into Perth, his coronation ordered at Scone. But on 4 February 1716, he turned tail and sailed for France.[12]

While all this was good news to the Whigs, tragedy of a more private kind lay in wait for the Spencer family. In April 1716 the young Countess of Sunderland developed pleurisy, and her doctors were sent for. When an incision was made for letting blood, it turned septic, the countess falling quickly into a delirium. At two o'clock on Sunday 15 April, the Countess of Sunderland was dead. In a paroxysm of grief, the Duchess of Marlborough blamed Dr Mead for the tragedy, saying he had 'as certainly killed my Lady Sunderland as if hee had shot her in the head!' The grief to Lord Sunderland and his children was beyond description, but Joseph Addison attempted to express it. In the name of 'Mr Chute', he wrote of 'the lovely orphans' that remained, saying:

If a Churchill weep, a Spencer die,
The sympathetic sorrow streams from ev'ry eye.[13]

The countess was laid in a coffin quilted with silken sarcenet, which was placed in a lead coffin lined with velvet. On 23 April it was carried out to the hearse, five women clutching a corner of 'ye best pall'. To the sound of a bell tolling from St James's church, the hearse was drawn from Piccadilly by six black horses plumed with 'best black feathers' on its last journey to Althorp. All the servants were given crepe for mourning: the housekeeper 'Mrs Sarah', the two kitchen maids, two laundry maids, two house maids, Betty Beasely the dairy maid, and Diana's nursery maid Judith. The menservants received hat bands and gloves, and ninety pairs of chamois gloves were distributed among the deceased countess's women friends. Five hoods and five scarves were presented to the 'women at the funeral', perhaps those who clutched the tear-drenched corners of the pall. The Duchesses Marlborough and Montagu, and the Countess Godolphin, Lady Frances and Lady Anne Spencer (now fourteen) remained in shrouded rooms receiving sympathetic callers. Frances, the late countess's stepdaughter (whose companion 'Mrs Corne' was given 'mourning'), joined her father and her half-brothers and sisters to live at Sunderland House. Her aunt, the Duchess of Newcastle,* had died in the previous December, leaving her, like cousin Charlotte, in need of a home. Diana and the two youngest of her brothers were watched over by their nursemaids in the nursery upstairs.[14]

It took two days for the funeral procession to reach Althorp, the gentlemen outriders and coachmen dressed in mourning cloaks. As the cortège passed through the town of St Albans another bell tolled from the Abbey church, as so often it must have done during Anne's childhood and girlhood here. At Dunstable help was needed to carry the lead coffin up the

---

* Margaret (neé Cavendish) died 24th December 1715. When her father Henry, 2nd Duke of Newcastle, died in 1691, her husband John, 4th Earl of Clare, was created Duke of Newcastle. John died in 1711 and having no male issue, bequeathed the bulk of his estate to his nephew Thomas Pelham Holles, whom we shall meet later, who in 1715 had the titles Earl of Clare and Duke of Newcastle-upon-Tyne conferred upon him. Margaret contested her husband's will in favour of her only daughter Henrietta, without success, who in 1713 married Edward Harley, afterwards Earl of Oxford and Mortimer.

notoriously steep chalk hill outside the town to save the horses, and also down into Hockliffe. From here the procession veered toward Woburn, where it was to stop for the night. The Woburn church bell tolled as the coffin was brought into the chapel hung with black crepe, and laid down before the altar, while wax candles were lit around it. Two women and two men were hired from the town 'to watch over the body', while twelve pages guarded 'ye hearse with truncheons'. On the following morning the sad cortège moved on to Northampton, where another bell tolled from the church, and so on to Althorp. Mrs Dixon, the housekeeper, was ready to bear witness of the interment, and having done the same for the late dowager countess only a year earlier, needed only 'trimming' for mourning. As with her mother-in-law, the young countess's body was laid to rest in the vault beneath the Spencer chapel of the Church of St Mary the Virgin, in the village of Great Brington above Althorp.

It was now time for the grieving Earl of Sunderland to break open the seal of the letter that his wife had written him in fear for her life. The letter began tenderly, hoping he would find 'comfort for the loss of a wife', knowing he 'loved too well not to want a great deal', and begged him 'not to make his circumstances uneasy' by living beyond his means. 'You will ever be miserable if you give way to the love of play', she chided him gently, reminding him that he had five thousand pounds of the money her mother had given her yearly, asking that Lord Spencer should have the income from it for his allowance. She went on to consider the younger children:

Pray get my mother, the Duchess of Marlborough, to take care of the girls, and if I leave any boys too little to go to school [them too,] for to be left to servants is very bad for children, and a man can't take the care of little children that a woman can.

She hoped 'for the love that she has for me, and the duty I have ever showed her' that the duchess would do it, and also 'be ever kind to you, who was dearer to me than my life'. She begged him to make sure the children were 'married with a prospect of happiness', to 'never let them want education or money while they are young', and 'not be so careless of the dear children as when you relied upon me to take care of them, but let them be your care, tho you should marry again, for your wife may wrong them when you don't mind it'. Though reconciled to the fact that she must die,

Anne found it hard to part with 'one so much belov'd' as her husband was, and 'in whom their was so much happiness'.[15]

The distraught Sunderland sent this letter to his mother-in-law so that she might see for herself 'the desires of that dear, dear angell', and have 'the comfort & satisfaction' of seeing that out of her own 'tenderness & goodness' she (Sarah) had resolved to do all that his wife had desired of her, 'even before you had seen it'. He promised to send her a lock of his wife's 'dear hair' as requested, and the cup she had used, adding, 'Poor little Dear Dye shall come to you whenever you order it.' Sarah wrote back that she was glad she had resolved to do everything her daughter asked of her, 'except taking Lady Anne which I did not offer, thinking that since you take Lady Frances home, who is 18 years old, she would be better with you than me, as long as you live, with the servants that her dear mother chose to put about her.'[16]

At eighteen years old, Frances was certainly of an age to keep an eye on her fourteen-year-old half-sister, but her grandmother's rejection of her was not taken kindly by Anne. Sarah would accuse her later of playing 'a thousand mean tricks even from fourteen', but just now there was no outward sign of animosity between them. The duchess promised the girl's father that she would be 'all the use that I can be in every thing that she wants me', and if it so happened that she [Sarah] should live longer than the earl 'though so much older', she would 'take as much care of her as if she were my own child'.[17]

Sarah had already taken one granddaughter, Lady Harriet Godolphin, into her care, even though she had both parents still living. According to Sarah, the child's mother 'never loved her . . . never let her eat with her, and shut her up in a garret'. Although Harriet appears not to have joined the Marlboroughs in exile as her mother had hoped she would, she had settled with them on their return. In the absence of any clear rules regarding adoption at the time, Sarah described it as coming to live with her 'as if she were married' to her. Sarah now had an excuse to pop into Godolphin House whenever she felt the need, one day calling on her daughter to find William Congreve with her, the two playing at cards with another woman Sarah did not know. She wanted Henrietta's opinion of Harriet's 'pinners' (the lace caps worn at the time), and whether they should have 'lappets' or not. The 'lappets' were broad lace ties attached to the cap, dangling like rabbit's ears at each side of the wearer's neck or tied under the chin; the other type, sometimes called a round cap, with a ribbon drawn through it, was pinned on top of the head. As Harriet was 'low', Sarah thought the 'pinner', as it was also called, more suitable for her, since it would lend her height, but could not decide on a matter of such importance without consulting the mother. Congreve had passed the peak of success he had enjoyed as a young playwright, negative criticism having led him to retire, but was determined to become a 'gentleman', taking more notice of Sarah the grand duchess than Henrietta did. Sarah, finding herself ignored by her daughter, turned on her heel and departed.

Not only had Sarah taken young Harriet under her wing, she was also considering taking in the ten-year-old Lady Anne Egerton. Since the death of her mother Elizabeth, Anne had been cared for by her paternal grand-mother, the dowager Countess of Bridgwater, who was now sixty-one and ailing. Sarah had found the child 'very ill cared for' when she returned from overseas, informing Sunderland that she proposed to take her as well as Diana into her care. The child 'went yesterday to Ashridge', she informed him, and she would send for her to come to St Albans 'as soon as you will let me have dear Lady Di'.[18]

Diana, with two months to go before her sixth birthday, was obliged to kiss her brothers and her sisters goodbye before being lifted up into the family coach beside her father, who made the journey with her. With them went two or three servants the earl was 'prepared to part with', one of whom was Jane Pattison who had been his late wife's personal maid. Diana took with her the pearl necklace and striking watch her mother had left her, and if she smiled bravely, must also have swallowed back tears. The coach rattled through the countryside through which she had often travelled with her brothers and sister on happier occasions, and which Defoe described as like 'a planted garden'. Bushey Heath he likened to a nobleman's estate where the 'enclosed cornfields made one grand parterre, the thick hedge rows, like a wilderness or labrynth, divided in espaliers', and was 'all nature and yet looked all like art'. One of the noble estates he pointed out was Ashridge, where Diana's cousin Anne quietly awaited her call to St Albans.[19]

St Albans Abbey had appeared on the skyline long before Diana reached the town, and was now in use as the parish church, one of its chapels housing a school for boys. Once in the town, the coach passed through orchards and by cottage gardens, the scent of blossom filling the air. Her grandfather (with his late friend Godolphin), had planted splendid gardens beside his house at the bottom of Holywell Hill, and an avenue of limes led to the newly built north wing that now formed the front of the house. The pediment under the roof was carved with military motifs celebrating Marlborough's many victories, and a flight of steps led up between neat sash windows to a smart front door. A liveried footman was on hand to lift Diana from the coach, and another to light them up the steps, where the child's grandparents and cousin Harriet waited eagerly to greet her.

Sarah described Diana as a 'pretty talking child of six' when she came to Holywell House, although if she arrived in May as planned, she was two months short of that. Before the tragic death of the child's mother the Duke and Duchess of Marlborough had arranged to visit places where 'one can't carry children', and since the duke's health was not good enough for Sarah to 'trust him by himself', she suggested to Sunderland that 'while the weather is hot I will keep them two and Lady Harriet with a little family of servants to look after them and be there as much as I can'. She also promised to provide for 'Lady Dye' as if she were her own child, without it 'costing her father anything'.[20]

Lady Anne Egerton was ten years old when she arrived from Ashridge. Like Diana, she was an attractive child, but with her mother's dark curls and her grandfather's deep blue eyes. Though Jervas's portrait of her belies this, Harriet, at fifteen, was described as short and plump and rather swarthy (like her Godolphin grandfather), and she had also inherited his wit and 'understanding'. The children may have been given rooms in the older part of the building, their grandparents living in the new north-facing wing, with its hall, drawing-room and dining-room on one floor, and two bedrooms and dressing-rooms above. There was also a 'handsome chamber between'. A summer parlour on the ground floor overlooked the garden to the east, onto which opened a cloister, a relic of the ancient Tudor building. Here the family took walks when it rained, or sheltered from the sun when too hot. Fine gravel walks ran between Sarah's decorative flower beds, and near the cloister was the 'holy' well from which the house took its name. At the bottom of a slope ran the River Ver from which Diana's grandfather had diverted a series of pools and a canal to provide 'trouts and other fish' for the table. The kitchen garden was stocked full of vegetables, the walls heavy with peaches, figs and pears in season, and in the main garden was a summer house, a dovecote and the bowling green where three years earlier the duke had put up his tent.

Above the old cloister had once run the long gallery and Queen's Chamber, where Elizabeth I had slept, and Queen Anne, too, when she had stayed with Sarah, both of which may have been preserved. The old nursery where Sarah and her sisters and brothers had played and slept as children, and then her own children, could now be brought back into use for the younger girls. Harriet would have a room to herself and her maid. In Sarah's childhood the nursery had been hung with wall hangings, and there were thick 'foot carpets' under foot; and like the nurseries at Althorp and Sunderland House, it was furnished with old furniture, a curtained bedstead, an old table and 'a few stools'. There was also a pair of little dressing-tables that Diana and Anne might now use if retained. The kitchens and other offices were behind 'the garden room', and as Sarah was inclined to 'stuff her attics' with guests, the servants may also have slept downstairs.[21]

Diana would miss her brothers and sister, to say nothing of her beloved and beautiful mother; and though Lady Anne Egerton had had three years to recover from her mother's death (when like her mother she suffered from smallpox) she must have been disturbed by her change of environment. Harriet, too, had reason to be homesick, for she adored her pert and frivolous mother; her brother's tutor (while praising her intelligence) agreed with Sarah that she was 'strangely bound and captivated with an excess of filial aw[e] and respect, which has hung upon her from her cradle like an enchantment'. Sarah, having lost her power as a stateswoman, and her remaining children having fully grown up, prepared to channel her energies into bringing these sad little 'orphans' up as her own. But not even she was prepared for the first hurdle.[22]

The Duke of Marlborough, even before his sixtieth birthday, had longed 'extreamly to be at quiet' for, he said, 'I grow very old.'[23] Eight years later, prematurely aged by battles and the ingratitude of his nation, he was only a shadow of his former self. Gazing at a portrait of himself painted when he was still a dashing young soldier, he sighed regretfully, 'That once was a man!' As a young father he had delighted in his small children, writing to his wife: 'You cannot imagine how pleased I am with the children, for they having noe body but their maid, they are soe fond of me that when I am att home they will be always with me, kissing & huging me.' He had adored Sarah throughout their married life, rushing home from his campaigns to 'pleasure her in his boot-tops'. He loved her still, and was doubtless pleased with his grandchildren, but the sight of them mirroring their dead mothers was almost too much for him. Soon after their arrival at Holywell House, coming down the stairs on 28 May, he collapsed from a massive stroke.

For three days the duke lay in a coma, Sarah caring for him night and day, perhaps rather to the exclusion of her grandchildren. She prided herself in her nursing abilities, often refusing the bleeding and blistering advocated by doctors, dosing her husband with 'Sir Walter Rawliegh's Cordial'. While this contained some doubtful ingredients – 'Muske and Ambergriese' ground by a 'strong man used to labour', and 'Salt of Coral' to be put in a 'glass furnace till it is white as snow' – it included many health-giving herbs and flowers. Either because of it, or despite it, the duke slowly came out of his coma, but was paralysed and unable to speak. As the weather grew warmer he gained strength enough to be carried into the garden in a chair on poles, his campaigning tent again set up so that he might take the air in it. It would be therapeutic to have his granddaughters talk to him. Though his mouth remained twisted, and he was unable to control the tears that fell unbidden down his cheeks, he gradually regained his power of speech. In June he was able to journey to Windsor Lodge, a place perfectly suited to children.

The two younger cousins may have remained here with the 'family of servants' when the duke and duchess left for Bath, taking Harriet with them. Sarah was anxious to find the girl a husband, and had one or two in mind; and because she danced well, she dressed her in fine silk petticoats and decked her out with diamonds. She knew her little grandchildren would be well cared for by Jane Pattison, and was touched when a letter from 'little Dear Di' came to her. From the start Sarah had encouraged the child to call her 'Mama', and her letter reads:

Dear Mama,
pray come back very soon or us we shant be happy all the time if you stay long. I hope you will send one [?] for us from Dear Mama . . . Your most Dutifull Daughter
Diana Spencer.

The letter was addressed 'To Dear Mama Duchess', and though now nibbled away by time, enough of the missing word is left to suggest Diana's request was for a 'hug', or a 'cup', such as her mother had left Sarah when she died. More than anything, Diana needed mothering just now, and since Mama was no longer with her, 'Dear Mama Duchess' must do.[24]

CHAPTER FOUR

Marlborough House and Blenheim Palace
'I drank your Health to day in Wine'

When the Marlboroughs and Harriet returned from Bath in September, Diana and her cousins went with them to view the Blenheim Palace works at Woodstock. The family stayed at High Lodge on the hillside, where the duchess, concerned for her granddaughters' entertainment, asked the keepers to herd the deer together so they could see them, thinking it a 'very pritty sight'. The deer were nervous, and Sarah, believing it was the stony ground that upset them (or that they were frightened the family had come 'to destroy them'), begged for them to be released. She had a soft spot for animals as well as for her grandchildren.[1]

The foundation stone of the palace had been laid twelve years ago, on 18 June 1705, yet the building was still unfinished. The duke had feared he might die before he could enjoy his 'present', given him by a 'Greatful Nation', and Sarah was so weary of the work it had entailed that she called it 'a heap of stones'. The workmen were now preparing the 'Grand Approach', which in Sarah's opinion was created merely to impress visitors, while the east wing, which was to be the family's private residence, remained unfinished. Her particular annoyance was with Vanbrugh's elaborate bridge, which she called a 'bridge in the air', since it went from 'nowhere to nowhere', and had only a trickle of water running under it. The duchess ridiculed the ancient palace ruin on the site (retained by Vanbrugh as his studio, and as an historical memento to the past), stomping about the newer building making lists of the things left undone.

Diana, if allowed to descend the stony slopes with her grandparents, would be given her first insight into the building of a great palace in the English Baroque style, while her grandfather sat morosely on his horse, unable to comment. Sarah would later send her list of complaints to a Mr Richards, whom she guessed would pass them on to Vanbrugh, not wishing to approach the architect herself. Vanbrugh, once a soldier and a highly successful playwright, had been employed not only to build the palace (among others – he was also building Castle Howard), but to negotiate a marriage between Diana's cousin Harriet and Thomas Pelham Holles, the

Duke of Newcastle-upon-Tyne, and Sarah became as impatient with his slow progress in that area as she was with the building. She had eventually employed a professional matchmaker to complete the marriage negotiations, thus overriding Vanbrugh's authority, and now, upon reading the complaints concerning the building, and stung by this 'double crewlty', Vanbrugh retorted:

When I writ to your Grace on Tuesday last I was much at a loss what cou'd be the ground of your having dropt me in the service I had been endeavouring to do you and your family with the Duke of Newcastle. But having since been shewn by Mr Richards a large packet of building papers sent him by your Grace, I find the reason was that you had resolv'd to use me so ill in respect of Blenheim as must make it impracticable to employ me in any other Branch of your Service. But to put a stop to my troubling you more, you have your end Madam . . .

This was not at all how Sarah intended Vanbrugh to take her criticism, aware that a breach with the architect would upset her husband deeply. Vanbrugh ended by saying he would never trouble her again unless the Duke of Marlborough 'recovered so far to shelter me from such intolerable Treatment'.[2]

It was while the children were at High Lodge that their grandfather suffered a second stroke. Three doctors were sent for, as well as the duke's daughters. Mary, Duchess of Montagu, wrote that she was unable to come, having sat up all night tending the Princess of Wales through a troublesome pregnancy, but Henrietta, Countess Godolphin, came at once. She brushed past Sarah as if she were no more than a 'nurse to snuff the candles', but for the duke's sake Sarah took her in her arms 'whether she would or no'. When they were alone together, Sarah asked if she had not 'dissembled very well', upon which Henrietta looked at her as if she would kill her.[3]

The lodge where the family was staying was 'a very little lodge where there were but three rooms to lye in & garrets', but this gave young Harriet and her mother a chance to communicate. Harriet was able to tell her mother how at Bath she had met Wentworth Woodhouse, heir to 'vast woods and a great estate in Yorkshire', and how when her grandmother asked if she liked him, Harriet had politely answered 'yes'. Then with no more ado Sarah had whisked her off in the coach to meet his family, explaining only on their return the reason for their visit. When told it was to propose a match between

Harriet and Wentworth, Harriet, who fancied Newcastle, burst into tears. Sarah had wept too, hugging her granddaughter to her and assuring her she need not marry the 'Emperor of the whole World' if she did not like him.

Sarah had been kind to Harriet, her first granddaughter, ever since she was a small child, never commenting on her plainness, but showing off her dancing skills to her friends. Because she danced well she had dressed her in 'a great many diamonds' for a grand ball at Somerset House, having 'nothing more in mind than to have her taken notice of in order to marry her well', and it is possible she met Newcastle there. The duke was a fussy hypochondriac, but at twenty-four was not altogether unhandsome. His vast riches had come to him while young from both sides of his family, one of them his uncle, the 2nd Duke of Newcastle, whose wife Margaret had reared Diana's half-sister Frances. He had used his money and influence to secure the succession of George I and the triumph of the Whigs, and raised a troop of horse to quell the Jacobite uprising. The Marlboroughs could not but be impressed by him. As Vanbrugh had sold his own 'box', Claremont, to Newcastle, and was improving it for him at the same time he was building Blenheim Palace, the architect was ideally placed to negotiate a marriage between the young people.

Sarah had changed her mind about Newcastle when he asked £40,000 with Harriet, four times the amount Marlborough had given with his own daughters, Newcastle giving as his reason his wish that Harriet's 'bodily perfection' was equal to her 'mind and understanding'. Sarah was incensed by this, declaring Harriet to be neither 'Cityson nor Monster', and had consequently directed her search elsewhere.[4]

Having failed to interest Harriet in Woodhouse, Sarah had hired a professional marriage broker named Peter Walters to negotiate a better deal with Newcastle. The duke listened to the new broker's proposals before sending for Vanbrugh. While Walters sat in the next room, Newcastle questioned Vanbrugh about Harriet's 'behaviour at the Bath', and other 'nice enquiries', then confronted him with Walters. The architect was deeply injured by this confrontation, saying he had never been 'fond of meddling in other people's affairs', and that matchmaking was 'a damnd Trade'.[5]

Harriet had not only the disadvantage of being plain, but also of being bright. Diana's aunt, the Duchess of Montagu, wrote to Sarah saying she was 'a little ashamed to find Lady Harriot has so much more sence then I had at her age', adding spitefully that she hoped it would be 'of use towards her happiness, & not always a hindrance to your disposing of her as you like!' In the end Newcastle married Harriet, accepting her with a mere £20,000 dowry, Vanbrugh persuading him that in a few years 'nobody would be better liked'. The wedding took place at Marlborough House on 2 April 1717, with family and friends from both sides invited.[6]

No expense had been spared to make Harriet the best-dressed person present, sparkling in silks and jewels. The gentlemen in their scarlet painted heels clipped across the black and white tiles of Sarah's magnificent saloon beneath Laguerre's freshly painted murals depicting Marlborough's Blenheim victory, while the ladies' satin slippers played 'peek-aboo' beneath their hooped silk gowns. The double doors were thrown open for eating, drinking, dancing and cards. Harriet blushed behind her fan, hardly daring to glance at her lord. Soon they would be undressed by bridesmaids and best man, then enclosed within the curtains of their four-poster bed. Next morning it would be time for Diana and cousin Anne to wave bride and groom goodbye. As the couple was about to leave, Sarah took Harriet in her arms, hugging her and begging her on the first occasion her lord failed to take her out in their fine gold chariot, to call on her and drive her to Hyde Park.

The couple spent the first part of their honeymoon at Newcastle House in Lincoln's Inn Fields, before departing for Claremont, and a week or so passed before Harriet called on her grandmother. Then it was only to sit in a 'dead way and be pumped for questions', asking, 'How does my grand-papa?' Sarah was convinced she had fallen again under the spell of her mother who affected 'to go often abroad with her only so people would think she was a good mother', whereas she, Sarah, had been a bad one. The duchess therefore decided to dismiss Harriet from her mind, placing all her hopes in Lady Diana and Lady Anne.[7]

While living at Marlborough House, the cousins enjoyed a ringside view of the comings and goings of the royal family at St James's Palace. As aristocratic contemporaries of the three little princesses, the daughters of the Prince and Princess of Wales, they would be invited to their parties and entertainments. Diana was a year younger than the eldest Princess Anne, and the same age as Princess Amelia, who was the prettiest and cleverest of the princesses, while Princess Caroline was three years Diana's junior. Because Diana's aunt was lady-in-waiting to the Princess of Wales, they enjoyed further access to the princesses; and the Montagu children in turn

often played with their cousins at Marlborough House. After one such gathering, the Duchess of Montagu wrote:

> I give my mother a thousand thanks for the pleasure she gave my chil-
> dren. Lady Mary is as you say very natural, and I shou'd have guessed
> would have been much offended if lady Dye pretended to be more
> young than she is . . .

Diana was now seven, Mary four, and her mother's letter suggests that
Diana had been a trifle patronising towards her younger cousin.[8]

The Duchess of Montagu had been up nights waiting on the Princess of
Wales, who had lost the baby prince born at the time of Marlborough's
second stroke, and had given birth to a third son in the following year. The
methods of delivery used by the German midwives employed by the
princess appalled the English ladies-in-waiting, Diana's aunt being 'very
uneasy sometimes', but on this occasion there was a live birth, giving cause
for public celebration. Cannon guns were fired in St James's Park, and
church bells rang, and there were bonfires and illuminations. There was
'great joy for the young prince', Diana's aunt informed Sarah, and the king
(who had been staying at Hampton Court) had called to see the princess.[9]

Some changes, meanwhile, had taken place in government, Diana's father
once more appointed Secretary of State, and Harriet's new husband made
Lord Chamberlain. When the baptism of the baby prince was planned, the
king reminded the father (George, the Prince of Wales) that it was traditional
in England for the Lord Chamberlain to have the honour of being godfather.
The prince was appalled, since he despised Newcastle, nicknamed 'Hubble
Bubble' on account of his being always in a hurry and always late, and
'Permis' because of his tediously repeated phrase: *'Est il permis?'* Also, the
prince had wanted his uncle the Bishop of Osnabrück to be godfather. When
Newcastle turned up for the christening, the Prince of Wales flew into a rage,
crossing the foot of his wife's bed to exclaim, 'Rascal, I shall find you out!'

Newcastle (having done his duty by the baby prince) rushed off to
Sunderland House where another celebration was in progress. Diana's half-
sister Lady Frances was marrying Lord Morpeth, heir to the Earl of Carlisle
the owner of Vanbrugh's splendid Castle Howard. The wedding took place
at night, and as a cousin of the bride, Newcastle was one of the guests. He
first sought the bride's father Sunderland, well into the task of toasting the

happy pair, and wasted no time in telling him that the Prince of Wales had challenged him to a duel. Sunderland, a little worse for drink, felt it his duty to inform the king. The king flew into a roaring rage.

In his role of Secretary, Sunderland was one of the two sent to interrogate the Prince of Wales. The prince swore he had not said 'fight you out', as Newcastle claimed, calling him a liar. This so incensed the king he gave orders for the Prince and Princess of Wales to be placed under house arrest. Sunderland and his fellow Secretary, Stanhope, had difficulty preventing the king from imprisoning his son in the Tower, or alternatively banishing him to America. The prince continued to deny a threat on Newcastle's life, but in time agreed that his behaviour had been unseemly. The king refused to forgive him, banishing him and his princess from the palace.

George (who prior to his accession had incarcerated for life his divorced wife Sophia Dorothea for adultery, while in time honoured tradition openly keeping mistresses himself) refused the prince and princess access to their children. The couple set up a rival court at Leicester House, but their tiny prince, also separated from them, died, it was believed, partly from neglect at Kensington Palace. The king also threatened to dismiss from his service the husband of any lady-in-waiting who followed after the princess, and since the Duke of Montagu was the king's lord-of-the-bedchamber, his wife was obliged to resign.

Time must have been spent watching 'neighbour George' (the name Sarah had given the king), as he took his daily airing in the park in his sedan chair, flanked by his Yeomen of the Guard, followed by his incredibly ugly mistresses. Madam Schulenberg was named the 'Maypole' on account of her tall emaciated figure, and the opulent Kielmansegge the 'Elephant', causing the mob great hilarity as they passed in their chairs, cooling their highly painted faces with fast-moving fans. When the king picnicked on the Thames in his royal barge that summer, Sarah's daughter Henrietta Godolphin and her granddaughter Harriet Newcastle were of the party, Handel's musicians following at a discreet distance rendering the *Water Music,* and if any coolness had existed between master and musician before, a reconciliation was clearly about to take place. The king was growing increasingly fond of Handel's opera, taking a permanent box at the King's Theatre to enjoy it. Sarah, eager for her grandchildren to experience the very best that society offered, borrowed a box from Lord Stair, the family climbing a rickety flight of steps to reach it. The box was ready to burst with the number of people in it, but once again Diana heard the sounds she had absorbed in her infancy, now able to enjoy the lavishness of the productions.

In the spring of that year the Duke and Duchess of Marlborough took the cousins to Blackheath, 'famous for its beauty and excellent air', staying at General Withers's house. Withers was a 'very brave and good officer', having headed a regiment in Marlborough's army, and though not considered a 'man of quality', was made Governor of Sheerness. With him lived his friend Colonel Desaulnais, known as 'Duke Disney' to friends; and though Swift thought him an 'old battered rake', he believed him 'honest'. John Gay, soon to be famous for his *Beggar's Opera*, admired both men, describing them as 'Withers the good, and (with him ever join'd) Facetious *Disney*'. Sarah appeared to like them, as did Diana, writing to her grandmother fifteen years later: 'I believe you'll be sorry . . . that Duke Disney is dead', and that 'every body that was aquainted with him, loved him'. Withers, who died some time before Disney and left his house to him, was buried at Westminster Abbey.[10]

Marlborough was able to attend military reviews on the heath, while the children took rides in royal Greenwich Park, Sarah entertaining guests in Withers's drawing-room. The children were able to take a look through the great telescope then kept in the garden shed of Flamstead House (now the Royal Observatory), and admire the gem of architecture known as the Queen's House, from which Sarah had illicitly brought the Gentileschi* ceiling paintings to decorate the saloon at Marlborough House. Below them the River Thames twisted like a serpent, tall masted ships with billowing sails skirting the Isle of Dogs. On the 'island' were windmills, and the children were able to spy through the telescope the bodies of grisly highwaymen swinging in their gibbets. Blackheath was a notorious venue for highwaymen, their grandfather being one of many held at gun-point there. Below, too, Charles II's palace was in process of being turned into a hospital for seamen by Vanbrugh, while Thornhill was employed to paint the ceilings.

Withers's house comprised two Restoration houses standing outside the Greenwich Park wall, now called McCartney House, and which General

---

* '. . . the painted panels by Gentileschi which were removed from the ceilings of the Great Hall [of the Queen's House] by the imperious Sarah Duchess of Marlborough in the early 18th century', Nigel Andrew *A View of Reproduction England, The Times,* 28 April 1990, p. 29. See also: George Chettle, *The Queen's House Greenwich,* Appendix II, pp. 89–91, The Trustees of the National Maritime Museum.

James Woolfe would call 'the prettiest situated house in England', and there were several other mansions close by. Captain Hosier's residence was soon to be known as the Ranger's House, as it is today, the 4th Earl of Chesterfield becoming the first Ranger to live here, the current Ranger living in the Queen's House. Closer to the heath stood the house belonging to Diana's uncle and aunt, the Montagus: here Caroline of Brunswick would live, as the estranged wife of the Prince Regent. The cluster of houses here attracted well-to-do officers and merchantmen with their families, for Blackheath was not only healthy, but close to the Greenwich harbour for ships too tall to pass under London Bridge. Sarah's business manager James Craggs lived a little way down the hill at the Manor House, and it was Craggs who introduced Sarah to Lady Cairnes.

Elizabeth, Lady Cairnes, was the wife of Sir Alexander Cairnes, Marlborough's banker. They occupied a pretty house just below Withers's home on Crooms Hill, now called the White House, and with them lived their daughter Mary. Mary Cairnes was a lively and observant girl of about twelve years, who later recalled how 'Lady Anne Egerton and Lady Diana Spencer lived with the Duchess', and how she, Mary, 'was always with them'. This put her in the position of being 'an eye witness to many things', and she and the cousins 'were always in her Grace's Drawing Room and the duchess talked upon all subjects without reserve'.[11]

Sarah took a liking to Lady Cairnes, inviting her and her daughter to stay with them at Marlborough House, and Windsor Lodge. As well as being in need of a pleasing woman to be her companion, Sarah coveted Mary's governess for her own grandchildren. This was Marie La Vie, daughter of a Huguenot banker of Bordeaux, whom Sir Alexander had brought as a 'relation' into his family. Described as 'equally mistress of the most correct French & English', La Vie was counted among the lively minded *'beaux esprits'* welcome at the table of the king's more intelligent mistress, Kielmansegge.

So it was that Diana began lessons with Marie La Vie, brother Johnny joining her for a time in the schoolroom. Both children proved eager and able pupils, La Vie reporting to their grandmother:

Your two children Madam have great capacities, and one shall not see children of greater hopes this is the truth. This is excellent canvas to work upon . . .

Sarah was determined that her grandchildren should not be spoiled, as she believed at least two of her own children had been, the governess agreeing with her that 'the melancholy experience' she suffered through the ill manners of her remaining two daughters made her 'double' her 'watchfulness' with Johnny and Diana. This, the governess concluded, would not let her 'yeild so much' to her 'natural temper' as she would otherwise have done, Sarah's true inclination being 'not to cross them in anything'. Marie believed it was 'a misfortune to have so much quickness & sence, as Lady Dy, & master Johnny have, and will be so, till they are twenty if they are not stricktly watch'd', and the answer was for their whole time to be 'imploy'd in usefull & various applications', for they 'must be doing', and the 'great art is to fix what it should be'.[12]

Being older, Anne Egerton continued to take lessons with Jane Pattison, but both she and Diana would be pleased to have Johnny in their lives. Sarah was by turns delighted and infuriated with this grandson, sending him from the room when he was naughty, only to collapse into laughter when he vaulted in again through a window. She copied from *Ecclesiasticus*: 'A horse not broken becometh headstrong', and 'a child left to himself will be wilful', blaming Johnny's high spirits on his sister Anne Spencer's influence. La Vie agreed with her that 'We are all animals of imitation from the cradle till our judgement is formed', and that 'bad company was worse than the plague to young persons'. When old enough, Johnny joined his brother at school, Charles writing to his grandmother:

Madam,
I have the honour to aquaint Your Grace that my Brother John and I are removed from Chelsea to a School at Hampstead, which we like much better, we humbly beg leave to present our Duty to our Grandpapa, and our service to sister Diana, and to Lady Anne Egerton. I am with the most profound respekt, Madam, your Grace's Most Dutiful Grand-Son Charles Spencer.[13]

Throughout that year Mary Cairnes spent time with Sarah's granddaughters, meanwhile closely observing the hostility that was growing between the duchess and her daughters. Diana and cousin Anne must have observed this too, but were too strictly trained to make comment. While Mary recognised that there 'must always be faults on both sides', she had 'seen such behaviour' from Henrietta, Lady Godolphin and the Duchess of Montagu towards their mother 'that young as I was it has shock'd me'. When they called at Marlborough House it was clearly to see their father rather than their mother, and though the Duchess of Montagu had the grace to curtsey and speak a few words to Sarah, 'the other did neither'. When Mary Cairnes and her mother were at Windsor Lodge in the summer, Sarah fell ill, and although Henrietta was staying in the little park near by, there was no 'how d'ye' from her. On the family's return to Marlborough House, Sarah grew worse, 'had an appearance of the gout, put on a poultice, was dangerously ill, kept to her bed'; and when she did recover, it was to be carried into her dressing-room 'to lye on a couch all day'. Mary recalled how:

> In this situation one evening the door opened & Lady Godolphin was named. She dropt a curtsey just at the door & said rather in a low voice 'I hope you are better.' It might have been anybody but the old Duchess, supposing it was her daughter, replied, what is it that you say? I do not hear you. The other *d'un ton acariâtre* & looking like a fury repeated I hope you are better. Yes I think I am [Sarah said], and so the conversation ended.

Henrietta went to sit by her father, and 'never went near the D[uche]ss'. Diana and her cousin were present during this interchange, and in a short time word came that 'Mr Firis the dancing master was in the next room, and so Lady Anne Egerton, Lady Dy. Spencer & your humble servant went to dance . . .'[14]

Mr Firis charged two guineas a month for Diana's dancing lessons, plus twelve shillings and sixpence for 'the hourboy' (oboe).[15] When the cousins and their friend skipped away to dance, the Duke of Marlborough went with them for 'he loved to watch', Henrietta following after him. After she had watched for a time, Henrietta went 'quite away', presumably without bidding her mother goodbye. All this after a 'summers absence, a dangerous illness', the duchess 'a parent [and] an old person centred in one', and Henri-etta 'dropping a curtsey at the door like a milliners' prentice with a band box that is afraid of going near a great lady'. It was all very shocking to Mary Cairnes, and she noticed that the aunts talked a great deal to her own mother, 'who had not the honour of being acquainted with them', only to show 'they did not speak to their mother'. She remembered how 'the Duchess us'd to say she had made them all such great Ladies that it had turned their heads'.[16]

Then came news that Diana's father was to remarry. The earl explained how he needed a woman to be 'a companion' to him, and to 'manage the concerns of his family in order to lesson his expenses', for which, Sarah observed, 'he chose a girl of fifteen'. The duchess thought 'no body could imagine those ends could be answered by one of Mrs Tichborne's age and that I should think the conversation of such a one could not be agreeable to him; and that it was marrying a kitten'. And how 'very odd', she added sarcastically, 'for a wise man of forty-five to come out of his library to play with puss!'[17]

As the niece of Baron Ferrard of Beaulieu, Diana's stepmother Judith Titchborne was not entirely devoid of graces. Seeing her at the King's Birthday, Mrs Pendarves described her as 'very fine & very genteel', and wearing a gown of 'the finest pale blue and pink, very richly flowered in a running pattern of silver frosted and tissue with a little white'. She was 'very pretty, tall, and of a good figure', and 'very sensible and agreeable, though so shy and bashful that she by no means did herself justice'.[18]

Sarah saw Judith as a 'woman unknown, without a shilling to her name', who would produce a brood of children that would be 'beggars with titles of lords & ladies – that can have nothing but what he robs his former children of'. For once her daughter the Duchess of Montagu agreed with her, saying, 'I hope, nay must think, he will be persuaded by my dear mother to settle what he can upon his children – the others are at least nothing to us . . .' The earl married in December 1717, having agreed to make settlements on his children, and also to let Sarah take care of Charles and Johnny. Once this was settled, he proceeded to give proof of his virility by producing two sons and one daughter in rapid succession.[19]

Although Diana was not living with her sister Anne, since their half-sister Frances had married and left home, cousin Charlotte was staying at Sunderland House, and they called often at Marlborough House to 'amuse the Duke'. When a masked ball was organised at the King's Theatre in the Haymarket, Lady Anne told her grandmother how a great many people going to the masquerade would like to 'come first to show themselves to her if she liked it'. Sarah, believing 'their comical dress might divert the Duke of Marlborough, as well as the young people', agreed. In they came in their colourful and amusing costumes, one of them dressed as a friar, who sat beside Sarah and offered her some advice. The duchess, ready to join in the spirit of the occasion, prepared herself to listen. The 'friar' said earnestly that he wondered at her agreeing to see the masqueraders, since her 'enemies might come as well as her friends', to which Sarah asked, 'Who are my enemies?' The 'friar' answered, 'The Duchess of Montagu or my Lady Godolphin may come, and not knowing them you may give them a cup of tea, or a dish of coffee . . .' As there 'were several people around that heard it', Sarah left the 'friar' without a word. It was one thing for her to complain of her daughters' behaviour, quite another for a complete stranger to voice his opinion. She suspected the friar was her business manager Craggs's son, who would one day become Secretary of State, but word came just then 'that the children were dancing, which the Duke of Marlborough loved to see'.[20]

Sarah was busy making curtains and covers for Blenheim Palace when a messenger came to Windsor Lodge telling her that the newly wed Duchess of Newcastle had taken ill 'from a sore throat coming over the water at four in the morning from Hampton Court', and would 'not live an hour'. Dropping needle and thread, and leaving her small granddaughters to care for 'Papa Duke', Sarah drove pell-mell in her coach to Claremont. Here she found the Duke of Newcastle 'weeping very much and really in so much sorrow' that she believed 'there was no hopes of her [Harriet's] life'. One of the doctors who attended the young duchess was Dr Mead, whom Sarah had accused of murdering her daughter Sunderland, and to whom she now refused to speak. Another doctor was Sir Hans Sloane, who had attended Queen Anne. Sloane claimed he was happy with Harriet's progress, commenting that she had no 'heat in her flesh [and] that something had broak in her throat', and though her hands were moist, she 'had sweat'. It was true that she had been 'a little light headed by fitts', but this had 'quite gone upon a Glister working very well'. When Sarah begged to be allowed to see her, she was denied entry to her room, and when she asked the Duke of Newcastle to go to her, he refused, fearing that Harriet would be obliged to talk to him, and that would do 'prejudice to her'. This seemed inhuman behaviour to Sarah, but reasoning that it was unlikely that 'one of seventeen could dye of such a distemper when blooded and the right things applyd to her', she left and drove home. Was this the time the seven-year-old Diana eagerly awaited her return, tending her grandfather in her absence, and obliged to go to bed before she arrived, left a note for her? It read:

Dear Mama,

I hope you are Come Very Safe. I longed all Day to see you papa eat & drunk very Well to Day at Dinner I drank your Health to day in Wine if I mite have had more I would have Drunk it fifty times . . . from Your Dutyfull daughter

Diana Spencer[21]

Time was spent at Althorp during the spring of 1719, Diana getting to know her new stepmother, and Lady Anne Egerton accompanied her there. The move to Blenheim Palace was meanwhile eagerly anticipated by the Marlboroughs' two little granddaughters, but only weeks before they were due to move in, tragedy struck. Lady Anne Egerton's fifteen-year-old brother Lord Brackley died of smallpox at Eton. Sarah had complained earlier of his apparent ill health, her Montagu daughter writing to say she was 'mightily concerned at his looking so ill' and would be 'sure to let my lord Bridgewater know it'. The concern of the two duchesses was to no avail, however, the boy's father, the Earl of Bridgwater, scarcely able to speak of his grief, writing only briefly to thank Sarah for her 'favours'. A Mrs Carter who had cared for the boy apologised for not describing his death in more detail, and on the back of her letter Sarah wrote scathingly: 'on the death of Lord Brackley, who died for want of common care'.

Eton School (as it was then called) was almost within walking distance of Windsor Lodge, and Sarah recalled how when Diana's brother Charles contracted smallpox at Hampstead school, she had rushed to his bedside, wrapped him in a blanket, and brought him to Marlborough House in her coach. Her 'strengthening cordials' and unstinted care may not have spared him pain but secured him an unblemished recovery. If only she had had the same power with Brackley! Anxious lest Johnny Spencer should fall sick of the disease, she wrote of her fears to his father, Sunderland assuring her that if 'poor little John happens to have the small pox (& which I wish he had when his brother had) or any other ail – he shall be entirely under your direction'.[22]

The family moved into Blenheim Palace in the summer. The painters were still at work in the State Apartments on the north side of the building, but the east wing was ready to receive them. The stairs, passageways, rooms, ceilings, were beautifully decorated, but were of more human proportions than the vast State Apartments, Diana sharing a bedroom with her cousin Anne. The windows and huge four-poster bed were hung with spotted curtains, the bed covered with a spotted calico quilt, edged with a pretty chintz border. Jane Pattison slept on a couch at the foot of the children's bed, and during the day prepared light meals for them, a 'gilt salt, two knives, forks and spoons' delivered into her hands for the use of 'ye Young Ladies' when they were at Althorp. There were also 'egg kettles', lamp and plates, patty pans, a cheese toaster and a 'large soup dish' provided for them. There was a walk-in closet, this and the bedroom (possibly) the two rooms shown above the 'little wood stairs' over 'Lady Kerns' room in Vanbrugh's plan, behind which was the children's schoolroom.[23]

Diana must have been delighted to see more of her sister Anne who was allocated a splendid apartment at the palace, Sarah hoping she would like the bed hangings chosen for her, of 'sprigg'd Indian calico with a border of striped green, red, and white', the window curtains of pretty 'white birds-eye dimetty'. She believed she had been kind to Lady Anne, saying she 'was welcome to my house either in Town or Country', and in the previous summer Anne had risen early to visit 'Dear little Dye' at Windsor Lodge. Her grandmother had sat with her on a bench in the garden discussing her future, observing that she was 'followed' by Henry Pelham. This was a younger brother of the Duke of Newcastle, for which reason (Sarah assumed) Anne said she had 'no thoughts of him'. It was not for Anne to know that one day Henry Pelham would become Prime Minister. Sarah put Anne's refusal down to her 'great passion for money even as a child', but in the end agreed to let her settle for William Bateman, heir to a rich banker. This was Sir James Bateman, late Lord Mayor of London, who had died in the previous year. Sarah found William's fortune not so good 'as the town reported', but considered it 'very well considering the plainness of [Anne's] person'. Anne's face and lips were narrow, accentuating her large nose; her lashes were pale, but her figure was slender and graceful, her flaxen hair falling lightly to her shoulders. She considered herself intelligent, a 'woman of parts'.[24]

Diana's father was with the king in Hanover when the Marlboroughs and their little family moved into Blenheim Palace, leaving Sarah to arrange Lady Anne's marriage. The duchess was careful to keep him informed of the arrangements she made, the earl writing that if she found Bateman 'a man of understanding', and 'Lady Anne herself dos nott dislike him', whatever she 'thought right in that' he would too. Anne had cried 'mightily' when William was ill, and her father agreed that it was 'a good sign when people mend upon aquaintance'.[25]

Diana celebrated her ninth birthday at the palace, riding with her sister and cousins in the grounds 'from morning till night'. The Marlboroughs drove together in a specially designed carriage for two, pulled by a 'safe horse'. Although they enjoyed separate apartments on the ground floor, they were interlinked. The duke's bedroom led into his 'Grand Cabinet' where he would (were he well enough) meet important visitors to discuss military procedure, and from his windows look out onto his Military Garden, designed by Vanbrugh and planted by Wise. The duke was carried along its walks in his chair on poles as if reviewing his troops. Sarah's favourite Bow Window room (the only room she liked since she had designed it herself) overlooked her flower garden, already a blaze of colour. It was in the Bow Window room that friends and family gathered to play cards and sing ballads, and were to put on a play.

Diana's sister was now sixteen, her cousin Lady Charlotte McCarthy eighteen, the two staying together at the palace. Although Charlotte was not Sarah's blood relation, the duchess had taken a fancy to her and was familiar with her family history. The girl's mother, Lady Elizabeth Spencer (the sister of Diana's father), had been married to the Earl of Clancarty when she was only thirteen, he sixteen, and the two parted immediately after the ceremony, leaving the marriage unconsummated. This had been a heartless move on the part of the girl's father (Robert, 2nd Earl of Sunderland) to gain possession of the Clancarty estate. Clancarty was sent home to his estate in Ireland where he became a Catholic convert, and during the Great Rebellion was a Jacobite rebel; he received James II at Kinsale, becoming his lord-of-the-bedchamber and colonel of the 4th regiment of foot. After a spell in the Tower following the capitulation of Cork, he escaped, leaving his wig on a head-shaped block in his bed with a note saying: 'This block must answer for me.' He then rejoined his regiment in France, but after James's army was disbanded, he returned penniless to England, making his way to the home of his wife's parents. This was the house in St James's Square then occupied by Robert the 2nd Earl of Sunderland and his wife, and daughter Elizabeth.

Elizabeth was now twenty-eight years old, 'her beauty youth and happiness gone to waste'. As her parents were at Althorp, Clancarty, using all his Irish charm (his castle home was Blarney), had little trouble easing himself into his wife's bed. A house servant warned her brother Lord Spencer (the man to become Diana's father), who was then living with his first wife in Piccadilly. Spencer, whose passions were easily roused, stormed his sister's bedroom with a posse of soldiers, dragging Clancarty off to jail. Elizabeth followed in tears, and with the help of her family and friends (including Sarah) appealed to King William. William, whose Queen Mary was now dead, refused to reinstate Clancarty's lands, but offered them each a pension on condition they left England for ever. The couple settled in Hamburg on an island on the Elbe, where Charlotte and her brothers and sisters were born. After Elizabeth's death the children, as we know, were sent to their Spencer grandmother in England, Charlotte's father remaining in exile. All this lent an aura of romance and sensuality to Charlotte, and when a rumour reached Sarah that the girl had married her cousin Robert, Lord Spencer, she flew into a panic. She wrote at once to Diana's brother, who was now at Utrecht enjoying the Grand Tour, demanding the truth of the matter. The indignant seventeen-year-old replied:

> I am extremely sorry to hear by My Dear Grandmama's letter which I receiv'd to day, that she should be put in any pain upon my account by so groundless and ill-natur'd a report as that of my being married to Lady Charlotte Maccartie. I assure my dear Grandmama that there is not the least ground for that report, but that it is as false and malicious a lye as could be invented. I hope my Dear Grandmama will be satisfy'd of the truth of what I say . . .[26]

Sarah adored this golden-haired grandson who signed himself his 'Dear Grandmama's most dutiful Son', and chose to believe him. Mary Cairnes declared Spencer to be not only the duchess's 'passion', but the passion 'of every person that ever saw him'. Blessed with his mother's looks, he was also a leader of fashion, Mary describing him as the very 'pattern on which the Youth of England dresst themselves'. His pearly white teeth, his soft complexion, and deep blue eyes, might have proved a temptation to Charlotte, and Sarah was doubtless keeping a close eye on her at the palace.[27]

On the back of a poem in Charlotte's hand Sarah wrote: 'Imitated by – Lady Char: Maccarty in a very little time after my shewing her Sir Sam Garths.' Garth had been Marlborough's doctor and physician-in-ordinary to the king, and had died that January. He was a known poet. His poem 'imitated' by Lady Charlotte ends with the verse:

Let Nature lye dissolved in night,
The powerfull sun forbear to rise.
The Spacious world needs want no Light,
'Twill flow from Lady Marlborough's eyes.

It is uncertain whether this was a parody of an actual poem by Garth, or another written in his style, but as Charlotte's name was to be linked with those of Ovid, Congreve and Sappho after her death, she obviously had poetic leanings. She was artistic in other ways too, counted as a 'Woman of great merit with whom I lived in much intimacy' by the literary blue stocking, Lady Mary Wortley Montagu. Just now Charlotte needed a guardian and friend, and Sarah took her under her wing.[28]

As well as riding in the grounds, the granddaughters and their cousin and friend Mary Cairnes breathed in the scent of lavender, roses, jasmine, honey-suckle, pinks, rosemary and lilies that grew in Sarah's garden, and the sharp scent of oranges from the Orangery, out of which little trees in tubs were trundled to blossom and fruit in the sun. The duke's garden would make a bracing walk for the young people, even under tightly laced hooped skirts. Steps led up to the Great Parterre, a thick wall forming a hexagon, with a round bastion at each corner, from where breathtaking views were had across to Bladon. Within its walls, the garden represented a fortified town. Sandy paths led through low box, yew and holly trees, and there were also summer houses, alcoves, fountains and 'everything that can render the place agreeable'. In warm weather the young people were able to rest here and learn their lines for the play they planned to put on to celebrate the Duke of Marlborough at last taking possession of his 'castle'. Around them figs ripened on the bastion walls, and sunshine flecked the grassy paths running under green espalier walks. The young ladies in their shimmering gowns could check the time at a sundial, or listen for the Townsend Tower clock.

The play the young people were to perform for the duke was *All For Love* by Dryden, a version of Shakespeare's *Antony and Cleopatra*. On the day of the performance the participants were draped in robes made from the rich brocades and velvets left over from the curtains and covers for the palace, and were decked with 'Jewels . . . in plenty'. Sarah's Bow Window (framed by Grinling Gibbons's elegantly carved pillars) made an ideal 'stage'. 'Great screens' were painted for scene changes, perhaps assisted by the artists at work in the north wing. There was evidence of type-casting, the sensual

Charlotte playing the fateful Cleopatra, and Sarah's page Captain Humphrey Fish, Mark Antony. For the performance Fish wore Marlborough's diamond-hilted sword, which had been presented to the duke by the Emperor of Austria in recognition of his greatest victory. But when Charlotte and Fish were discovered displaying too much ardency during rehearsal, Sarah went through the script and 'scratched out the most amorous speeches'. This may have had more than the required effect, Sir Richard Steele (newsprint publisher, playwright, and supervisor of the Drury Lane theatre) commenting to Bishop Hoadly (who wrote the prologue), 'I doubt Fish is flesh!'[29]

Mary Cairnes played the High Priest Serapion, wearing an exquisitely embroidered surplice which was designed for the chapel, it being 'no sacrilege' as the chapel was not yet consecrated. Marie La Vie played the eunuch Alexas, and Diana's sister Mark Antony's embittered wife Octavia. Diana and cousin Lady Anne Egerton must have delighted in playing Octavia's small daughters, the air surely charged as the betrayed wife pushed Agrippina and Antonia toward their faithless father, bidding them:

> . . . Go to him children, go;
> Kneel to him, take him by the hand, speak to him,
> For you may speak, & he may own you too,
> Without a blush; and so he cannot all
> His children. Go, I say, and pull him to me,
> And pull him to yourselves from that bad woman,
> You Agrippina, hang upon his arms;
> And you Antonia, clasp about his waist:
> If he will shake you off, if he will dash you
> Against the pavement, you must bear it, children,
> For you are mine, and I was born to suffer.

The sound of Diana and Anne shrieking their one line 'Father!' must surely have brought down the house.[30]

The Duke of Marlborough was so moved by the performance that he asked for it to be played two more times. Sadly Diana's brothers were not present, being at school, and their father was in Hanover with the king. The earl wrote to Sarah: 'I am mighty glad to hear the Duke of Marlborough has

been well all this Summer at Blenheim, & that he has had so much satisfaction in seeing it made habitable', and he prayed to God he might live long
'to enjoy it'. He was also glad that the 'Dear children' were well, and those
'at Hampstead I hear are so too'. He ended by wishing he had 'the happiness of being with you at Blenheim', and 'to have seen the play acted . . .'[31]

Diana's grandmother was now queen of her castle, riding with her 'king'
in their chariot, and could rightly call herself 'princess'. She told her grandchildren and Mary Cairnes how the Emperor Leopold of Austria had
presented their grandfather not only with the diamond-hilted sword but
also with the principality of Mindelheim in Bavaria. The principality had
since been restored to Bavaria in accordance with the Peace Treaty, but the
title remained with the Marlboroughs, as it does to this day. Although Sarah
professed not to care a jot for titles, her story struck a spark with Diana.
When again parted from her grandmother for a short time, she addressed a
letter to 'Her Royal Highness the Princess of Mindleheim at her Villa near
Windsor', and continued:

> Dear Mama,
> I love you better than anybody in ye world and shall always do so for
> if I did not I should be very ungratefull. I hope both papa Duke & you
> are very well for I am sure no body wishes them so well as your
> > Most Duttyfull Daughter
> > > D Spencer

And in a postscript:

> I have so many obligations to my dear grandmama that I dont know
> which way to show my thankfullness and express my gratitude.[32]

CHAPTER FIVE

A Wedding and Two Funerals

'Dye I thank god is well . . .'

In the spring of 1720 Diana's sister Anne married William Bateman at Blenheim Palace, and after the ceremony (which was conducted by special licence), and they were 'put to bed together', the young couple drove to London to spend the first part of their honeymoon at their town house in Soho. This magnificent mansion had been built for the Duke of Monmouth, Charles II's illegitimate son, Bateman's father having bought it from the duke's widow following his decapitation on Tower Hill after the Great Rebellion. Sir James had completed the building, and added stables to it. After a week or two making and receiving courtesy calls here, the couple spent time at their hunting lodge at Totteridge, celebrating their nuptials with servants and neighbours, before setting off for their country seat of Shobdon in Herefordshire. As soon as they arrived here the bride wrote dutifully to her grandmother:

Dear Grandmama,
We are at last after a very tedious journey safely arrived at Shobdon. I was so tired the day I came here & it has been such very bad weather all to day, that I have hardly been out of doors, so can give you no manner of account of anything but the house. The partition that you took notice of in the plan, I find pull'd down as several others are to be very soon, which will make the house considerable deal better, indeed every thing withinside of the house must be new done, as painting & new wainscoating, most of the rooms, & cieling them, & all the floors in general to be new laid, and the house to be new sash'd, and after all this to be furnish'd that there really is nothing in the world done yet but the walls. The situation is extream good & the prospect is the finest four ways that it is possible to imagine. One is mighty apt to be partial to anything that is ones own but I think it is as pleasant a place as much as I have seen of it as ever I saw.

Anne had brought Lady Anne Egerton with her, for whose company she thanked her grandmother, 'for she is so good humoured & so easy that she makes every body cheerful''. Her husband had sent a gift of beef and mutton to Blenheim, which she hoped would 'be as good as ours is here which he says is the best in the world'.[1]

Prior to the wedding Sarah had quarrelled with Diana's father, having threatened to send 'little Di' back to him if he refused to make a proper settlement on his children, and withheld the full marriage portion she had formerly promised Anne, offering only half the sum. To raise the needed balance, Sunderland had meant to sell off his fast-rising South Sea stock, putting off the wedding as long as he could in hope of a better price.[2]

One day after Anne wrote her letter, the Marlboroughs visited Richmond Palace Lodge, the summer residence of the Prince and Princess of Wales, taking Lady Charlotte McCarthy with them. The rival royal courts of St James's and Leicester House had become reconciled to each other at last, which meant the Marlboroughs were able to accept this invitation without offending the king. Sarah was touched by the princess's reception of her, saying how very kind she was 'to the Duke of Marlborough and poor me', and when the party was about to leave, the princess had called Lady Charlotte back, bidding her 'hold up her head' – something Sarah said she was always telling her about. Sarah was now busy arranging a match between her and Lieutenant-Colonel John West, verderer of Windsor Park, and heir to Baron De La Warr.[3]

On 16 August Diana was again at Blenheim with her grandparents, a letter arriving from her father to remind Sarah of a promise she had made to have Johnny and Charles to stay:

Your Grace sometime since was so good as to tell me that you would have my two little boys come to you at Blenheim when they break up school. They have sent me word that will be tomorrow Se'nnight. If you would please therefore to lett me know yr commands, when you would have them come I will order my Steward Hooker to go with them, to see them safe there, and when they have staid there as long as you would have them, he shall go again to bring them away, and carry them to Eaton which place I think better for them now, they being grown to big for the school at Hampstead. Their brother dear Lord Spencer did just the same, & it succeeded very well with him.[4]

Lime trees had been planted about the ninepin alley where the boys would play, and the gardeners had rammed and rolled the bowling green in preparation for the general influx of summer visitors. As before, Diana would ride and play between schoolwork, joined by cousin Anne when she returned from Shobdon. Gambling being a staple preoccupation of the leisured eighteenth-century aristocracy, there were endless games of cards for the grown-ups, and between informing Sarah of his boys' intended visit, Diana's father referred often to South Sea Stock. The words 'South Sea' echoed along the stone passages of the palace, wafting up the marble staircases, and drifting across the clipped box hedges of the duke's and duchess's private gardens.

As First Lord of the Treasury, Diana's father was at the peak of his career as Prime Minister (a name not in common use till Walpole's 'reign'), and in a position to write to Sarah: 'I have sent Mr Knight the names your Grace sent me and directions to take care of them if there is to be another subscription.' Mr Knight was Cashier of the South Sea Company, which had ostensibly dealt in the slave trade, and in a bid to compete with the Bank of England had taken over much of the National Debt. Sunderland (with other senior government members) was bribed with free grants of stock to secure his compliance in the dubious methods used to promote the scheme, the success of which depended on the stock's being promoted to an artificial height. As the market soared, there was a public rush to subscribe, Sunderland writing to Sarah: 'If there be another Subscription, as I believe there will, I shall take care the Duke of Marlborough's persons, shall be in, as he desires.'[5]

Countrywide, rich, and not so rich, people were investing in South Sea stock. As it was perceived to be approved by the royal family as well as the ministry, many of those who had formerly put their trust in safe government annuities, were exchanging them for South Sea stock. Stock had risen to 128 in January, and in March stood at 330 (when Sunderland was obliged to sell some to finance his daughter's marriage). By May it had risen to 550, and when in June it rose to 890, Sarah became suspicious of ever rising prices from a company whose profits were so pitiful, and sold out, advising her duke to do the same. The £30,000 worth of stock she had purchased in 1717 brought her a profit of £100,000, and when stock rose to 1000 in August she was convinced the scheme must end in disaster.

Letters from family and friends continued to arrive at Blenheim Palace asking Marlborough to use his influence to buy stock, Charlotte McCarthy and her brother Justin among the many to be caught up in the craze.

Though Sarah was willing to lend money for the purpose to those she trusted, she continued to speak out loudly against the scheme. Diana's father was meanwhile promising to have 'ten thousand more subscription reserv'd for such as yr Grace shall send the names of', while sending further information regarding his sons' visit:

> My two little boys come home from school on friday morning so that I shall be sure according to your orders to send them on Saturday on their way to Blenheim. They shall set out in the morning, so that they will be with yr Grace on Sunday. You will please to lett Mr Hooker know when they shall go to Eaton that he may take care of it as you shall order.

And he added in a postscript:

> I am very glad to hear Ld Marlborough continues so well & that Dear little Dye is to[o].[6]

As Eton was just across the little wooden bridge from Windsor, Sarah was almost sure to approve of Diana's brothers being sent there. She had heard 'fault found with Hampstead', and 'Eton commended', and if her grandsons were sent there she would 'have opertunitys of seeing them oftener then at any school'. She feared Eton might not be 'a wholesome place', however, since Lady Anne Egerton's brother Brackley died there, begging Sunderland to arrange things so that if Johnny caught smallpox 'hee may not bee murderd as poor dear Ld Barkely [sic] was', and went on to describe his being 'blooded & removed after the smallpox was on & had not the least cordial to support such an extremity'. Charles was over that 'terrible distemper', but 'Poor little John has not had it', and if Sarah was at Windsor he 'may as easyly bee brought to me as his brother was to London'. As to Windsor Lodge, Sarah found it 'a thousand times more agreeable than Blenheim', and intended to 'pass the greatest part of my life there'.[7]

The Earl of Sunderland was on a high, his script careering across the gilt-edged pages he sent Sarah, resembling a string of runaway horses, each word linked to the other. As stock rose so his handwriting sped faster, but in September, when stock that stood at 1000 fell to 150, he was obliged to draw in his reins.

Mr Knight fled to the Continent, taking valuable South Sea evidence with him. Holders of stock countrywide flocked to London to besiege the South

Sea Company offices, finding the 'disproportion between paper promises and the coin wherein to pay' too great. Many investors were reduced to beggary, some committing suicide. A cry of resentment went up, not only against the directors of the company, but against the Treasury, of which Diana's father was head. The government, the king and the king's mistresses were all more or less deeply involved, as were the Prince and Princess of Wales. Sarah continued to speak out against the scheme, saying she had always been 'mighty averse' to it, and hoped the directors would be punished. King George, on a visit to Hanover, was called home. Sunderland looked on helplessly as stock became worthless.

Sarah meanwhile, having found a husband for Charlotte, was now searching for a suitable mate for Lady Anne Egerton. The child would be fourteen in December, a pretty girl with red cheeks and the deep blue eyes and black curls of her grandfather. For her birthday Sarah had given her a masked ball at Marlborough House, with forty young guests invited; and in the summer James Bridges, aged seventeen, found himself at an impromptu ball at Blenheim Palace. James, his title Marquis of Carnarvon, was heir to the Duke of Chandos, and studying at nearby Oxford. Sarah wrote to her friend Mrs Boscawen:

Saturday last the D: of Shandows [sic] son dined here and wee had a sort of a ball with a scraping fiddle which kept him till late at night. The Town has in this particular been good to me in giving this young man for one of my grandchildren, but I doubt the Duke of S: does not think of it, for I never heard of it from him, but I must own I should like it extreamly, for I never in my life saw a young man of 17, that is yet at Oxford, & before that only at school, so very well behaved, & so promising, & like him so prodigiously that if his father should think of my little children I should think I could not make a better use of my own money than to contribute towards such a match.

Lady Anne was 'within three years of my Lord Car[narvon]', and looked to have ten thousand pounds her father must give her 'besides what the Duke of Marl[borough] may add to it', and in Sarah's opinion, a 'better natural child was never born'.[8]

Carnarvon's father, Chandos, had made his enormous fortune during Marlborough's wars as Paymaster General of the Forces, and now lived in stupendous style at Cannons, his villa at Edgware, described as the 'wonder of England'. Handel was at work on his 'Chandos' anthems here, as well as composing his first English oratorio *Esther*. Guests and family were entertained by his choir at dinner, waited on by a hundred and twenty servants. Should Anne marry Carnarvon, she could look forward to a life of tremendous style. At the end of May the Duke of Chandos wrote to Sarah:

> There is nothing I have been more desirous of, for L[or]d Carnarvon, than ye gratyfying his inclinations, by procuring him an acceptable match as is in my power to make him, to this Young Lady, of whose person & temper he hath received so just an impression.[9]

South Sea stock had meanwhile tumbled to 124, Chandos being one of the many to suffer acute losses, making Anne Egerton's fortune appear to him at least as attractive as her 'person & temper'. Diana's father stood in fear of prosecution, furious at Sarah's outspoken criticism of the South Sea Company, and in order to put a stop to it invited the Duke of Marlborough to his London house. The earl's library extension had been completed, stretching almost the length of his garden, and was two stories high. A gallery ran round the inside of it, the whole lit by large sash windows, and described as the finest in Europe 'for Disposition and books'. It may have been here that Sunderland, in a 'very mad fit', accused Sarah of remitting a great sum of money to the Pretender during the 'last fright of a Scotch invasion', telling Marlborough that the king knew it, and he, Sunderland, could prove it. As Head of the Secret Service Money, this was something Sunderland might indeed know, were it true, perhaps hinting at Marlborough's own advance of money to the Pretender. Certainly the Duke of Marlborough was deeply disturbed by the earl's accusations.

When the duke returned to Marlborough House, he looked 'half dead', Sarah dismissing her card-playing friends in order to dose him with 'a great glass of strong wine and toast'. She sat 'up with him two or three hours' that night, administering 'a double dose of Sir Walter Rawleigh's cordial' while gathering from his incoherent speech that she was accused of some heinous crime.[10]

Next day Sarah asked Diana's friend's mother, Lady Cairnes, to accompany her to the king's 'drawingroom', and since she was herself short-sighted, asked her to observe the king's face 'very closely'. Sarah then sidled up to the king's mistress Schulenberg (by now promoted to Duchess of Kendal), asking her if she would obtain for her 'a very short audience of His Majesty'. The duchess promised she would try, and on her return to Marlborough House Sarah wrote a letter to the king protesting her innocence, and afterwards asked Diana's governess La Vie to read it very 'attentively', and to 'enter into the spirit of it', and 'put it into proper french'.[11]

An audience was granted Sarah, and she bustled into the royal presence. Here she found the Duchess of Kendal with the king, who 'looked very good-natured'. As neither the king nor Sarah spoke the other's language well, Kendal offered to translate for them, but Sarah refused to accept her offer, handing her instead her translated letter to the king. She then made her curtsey and withdrew.[12]

The king's reply was to assure Sarah that whatever he might have been told on her account, he would always judge her and her husband 'by the behaviour of each in regard to his service', and prayed God to preserve her in all happiness. Sarah felt dismissed and humiliated by this, believing Sunderland was behind it, and promptly sent the king another letter. This was likewise courteously answered, her concerns dismissed.

Diana's father was to be hauled over the coals by a House of Commons committee, along with other chief ministers and directors of the South Sea Company. Faced with the prospect of a period in the Tower, and his lands confiscated, Sunderland allowed Walpole to defend him. This Walpole did stoutly, saving the earl from a fate worse than death, but taking for himself Sunderland's high office at the Treasury by way of reward. Although Sunderland had been reprieved, and made Groom of the Stole, he must now pin his hopes for preferment on the coming elections.

Among Sarah's card-playing friends was Lady Burlington, Diana's onetime neighbour in Piccadilly. Other friends included Lady Cairnes, Miss La Vie, the king's mistress Kielmansegge (now Countess of Darlington) and Lady Mary Wortley Montagu. The last three were here to be as it were 'in the clouds together', Burlington and Cairnes 'to talk sense with'. As there was a severe outbreak of smallpox in London at the time, Wortley Montagu (just returned from Constantinople) had a fine opportunity to air her observations on how Turkish women dealt with the disease. She told how the Turkish children were gathered together for the purpose of 'engraftment', a little 'good smallpox' taken from a known sufferer and applied to the children by means of a needle. The incision was then bound with leaves till it 'took', and after three days of fever the children were up and well again, immune from further attacks. So convinced was Wortley Montagu of its success that she had her own son 'engrafted', with total success. On her return to England she had doctors perform the same operation on her small daughter, and after two days the doctors witnessed the child playing about her room 'in her nightcap' with the smallpox 'raised upon her', but perfectly well. The Prince and Princess of Wales were so impressed by the experiment that they had it tested on volunteer prisoners, and when it succeeded the prisoners were set free. The poor children of the parish were the next guinea pigs, and again engrafted with total success. Pleased with the results, the royal pair had the two youngest of their little princesses engrafted (Princess Anne had had smallpox already), as well as their latest born Prince William. So it was that William survived to become a smooth-faced 'Butcher Cumberland'.[13]

For all this, Diana fell ill with smallpox in 1721, but whether from infection by the prevailing disease, or by use of the experiment, is uncertain. Sarah as we know disliked doctors, priding herself on her own nursing skills, putting her trust in Sir Walter 'Rawliegh's' cordial. Yet when Diana's aunt, the Duchess of Montagu, called at Marlborough House, she asked if 'Lady Dye was well Though She was in a Night Cap' – words redolent of Wortley Montagu's description of her own daughter's recovery. A letter sent to Sarah after Diana's recovery, though positive, remains ambiguous as to the cause:

> I rejoyce when I reflect your Grace has no fears for Lady Die. That cruel Disease has left her both her life & Beauty; which is featuring two points. Tho' there are many Doors to Death, yet ye small pox, is ye Door that opens ye most, & that being Bar[re]d is a great security.

Diana's half-brother William (her stepmother Judith's child), aged two and a half, was one of two to die from the experiment, and his little sister Margaret was buried in the same month. As the experiment became popular, less care was taken in sterilising the instruments, leading to more children dying, and the practice falling into disuse. Not until the discovery of 'cow-pox' was inoculation to be used again.[14]

The South Sea Bubble crisis was meanwhile causing other related deaths. The Secretary of State, James Stanhope, died of 'apoplexy' after making a speech in his own defence in the House of Lords; and Sarah's old business manager Craggs died from an overdose of laudanum following his South Sea losses and the death of his son from smallpox. Rumour had it that the younger Craggs died not from smallpox but from a 'great debauch' at the

Duke of Newcastle's house, where 'tokay, champagne, visney and barba water' was drunk for thirteen hours together.[15]

On 22 April 1722, Diana's father, too, lay dead. So sudden and unexpected was his death that an inquest was ordered into the cause, and death by poison suspected. As well as Walpole and Townshend wanting him out of the running for the elections, in his capacity as Head of the Secret Service Money, Sunderland had investigated the activities of the Jacobite sympathiser, Bishop Atterbury, either of whom might welcome his demise. Sunderland had died surrounded by members of his family, his wife Judith, her sister Margaret Pultney, and his daughter Frances Lady Morpeth. Margaret and Frances sent at once for their husbands, Daniel Pultney arriving first, followed by Lord Carteret, the Secretary of State, Townshend and the Duke of Newcastle following in the rear. Between them they gathered up the earl's papers, bundling them together in one room. When Frances's husband Morpeth arrived after the others he found these men locking the doors and putting their seals on them in order to stop unauthorised persons entering. It was Newcastle who thought to send the late earl's steward Hooker to Marlborough House.

The Marlboroughs were at dinner when Hooker was announced, Sarah's first thought on hearing of the death being for Diana's elder brother Robert, who was still away on the Grand Tour, cut off from any knowledge of his father's death, unaware that he was now 4th Earl of Sunderland. On his behalf Sarah asked that her own and the Duke of Marlborough's seals be added to those of the ministers on the doors, since 'it might be very dangerous to leave things of consequence without securing them'.[16]

Diana's grandmother was surprised to learn later that the government ministers were to investigate the earl's papers since he was 'only Groom of the Stole'. Pultney, who was 'deep in the Earl's secrets', told her there was to be a council of the king's ministers that afternoon, which would certainly 'make a big noise'. Sarah asked him to inform the ministers that while she and other members of the family would comply with 'anything reasonable', they should have 'some person in the room representing the Duke of Marlborough to secure the fortune from any loss'. After this she ordered Hooker to stand guard at the sealed doors, and to let no one through them without first informing herself and the duke.[17]

After the ministers had called at Sunderland House, a 'Mr Clagett' called on Sarah, introducing himself as the late earl's chaplain, having replaced Trimnell. Clagett told Sarah how, despite Hooker's valiant attempts to stop them, the President of the Council, the Lord Privy Seal and two Secretaries of State had broken open the seals on the doors to take away the earl's papers, and had chosen Clagett to watch in place of the family. The ministers had taken papers out of the drawers, and if found to be Secret Service papers, had put them into a bag.

> They seem'd to be very well instructed where the papers lay for they were not above half an hour about it, and some of the drawers they did not look into at all, and others very slightly, and a cabinet that was seal'd up, which had papers that belong'd to the Secretaries Office they did not so much as open, but said perhaps those might be one time or other an Entertainment to the present Earl of Sunderland.

The only letters they 'directly shewed' to Clagett were one that was sealed and addressed to the king, some cyphers, and papers from which they 'read the Endorsements'. During their search they had come across the will and, the seal being broken, one of the Secretaries asked Clagett to 'take notice that they did not break it'. After this the ministers put their own seals on the door and departed.[18]

Because of the 'very great alteration there was in the late Lord Sunderland's effects, so infinitely short of what he must have had when he made his will', Sarah was convinced that the earl had used his own money to pay Parliament during the South Sea alarm in order to 'stop that enquiry as much as was possible'. Had he lived, that money would have been repaid to him. As it was, she believed Diana's brother would have not so much as 'a silver spoon without paying for it' himself.[19]

Robert was meanwhile kicking his heels in Vienna awaiting a letter from his father to tell him whether or not to join him at Hanover (where he was due to arrive with the king), or to go on to cousin Willigo in Italy. As it took several days for a letter to cross the Channel, and still more to reach Vienna on horseback, Robert remained oblivious of his changed situation. When the news did reach him he was deeply shocked, writing to his grandmother:

> I received last Monday with a vast deal of grief the melancholy news of my Dear Fathers Death. As I believe my being in England now must certainly be very necessary I shall set out the beginning of next week. I would have set out sooner but that I have had a fall which hurt my side, and which has obliged me to keep my room some time, but I

hope in three, or four days to be able to begin my journey without danger. As soon as I arrive my Dear Grandmama may be sure the first thing I shall do, shall be to pay my duty to her, and to beg her directions in everything I do . . .[20]

The young Earl of Sunderland reached Dover five days later, more than a month after his father's death. A message from his grandmother awaited him at Dover, urging him to go straight to Windsor rather than London, and to speak to nobody. His brothers Charles and Johnny, and 'little dear Dye', were at the lodge awaiting him, as well as cousin Anne, Mary Cairnes and his sister Anne with her new baby. The Bateman baby was named John after his great-grandfather, who stood godfather to him.

By going straight to Windsor, Diana's brother avoided a great outcry in London as news broke of a Jacobite conspiracy to assassinate the king. This was partly a result of their father's Secret Service investigations, Walpole as new Head of the Treasury proclaiming a state of emergency. He had ordered all Catholics from the city and troops to be assembled in Hyde Park, while habeas corpus was suspended. The visit to Hanover planned by the king had been cancelled. Meanwhile a post-mortem of the late earl's body proved he was not poisoned as feared, but had died from pleurisy and heart disease.

The dazzled Mary Cairnes described the fashionable Robert as being 'what Shakespeare makes Lady Piercy say of her Lord: ". . . the Glass, the Picture & the Book, in which the Youth of England dresst themselves" ', but his father's debts must have sobered him somewhat. The prized book collection had to be packed up and sent to Blenheim to offset a mortgage Marlborough had granted him, Robert declaring that it would break his heart to see it broken up and sold to strangers. Money was still owing on the library building, and the booksellers' bills alone added up to £3000. In place of an offer made to Robert by the court to make him a gentleman-of-the-bedchamber, Sarah offered him £1000 there and then, and to pay the ground rent of Sunderland House. Furthermore, if he continued to behave in a manner she approved of, she would make him heir to her private fortune. Meanwhile he would receive £10,000 from his father's will, as well as the Althorp estate, while Charles and Johnny were each left £15,000, and Anne Bateman and Diana £2000 pounds each. Lady Frances was to have £15,000. Diana's £2000 was increased when her half-brother and half-sister died that summer, bringing her an additional £1600.2s.7d. Her grandmother deducted a quarter of the interest for her subsistence, the rest to be used as pin-money. The widowed countess received £30,000.[21]

The widowed and childless Judith, dowager Countess of Sunderland, was hustled from her town house in Piccadilly, taking in her hurry a length of furnishing fabric. Writing to her executor, she pleaded:

> I never had any thoughts of taking the Crimson Damask, the mistake I found is made by their haveing put it in the trunk among those things I desir'd to have; however though I think they are extravagantly rated if my Lord Sunderland has chang'd his mind and wont take it, rather then give the trouble to have them apprais'd over again I will take it in the lump with the other things . . .

Being 'naturaly a Squanderer as you know', Judith suggested that her inheritance be 'laid out' in South Sea Annuities, as well as in 'civil List Annuity', evidence that the South Sea Company still thrived, thanks to a timely intervention by Walpole. The still beautiful widowed countess moved with her sister to the highly fashionable Chiswick, to be 'persecuted with lovers and with poetry by the penny post'. She was soon remarried, this time to Sir Robert Sutton, KB, Privy Counsellor and diplomatist of the first rank, as well as MP for Nottingham.[22]

Charlotte McCarthy had meanwhile married Lieutenant Colonel John West, Diana's grandmother furnishing their home in Windsor Park, where he was verderer. Described later as a 'long awkward person', West was doubtless presentable as a young man, any deficiencies balanced by his prospects. He would become Baron De La Warr at his father's death.

The Duke of Chandos had meanwhile proposed a match between Diana's cousin Lady Anne Egerton and his son Lord Carnarvon, suggesting to her grandmother that if it should 'meet with Your Graces' approbation & this Match hath success I so much wish for, I shall esteem it such an hon[our] & advantage to my family as can leave me no room to doubt of its future prosperity'. But when Sarah approached Anne's father for her dowry, Bridgwater claimed he had invested it in land, and would need to raise a mortgage to release it. To save time, Sarah thought of advancing the money herself, but fearing endless litigation before it would be refunded to her, hesitated. She was also aware that Chandos's estate was 'too much ingaged in South Sea and other prospects' to be relied on, Swift saying that all Chandos 'gained by fraud' he 'lost by stocks'. On top of all this, Sarah found Chandos too full of 'compliments' and 'prodigious professions' towards her that 'meant nothing', for him to be altogether trustworthy. In the end she decided to call the marriage off, excusing herself by saying that as Anne was still very young, and 'appeared much younger than she was', it might be better if the couple did not 'live together' just now. But if 'as they grow up they should by chance like one another, and all difficulties removed, it might still be a match'.[23]*

And now the Duke of Marlborough himself lay dying at Windsor Lodge, his grandchildren grouped about him, Sarah kneeling by his bed. The duke had been ill for several days, the doctors at last pronouncing themselves unable to do more; and when a coach was heard rattling over the cobble-stones carrying her daughters and young Harriet Newcastle, Sarah sent Captain Fish to meet them. He was 'the first person they saw & that helped them out of the coach', Sarah recalled later, and 'Little Di' went with them to the dining-room, where she 'asked if they would have any wine or bread', which they refused.[24]

The ground floor room where the duke lay, with surgeons, doctors, apothecaries, the duke's chaplain, several grandchildren and Sarah's new companion Jane Kingdon, to say nothing of the servants, was 'pretty full'. The daughters curtsied to their mother as they entered, asking how she was, Sarah sniffing at their 'how dy'es' after a silence of three years. Soon the duchess found she could not bear to be in the room with them, and left. After what seemed a long time away from her dying husband, she grew impatient, asking Jane Kingdon to beg her daughters to not 'stay long in the room because I could not come in while they were there, being in so much affliction'. Jane whispered Sarah's message to the Duchess of Montagu (who though the younger of the two sisters was of superior rank), who answered that she did not understand what Jane said, but if she meant they were not to see their mother 'they were very well used to that'. At this Sarah asked for all her grandchildren to be dismissed, except Harriet, and went into the room although her daughters and Harriet were still there. The three women rose to their feet as Sarah entered, and 'made curtseys', but did not speak to her. After kneeling beside her husband for a time, Sarah called for prayers, and after they were over asked the duke if he had heard them. He murmured 'yes', and that he had 'joined in them'. After this the dying duke was carried to his own room, followed by his daughters and Harriet.[25]

---

* Carnarvon was to die unmarried of smallpox five years later, his younger brother Henry inheriting the Chandos title and estate. So great were his father's debts, however, Canons had to be demolished for what could be made from the sale of the materials.

Diana, as one of the grandchildren and a very helpful one at that, must have been aware of the conflict between her grandmother and her two aunts. Sarah said she would have had a great deal to say to her husband if there had not such 'cruel people been by', and had eventually asked her maid Grace Ridley to 'go to the Duchess of Montagu & tell her that for many days I had been mightily harassed & must lie down, & I desire her to go into another room'. To this the duchess answered, 'Will our being here hinder her from lying down?' Upon this Sarah instructed Jane to ask Montagu 'if she had such an affliction & was in my condition whether she would like to have me with her?', to which Mary promptly answered 'no'. The sisters and Harriet continued in the room until Sarah sent to them a third time, upon which 'all three went out of the room & the Duchess of Newcastle went quite away'.[26]

When Harriet called at the Lodge next day, it was to find her grandfather was dead, her grandmother sending a message to her that she could not see her. Instead she visited her 'Cosens Lady Anne Egerton & Lady Di Spencer'. Harriet would learn from them that her mother and the Duchess of Montagu had 'staid in the drawingroom & hall till four in the morning', and when the duke died, had left. Harriet's mother was now Duchess of Marlborough in her own right.[27]

Diana's 'Papa Duke' had died on 6 June 1722, two months, two weeks and two days after the death of her father. Sarah's friend Jane Kingdon (who was once maid of honour to Queen Anne) must have been a comfort to the cousins, for Diana would always have an affection for her. Jane had remained sitting in a window seat near Sarah till ordered off to bed, returning to the duchess when the 'terrible stroke was given'.[28]

Diana and cousin Anne would stand in for Sarah's daughters, of whom custom demanded they sat at the foot of the deceased's bed while the widow sat seated under a crepe canopy receiving visits of commiseration from women friends. The room would be draped in black and lit by a single taper, but more lights must have been brought in between calls to enable Sarah make her endless lists of funeral preparations. She had planned for the duke's body to lie in state at Marlborough House, but when news came that Henrietta, Duchess of Marlborough, planned to take friends there to pay homage to her father, Sarah sent word that the house was to be locked up, and 'no person what soever admitted'. She could not prevent her daughter from presenting herself at the rehearsals of Bononcini's funeral anthem at Westminster Abbey, however, taking Johnnie Gay and William Congreve with her. Sarah found this 'very provoking'.[29]

It was in Diana, almost twelve, that Sarah confided her annoyances, though Anne was four years her senior. The late duke's chaplain, Dean Jones, who had played cards with Marlborough and sometimes made him laugh (there is a caricature of him in Laguerre's wall fresco in the Great Saloon at Blenheim Palace), had the temerity to write to Walpole to suggest that the king should pay for the duke's funeral. Upon hearing this, Sarah had promptly sacked him, enlisting 'little Di to write the truth of the matter that it might be given in order to contradict it'.[30] Diana's uncle, the Duke of Montagu, rode as chief mourner at the funeral, her grandfather's black suit of armour laid on his coffin 'as if he were lying armed himself'. Eight black horses drew the carriage through the winding streets of St James's to Westminster Abbey, and seventy-two Chelsea Pensioners walked behind in the procession, one for each year of the duke's life. Soldiers marched on foot leading their horses, the richly caparisoned Horse of Honour led by Captain Fish wearing full Military Mourning. Noblemen and bishops followed to the sound of muffled drums. Although King George did not present himself, the Prince and Princess of Wales, together with the young princesses, looked down from a balcony.[31]

It fell to Atterbury, Bishop of Rochester (in his capacity as Dean of Westminster), to murmur 'dust to dust and ashes to ashes' as Marlborough's coffin was laid in the Westminster Abbey crypt, the Blenheim tomb being not ready to receive him. In August this same bishop would be arrested on a charge of High Treason, one of the results of Diana's father's investigations.

Diana's grandmother was not to be shuffled out of Blenheim Palace into a dower house, as was the fate of most rich widows, but left a generous allowance with which to finish Blenheim Palace 'in her own way'. She also had £20,000 a year on top of her personal income. Her grandchildren were to be her chief concern as she climbed from her crepe-canopied bed to continue with what was left of her life. Diana was to be taught to paint in watercolours, and would show real potential, producing a 'View of Windsor' in the following April. Though nothing is known of her teacher, or how much help she had with this, her competence was enough to persuade Horace, son of Walpole, to purchase the painting, keeping it in his private collection at Strawberry Hill. We know that when his 'little Gothic castle' came to be auctioned in 1842, this painting was sold in a lot with one by Samuel Lyson, the two going for £3.13s.0d. With cousin Anne she also learned to ride side-saddle, the saddles and 'furniture' for the horses being ordered by Lady Elizabeth Rich. Elizabeth was a distant relative of Sarah's through the first marriage of Sarah's brother-in-law, Edward Griffith. Elizabeth, the daughter of his second marriage, had married Sir Robert Rich in the year Diana was born. Now thirty, with bright auburn hair and an 'unsully'd complexion', Ellizabeth considered 'herself young'. Sarah wrote to cousin Anne's father asking if his daughter might have the little horse her brother Brackley had ridden before he died, and this request was granted. Although Anne and Diana had ridden since they were small, they must now learn to ride side-saddle with elegance.[32]

Four months after their father's death, Sarah asked if Diana's brothers Charles and Johnny might come into her care, their designated guardians being only too willing to agree to this. Not too pleased with their education at Eton, Sarah removed them, placing them in charge of a tutor at Windsor Lodge. The person she chose for this duty was James Stephens, a brilliant mathematician who would later become a doctor of medicine. So much did Sarah trust this man, and so agreeable was he, he was destined to remain in her household for thirty-five years.

While Diana rode and painted, Sarah circulated an account to her friends of 'the cruel usage from my children', which in time became known as her 'Green Book'. She had dismissed her friend Jane Kingdon, accusing her of shrugging her shoulders when delivering her message to her daughters. Jane protested that all 'that malice can invent is that I made some motion that they interpret their own way', and remembered no 'such motion I made'. While Sarah found Jane 'more agreeable than most people', she insisted she should go.

As Lady Cairnes was in Ireland arranging a marriage for her daughter Mary, Sarah was left alone with her grandchildren, coming more and more to lean on Diana. Writing to Lady Cairnes, she reported that 'Dye I thank god is well & has almost regained her looks', and begged her to send cloth to make 'mantoes and petticoats' for her and Lady Anne, but only 'if you can get it in grey for it must bee mourning'.[33]

CHAPTER SIX

The Best Match in England

'. . . nobody to marry but Dye'

When Lady Anne Egerton's father, newly created Duke of Bridgwater, wrote to tell the dowager Duchess of Marlborough he was to remarry, she chose to ignore him. Receiving no answer to his letter, he wrote another to his daughter, wanting 'mightily' to hear how she did. When Anne dutifully showed this letter to her grandmother, she was told to leave it unanswered. Five days before Marlborough's funeral the duke married Lady Rachel Russell, sister of the young Duke of Bedford, abstaining from attending the funeral itself; a fortnight later he wrote to his daughter again. This time he sent the letter with his servant in a coach, to make sure she received it, saying now that 'ye hurry of our visitors is over' he was impatient to see her. He desired her to ask her grandmother leave 'to come to Ashridge to wish me joy', and believed her 'so discreet a woman' he could trust her to 'come alone'.[1]

Bridgwater's letter was written on 'Sonday night', and arrived at Windsor Lodge on Monday morning. Anne, under Sarah's instructions, wrote wishing him and his bride 'all ye happyness that you can desire', but said her grandmother could not send her just now as she (Anne) had 'so great a cold & pain in my ear that my head is now wrapped up in flannel'. Her grandmother was also in a 'meloncholy condition' which made her unwilling to part with her granddaughter just now, but as soon as Anne was well the dowager would send her 'half way to any place you will please to appoint so that [she] might waite upon you & upon my Lady Dutchess'. She must, however, 'return to ye lodge at night'.[2]

Lady Anne had been left £10,000 by her grandfather the Duke of Marlborough, in addition to the £10,000 left her by her mother – which made Sarah fear that Bridgwater designed to take her away in order to gain control of her wealth. The dowager had cared for the child for seven years, educating her and bringing her up 'in every particular as her own', but when she consulted her lawyer friends, she was told the Duke of Bridgwater had every right to resume custody of his daughter.[3]

Sarah's suspicions increased further when Bridgwater's servant was discovered snooping around the Windsor Lodge stables, saying he had orders to take away Anne's 'little horse', and the situation worsened when Bridgwater came in a 'passion the next morning, at five a clock', obliging Sarah to send his daughter out to meet him. The duke questioned Anne as to how long she had been ill, his daughter answering that it was 'two or three days', upon which the duke said, 'I believe you have not been very bad, for my servant told me that he saw you yesterday.' When Bridgwater presented himself to Sarah his temper had reached boiling point, she attempting to assure him that his daughter would visit him just as soon as she was well. But this would not do; Bridgwater insisted that Anne should go with him at once, believing 'she might do very well'.[4]

This conversation continued for about three-quarters of an hour, the duke growing 'pretty warm in his complexion', insisting that his daughter did not need a maid sent with her as Sarah wished, as he had servants at home, until she, unable to make 'any impression on him' thought to ask if she might accompany Lady Anne to Ashridge herself. The effect of this was to make the duke agree 'he lik'd very well to have a servant sent with Lady Anne', indeed 'he lik'd it better!' After this there was 'nothing but civilities & common discourse till dinner was serv'd', Lady Anne waiting on her father 'wrapt up in flannell & a night-cap'.[5]

Diana must have been intrigued, if not alarmed, by her uncle's appearance so early at the Lodge. The thought of losing Anne must have worried her, since her cousin had taken the place of a sister for seven years, sharing her bed, her maid, and even the same friend, Mary Cairnes. Indeed, while Anne was busy attending her father, Diana wrote Mary a letter:

Dear Miss Cairnes,
I can't help troubling you with a letter, (as you desired me,) to let you know, that, I have often wished that we were going to meet you on the road from Ireland, tho I am afraid I shan't have that happyness a great while. I have no news to divert you with, but that Mrs Lavie is learning me Italian, and I hope in a little while to be able to write you a letter in it. Pray, present my humble service to my Lady Cairnes, who I hope is well. I am dear Miss Cairnes,
Your most humble servant,
D Spencer

In a postscript Diana added: 'Lady Anne, presents her service to you and Ldy Cairnes', and 'Pray answer this as soon as possible'.[6]

Mary Cairnes was to recall later how the Duke of Bridgwater was apprehensive that Sarah intended 'to marry Lady Diana Spencer to the Duke of Bedford which she certainly wish'd', and Sarah in her turn suspected Bridgwater had 'got it into his head to make a cross-match between the Duke of Bedford & his daughter' Anne. The Duke of Bedford, brother to Bridgwater's new wife, was fourteen, a young man of immense wealth. Sarah consoled herself that his mother Elizabeth (Howland), the widowed Duchess of Bedford, was 'so averse' to her son marrying Lady Anne Egerton she had told her father 'he must not think of it'. When the agitated Bridgwater returned to Ashridge after seeing his daughter he sent a polite message thanking Sarah for her 'kindness to my daughter', and said he would send his coach to meet her at 'what place yr Grace shall appoint', signing himself off as her 'obedient Son'. He added that his wife and his mother-in-law, the dowager Duchess of Bedford, sent their 'humble service'.[7]

Rumour soon spread to London that the Duke of Bridgwater had 'taken away Lady Anne', Marie La Vie writing anxiously to Diana for the truth of the matter. Diana allowed some time to elapse before answering her governess's letter, excusing her delay by saying:

I have been so taken up (dear Mrs La Vie) with your lessons & something else that seemd to me business that I neglected to shew my Mama Duchess your letter till last night, & now she bids me not only thank you for the favour of yours to me, & the very fine Housewife which you were so good as to send me, but she says I must thank you for the favour of your letter to her because she thinks you will like it better than if she writ to you herself.

The gift of a 'Housewife' was a linen pocket containing the essentials for needlework, considered necessary equipment for a young woman, which at twelve Diana had officially become. Diana went on to say that her grandmother 'wondered at people being able to give an account of herself and Lady Anne Egerton' since she 'sees nobody', and 'if such things has been writ, it must be a miracle to have them known'. As to Lady Anne's being taken away, 'there needs no answer to that because she is here, and you heard that the Duke of Bridgwater desired to have her but three or four days, which was very reasonable'. Diana further observed that 'Mama Dutchess' did not believe the Duke of Bridgwater had 'any thoughts of taking Lady Anne away', and if he should have any such inclination he was 'certainly Master of it'.[8]

This was a masterful letter from a twelve-year-old, even if largely taken from dictation; and after mentioning other snippets of 'extraordinary gossip', Diana put forward her grandmother's view that if 'anybody will give themselves up to a lye without examining whether it is possible to be true or not', there was 'no remedy but patience', signing herself off with the more girlish: *'Io Sono Cara mia Signora / Humilisima Serva Suu'*.[9]

Anne's return from Ashridge must have been a great relief to both Diana and her grandmother, Bridgwater sending a letter to Sarah thanking her for his daughter's visit, and hoping 'she got safe to ye lodge as she did to Beaconsfield'.* But the sixteen-year-old's short absence had the effect of firmly establishing Diana as her grandmother's 'little secretary', on whom henceforth she was to pin all her hopes. When Miss La Vie wanted news of her grandmother it was to Diana she wrote, since no one but the duchess herself 'can so well inform me how she does'. Sarah was suffering from 'Anthony fire', a painful flushing in her face, as well as from gout, stones in the kidneys, a weakness in her hands and legs, and fainting fits, doubtless exacerbated by her husband's death.[10]

Blenheim Palace must now be completed, Sarah taking the cousins, including Charlotte and her new husband, to Woodstock, where Nicholas Hawksmoor had taken over from Vanbrugh. The duchess found this architect 'much honester as hee is more able than Sir John', writing to Lady Cairnes that she was confident the building and the park would be even finer than 'ever any body imagined it would bee', though 'more melancholy here then any where else' when she thought where he was 'for whom it was built'. She had completely alienated herself from her daughters, the 'young' Duchess of Marlborough saying she would never set foot in the palace dead or alive; and when the Duchess of Montagu attempted to visit, she was denied entry. Sarah's hopes were pinned firmly on her Spencer grandchildren, in the belief that the 'whole branch and La: Ann Egerton' would be good to her, not only because it was in their natures, but because they would want her for her fortune, which was in her own power.[11]

* Anne would change coaches at Beaconsfield.

Having left Hawksmoor to design the Triumphal Arch for the Woodstock entrance to the palace, Diana and Anne were then taken to Althorp with Diana's brother Sunderland. While Sarah was fond of Robert, finding him 'as easy with me as I can desire', she felt she could 'never love him as she had her own children' (meaning those that were dead). She was delighted with Althorp, finding 'room enough to entertain a king if one had such bad taste as to like them', and 'so contrived that one could live mighty comfortable with a few friends'. After a short stay the family returned to Windsor Lodge, stopping off at St Albans on their way. Here they found Charles and Johnny, now aged fifteen and fourteen, fresh from attending an equestrian academy in London. They were learning to fence and to draw, as well as to ride well, and taking dancing lessons with Mr Firis.

The winter was spent making up furnishing fabrics for cousin Charlotte's house, Diana's 'Housewife' doubtless put to good use. In the following summer Lady Anne Egerton went to Totteridge to spend time with Diana's sister Anne, helping her pack for a trip to Paris. Lord Bateman had sailed ahead of her, and it was rumoured that the young couple were not happy. While at Totteridge, Anne Egerton received a note from her father telling her he was planning to leave for Ashridge on Thursday, and would she dine with him? He thought Lady Bateman might drop her 'when she goes to France', or he would send his own coach to fetch her. On the reverse of his invitation Anne's grandmother wrote later:

A foolish contrivance of the Duke of Bridgwater to take Lady Anne Eg[erton] from me in a mighty unhansome & rude manner when he had a mind to marry her to the Duke of Bedford, but he was such a fool that he would not let me know it, tho I had kept her as my own child from the death of her dear mother & had been upon all times kind to him.[12]

While Bridgwater entertained his daughter at Bridgwater House in London, Diana and her grandmother were visiting friends. When they returned to Marlborough House it was to find Lady Anne Egerton 'all in tears', saying her father had ordered her to go to him 'at 7 a clock to go into the country with him'. She was ordered to take her 'gold watch, all her coloure'd cloaths, as well as mourning, all her jewells, and linnen', and to 'tell Mr Read that he must send her horses to Ashridge'. Her grandmother observed that he seemed very well informed of what Anne possessed considering he had 'never given her anything in 8 years but a box of Shrewsbury cakes, a hat, & a whip, and a little string of diamonds that was her mother's', and only 'one [horse] that was his'. Even when he sent her the string of diamonds he said 'he only lent it her'. This was 'so strange a manner of taking his daughter away', and the child was 'so much griev'd at it' that Sarah sat her down to write to her father telling him 'it was extra inconvenient to send her so soone as the next morning', but that she would be 'sure to wait upon him in a few days'. Apart from the place, this was an exact repeat of what had happened at Windsor Lodge, Sarah hoping to persuade someone who was enough his friend ('if such a man had any!') to convince Bridgwater of the 'prejudice he was doing to his own child'. Anne's letter was no sooner delivered to Bridgwater House than the duke sent his steward telling her he 'comanded her to come the next morning'.[13]

Though late at night, Lady Anne was once again bidden by her grand-mother to take up her pen and write to her father, but before she could begin 'there came two footmen to fetch away her trunks, and in less than a quarter of an hour after that (when it was near 12 a clock) my Lord [Bridg-water] came in to the court with a candle and lantern, his steward, & two footmen'. The first person to see the duke was 'Lady Anne's woman', who hurried to warn Sarah so 'she might not be surprised'. Bridgwater chased after her (the woman servant was doubtless Jane Pattison), telling her to inform the duchess that 'he desired she would not make his child ungrateful to him'. Fearing he might come into her bedchamber, Sarah made 'all the hast[e she] could to send the woman out to him to tell him his daughter should obey him'. Upon this 'my Lord Duke order'd Lady Anne's woman to pack up all her things, and linnen, *foul* as well as clean'.[14]

Although so much younger, Diana must have helped soothe her cousin as she wrote, Anne managing to complete her letter to 'Dear Papa':

I am in the greatest affliction imaginable not only at the apprehension I am under of leaving my Grandmama, but at the manner of leaving her, who has been so tenderly kind to me for so many years, and so very careful of me in all respects that my own Dear Mother could not have been more so, for whose sake I beg you to let me continue with my dear Grandmama, which I am sure will be very much to my advantage to do, and if I leave her, or am in the least ungreatfull to her, (to whom I owe so much) it will make me very unhappy as long as I live, which (I am sure) you would be sorry to have me be.[15]

Bridgwater 'walk'd about in the Hall like a madman with the most ill natur'd countenance that ever was seen in any humane creature', refusing to go into any room, though 'he was desired to'. In the end he sent his servant into the duchess, although she was 'in bed', to tell her that 'if Lady Anne was sick, it was she who had made her so & that he would have her away!' In the end Sarah said, 'For God's sake let him take her.' Lady Anne went down to her father 'half dead with grief', the servants giving her 'some water & drops', after which he took 'her away in his coach'. Describing this scene many years later, Mary Cairnes told how the duke came dressed 'in a chairman's great coat helping to carry a chair & carry'd off his daughter'.[16]

Diana, severed from her cousin, had few young companions save Charles and Johnny when they joined her on leave from their academy. Some of the boys' time was spent at Sunderland House with their brother Robert, and Charles was already preparing for the Grand Tour. While Sarah thought Charles 'perfectly honest' and 'good natured', with 'many vertues', she found him awkward. She recalled later how 'when he was a very great boy' he 'burnt the hair of his head almost down to his forhead', and she being so 'frightened at it' asked how it came like that. Charles repeated for 'half an hour together' that he 'knew nothing of it', Sarah insisting that he tell her 'who had cut it to hide its having been burnt or cut?' In the end she had tired of it and 'let it drop'. The boy may have shaved back his natural hair to accommodate a wig, a fashion of which Sarah strongly disapproved. She meanwhile thought it a 'very bad sign of the nature of a boy when he will so obstinately deny truth', and that there was 'a great addition of folly, as falsehood in it'. Johnny, on the other hand, could do no wrong.[17]

Diana's grandmother, though confessing to be a 'little of the fattest', was still considered beautiful at sixty-three, looking 'mighty well for a grand-mother'. Wortley Montagu would describe her even later as having the 'most expressive eyes, and the finest hair imaginable', which she kept golden with the use of 'honeywater'. Only months after Marlborough's death the Earl Coningsby was besieging her with proposals of marriage, living in hope that the 'Great & Glorious Creator of ye World . . . will direct you to make mee ye happyest man upon ye face of the earth'. Sarah thought him quite mad, and though she invited him to Blenheim, afterwards went out of her way to avoid him. A more fascinating and desirable suitor was Charles Seymour, 6th Duke of Somerset.[18]

Named the 'Sovereign', on account of the blue blood he believed coursed through his veins, the so-called 'Proud' Duke of Somerset instructed his servants by signs rather than speak to them, and had the signatures of artists removed from their works. Roads were scoured by outriders 'to protect him from the gaze of the vulgar', and he disinherited a daughter for sitting in his presence while he slept. His red-headed duchess (she who had refused to sit at Sacheverell's trial) had died five months after Marlborough, and having struggled under an 'unalterable love and admiration' for Sarah for many years, the duke declared there was 'noe person on earth I doe love and desire more than you'.[19]

Diana may have been amused by the passionate pursuit of her grandmother by this sixty-five-year-old oligarch, but pleased when Sarah declared she would not marry him, nor the 'Emperor of the world if I were but thirty yeares old'. All the same Sarah was willing to continue the friendship, since Somerset had experience in building. He had rebuilt Petworth House with his late wife's fortune, and Sarah needed advice on finishing Blenheim Palace. Another reason for encouraging the duke's interest was that his grandson, Charles Wyndham, was Diana's age, and might make her a suitable husband. As the son of Somerset's eldest daughter Katherine and Sir William Wyndham, he looked to inherit a considerable fortune. He appeared to be intelligent, attending Westminster School, and would later matriculate at Oxford.[20]

The summer of 1723 saw Diana and her grandmother at Blenheim Palace, Lady Burlington and her son the Earl of Burlington among those invited to visit. Since Diana had left Sunderland House, the next door Burlington House had been improved beyond recognition, and as an up-and-coming leader of the Palladian school of architecture, Burlington also planned to build a splendid villa at Chiswick. Diana had been surrounded by talk of building since her early childhood, and at dinner was able to listen to the ideas that Burlington had brought from the Continent, the seeds of a growing interest in architecture planted in her young mind. It amused her grandmother to hear Burlington criticise Vanbrugh's work, while praising Hawksmoor. This new architect had completed the Triumphal Arch, and Sarah was composing an inscription to be put over it. It was to be inscribed in English on one side, and translated into Latin on the other, informing visitors that the arch had been built by order of Marlborough's 'beloved wife', and that details of his heroic deeds were to be found 'on a pillar' in the park.

The pillar, or Column of Victory as it came to be known, was not yet designed, let alone completed, and as Diana had a talent for drawing she was called upon to sketch ideas for it from suggestions by her grandmother. The pillar was first conceived as an obelisk, and Somerset had promised to talk to the poet Alexander Pope regarding an inscription for it. Meanwhile Diana and her grandmother produced ideas of their own, showing them to the Countess of Burlington, who wrote:

> I found I was so charmed with dear Lady Dies' performance that it made me forget to tell your grace my thoughts on the subject I admire her so much for; but think nothing can be better or more proper than the inscription, and without flattery I may add that I think the same of everything you do . . .

Grandmother and granddaughter had grown very close since Marlborough's death. Sarah started to dictate a history of England to Diana, but what with the 'gout and "perpetual interruptions", both resented, grandmother and grand-daughter never got very far'. Johnny was staying with them for a while, Lady Burlington sending her 'humble service to the dear brother, and sister', Charles having left for the Continent. After the Burlingtons' stay at Blenheim, Sarah decided to try the waters at Bristol, taking Diana along with her.[21]

The 'Hotwells' of Bristol were quite primitive compared to those of Bath, but offered the hope of peace and quiet, and relief from the dowager's infirmities. There were several grand houses where grandmother and granddaughter might lodge, those in Queen's Square having been built in honour of Queen Anne's visit there twenty years earlier. Most houses were built high on a ridge, Sarah being obliged to jolt down 'a long suffering road' every day to 'pick up a little hazard', her hair piled under a 'dowd', while Diana helped carry her 'large bag of silver to distribute to the poor'. The Assembly Rooms were built on stilts above muddy water that bubbled up at 70°F, and had long been considered a cure. When Diana did not accompany her grandmother, she busied herself learning Italian, and sketching designs for the obelisk.[22]

Sarah had chosen Bristol as a place most suitable for mourning, but news of her solitary state soon reached Bath, Beau Nash taking it into his head to ride over to see her. The Master of Ceremonies had lost £14,000 at cards within the last few days, and was hoping to recoup his losses. According to

Lady Bristol he proved 'indifferent company', and found Sarah disappointing in play, cutting 'whenever she has picked up a pair of pieces'. Nash was a colourful character, his large white hat cocked over a curly black wig, tall and of the 'finest shape', his 'black-brown complexion' brightened by a 'scarlet countenance'. Though he could be crude in respect to women, he added the 'greatest politeness' to his 'natural wit'. Nash spent two days with the duchess and her young granddaughter before returning to Bath.[23]

Sarah and Diana kept to a healthy routine, rising in the morning at six or seven, taking the air twice a day, and retiring to bed at nine. When a package arrived sealed with the Bull and Unicorn, Diana would guess at once it was from Somerset. Inside was a snuff box for Sarah, 'very fine & very pritty', and a 'fairing' for 'little Dye'. Her grandmother wrote to the duke at once to say how pleased they were with them, and that Diana would thank His Grace when she 'has the honour to see you at London'. After marvelling at the careful way the duke had packed her present, Sarah ended her letter: 'I have sent you an obelisk of Dye's drawing but I must have a great consultation about that before it is determined.'[24]

The Hotwells turned out to be less than beneficial for Sarah's infirmities, Somerset suggesting it was because she took a 'larger quantity of the waters at Bristol than any discreet body ever did'. Worse, Sarah found the town was intolerably dull, her patience 'quite worn out'. At last she decided to move to Bath, sending word to Lady Bristol to meet her and Diana at a 'halfway house'. Lady Bristol (wife of John Hervey, first Earl of Bristol, whom the Marlboroughs had helped to his title) arrived at '11 o'clock' sharp, both parties 'so exact we met at the door'. They had dinner here, before moving on to Bath, where grandmother and granddaughter received another letter from the Duke of Somerset, sent on to them from Bristol. He wrote:

> The stroaks of Pretty Ldy: Di's pencill must have a fruitful return, which I presume to send for your amusement, to correct, & amend at leisure hours . . .

He had spoken to Pope about the inscription, the poet saying he would be pleased to write something, just 'so long as it was not known'. But finding his notions 'so different from ours as to liberty', Sarah eventually turned him down. Her only wishes now were to commemorate her husband's life with a fitting monument, and to marry off 'poor little Dye'. This she expected to do in a 'verry few years'. Somerset responded by saying he hoped she would 'contract to marry Pritty Lady Di when ever you please', and with a marriage to the young Charles Wyndham in mind, would be happy to 'have her in my family'.[25]

Sarah was coming increasingly to depend on Diana, believing she had 'more sence than any body that I know of my own sex'. Her friend Mrs Boscawen wrote a letter to Diana herself, saying she was persuaded 'yu are as good as yu are prettie'. Meanwhile Diana's cousin Bella Montagu had married the Duke of Manchester. Lady Mary Wortley Montagu wrote to her own sister in France: 'Belle is at this instant in the Paradisal state of receiving visits every day from a passionate Lover who is her first Love, who she thinks the finest Gentleman in Europe.' Sarah thought it wrong that Bella should be married when she was 'like a bird out of a cage & knew nothing of the world', and that in 'half an hour's conversation' her mother the Duchess of Montagu should have seen 'any woman that had sense must be very miserable with him'. Although Manchester's estate included Kimbolton Castle in Hunting-donshire, and a large house on the site of London's Manchester Square, Sarah thought it very small, and was determined that Diana should do better.[26]

Diana's brother Charles passed through Paris on his way to Geneva, and wrote to apologise for wearing 'so fine cloaths' there, and promising to spend 'not so much [in] the future'. His sister Anne Bateman arrived in Paris just after he left, writing that she had heard good reports of him, and that he was 'extreamly beloved by everybody'. She sent 'dear little Dye' a pleated 'head' and four heads 'Alamode' for dear 'Grandmama'. Anne admitted she had grown very thin, but denied it was because her husband was 'unkind' to her, promising to drink ass's milk which 'always makes me fat'. Whenever Anne wrote to her grandmother she apologised for any faults she might have, begging her to love her as she used to. But she told tales of cousin Willigo, who was idling in Paris, informing her grandmother that Walpole 'flatters him & makes court to him which Ld Blandford [as Willigo now was] does not seem in the least displeased with'.[27]

In November 1723 the Duke of Somerset was invited to Blenheim Palace, but ordered to bring a chaperon. With the country lanes scoured well ahead of him, he left Petworth in a jingle of bells and harness, and once at Stock-bridge passed in his coach through Hawksmoor's Triumphal Arch, observing the river to the right pouring into a splendid cascade. His heart may have missed a beat as he approached the golden palace itself, the

November light gleaming on the stone and copper balls on the skyline. Was the 'Darling of my soul' awaiting him on the north steps, or, if the weather was chilly, seated in the grand entrance hall with little Diana beside her? With silver-tipped cane in his hand, scarlet painted heels clicking across black and white marble, the duke must have paused to contemplate Thornhill's splendid ceiling. Was his grandson Charles Wyndham his chaperon? If Sarah served dinner in the state dining-room he must contend not only with the signatures of artists, but a caricature of the artist Laguerre himself, peering impudently down upon him. After dinner Sarah retired to her bed with toothache, Diana following her, then sending the duke a 'terrible account of the humour moving from my Lady Duchesses tooth into her stomache'. Somerset sent out a servant at once for the 'best medicine', and next morning wrote anxiously to Diana asking if 'Her Grace hasse had a good night'? The medicine may have been laudanum, soaked on a cloth and laid on the tooth – a cure Sarah would recommend to Johnny. Meanwhile the duke hoped it would make Sarah 'easy from those violent pains'.[28]

Somerset scribbled a second note to Diana next morning, addressing her as 'Madam':

The naturall affection your Ladyshp hasse for your Dear Mama Dutchesse gives mee confidance to believe that I ought not to think it a trouble to you to answer this enquiry after my Lady Dutchess's most precious health.

He asked her plaintively 'how shee slept, & how the pain in her stomach is abated, & whether the medicines have had those wished for effects'.[29]

Not only was Diana's grandmother suffering toothache, she was desperately suppressing the disappointment she felt in having Somerset at close quarters, her feelings for him made worse by the contrast he made with her lamented Marlborough, and also her maternal anxiety for her elder daughter. Henrietta had become pregnant at forty-two, after a gap of twenty years. Wortley Montagu wrote to her sister in October that 'My poor friend the young D of Marlbro is as much embarrassed with the loss of her big belly as ever Dairy maid was with the getting one.' Henrietta did not in fact give birth till 23 November, to a little girl Mary whom many believed to be Congreve's child. Whatever the truth of this matter, Henrietta's husband Godolphin accepted the child as his own. He wrote delightedly to his daughter Harriet:

You will I dare say, my Dear Child, be glad to hear that your Mama is very well after having been brought to bed, about two hours ago, of a little girl, who is likewise in a prosperous way.

Godolphin continued to be tender to this child, named Lady Mary Godolphin. It is uncertain how Harriet felt about a new baby sister, especially as she herself was childless.[30]

While they were at Blenheim, Sarah and Somerset discussed the possibility of the marriage between their two grandchildren. Sarah recorded that the duke was 'so obliging as to say all that was possible upon the subject of Dye & Master Wyndham', receiving it 'with a great deal of satisfaction'. For her own part, she saw nothing that was 'more desirable than that match upon all accounts, supposing that they should happen to like one another', but felt just now they were of an age when 'they cant have any notion of what can make them happy'. She had married for love herself, and genuinely believed 'young people must have the satisfaction of liking each other before they put on their bonds'. Whether Diana voiced a dislike of the young man is uncertain; Sarah said that she and Wyndham were 'much too young to judge that matter' and it must be left to 'time and chance'.[31]

In her heart of hearts Sarah was still set on marrying Diana to the Duke of Bedford, and profoundly irritated by Lady Anne Egerton's present proximity to him. Once Sarah had returned to the St James's card tables, there were several more contenders for Diana's hand, Somerset writing that he had it from 'a Sure Body that the Hawk hass undertaken to marry Lord Weymouth to Lady Di'. Like Wyndham, Viscount Weymouth was born in the same year as Diana; his name was Thomas Thynne and he was lord over Longleat. 'Hawk' was a play on the Countess of *Ork*ney's title (otherwise 'squint eyed Betty'), mistress to the late King William III. She was Weymouth's great-aunt and official guardian. Like Bedford, the young viscount had come into his title and estate as an infant, inheriting from an uncle. His mother had remarried after his father's death, the boy's education being left to trustees. With his mother and stepfather, Lord Lansdown, elected his guardians, the boy had followed a strict regime until the age of twelve; but while he was at Eton his stepfather chose to desert his mother, and she was left to cope with her son alone. Weymouth became arrogant, obstinate and unruly, choosing his companions from 'grooms and stable-boys', informing his trustees he no longer needed a tutor, wanting his mother to be his sole guardian. His wishes were not granted, the 'Hawk' sharing the guardianship with his mother.[32]

If the 'Hawk' considered Diana a fit match for her charge, Sarah did not comply with her wishes. Weymouth was described as 'short and thin, with an angular nose and sallow complexion', so unlikely to appeal to Diana. Another female card-playing friend put forward her son Anthony Ashley Cooper, 5th Earl of Shaftsbury, who was also of an age with Diana. The boy's mother, who idolised her son, put Sarah in mind of 'myself and Dye, for if she is speaking and her son begins to say anything, she leaves off to hear him, & seems to think that all the company should give attention to him'. This was an enlightening picture of the pride Sarah took in Diana, and of her place at the card tables, but nothing was to come of the match.[33]

Sarah meanwhile struggled to come to terms with the scandal surrounding her daughter and baby granddaughter Mary, whom she referred to as 'Congreve's Moll'. At fifty-three the playwright was suffering from gout and blindness, having long given up writing plays, concentrating, as has been said, on becoming 'a gentleman', something well within his grasp now that Henrietta was a duchess. And as Mary would inherit jewels with his initials 'WC' on their clasps, rumours of her paternity may well have been founded on truth. Sarah handed Somerset her 'Green Book', her journal on 'the cruel usage of my children', of which he was gratifyingly sympathetic:

> Your Grace dosse show throughout the wholle a more than ordinary tenderness for all your children, while your children in return doe seem to effect a most Unnaturall & Barbarous part to the best of women.[34]

No one understood Sarah better than did Diana, but with Christmas coming it was the duke who sent Sarah a 'very young suckling pig of the Indian kind', reared at his villa called Syon. If the pig proved 'agreeable', he wrote, he would send more 'day by day as they become fitt for eating', and he sent more romantic gifts of orange flower water, and a portrait of 'Fair Rosamond'. These attentions were flattering and comforting to the widow, but when a draft marriage contract arrived at Marlborough House, declaring that Somerset would renounce all claim to Sarah's wealth should she agree to marry him, the dowager duchess withdrew. The Proud Duke, 'struck to the heart', searched for Sarah 'at my Lady Burlington's house' without success, then came to Marlborough House itself. He came 'unexpected', and 'unseasonably', on Boxing Day, fearing to interrupt her 'soft slumber'. He left a note saying he would never have 'one moments happiness' if he could not gain her love, and begged her to tell him her thoughts on this, and 'whether I may not stay long this night & how long . . .?'[35]

On his way out Somerset picked up a prayer from the duchess's table, and being 'in need of such a prayer', slipped it into his pocket. When he discovered it was composed by Diana, he was mortified, sending her a gift of sweetmeats with an apology. His letter, dated 'Dec: the 26th 1723', read:

> That I may not lye under your Ladyp's youthful censure, that an old man is a Heathern, I doe want a Prayer, & all other good things and when I stole yours the other night off from your Mama Dutchess's table, I confess I did want that very prayer. I doe admire it, in return I send some white innocent Rocks, their sweetness are of a more dissolving nature then the substance of Diana the Great Diana's Prayer will be to your Ladyp's most ffaithfull humble servant.

Sarah advised Diana to make a copy of the prayer for the duke, and to sign it with her own name. Yet another note arrived, this time for Sarah, saying: 'I have sent my complements to Lady Di – for writing out the Prayer & for changing leaving out the word Amen & in that place writing, Diana'. He also sent a turkey, hoping it would prove 'more to your tast than the pig dide'.[36]

Sarah was still pinning her hopes on the Duchess of Bedford's aversion to her son marrying Lady Anne Egerton, and that he and Diana might still be a match. She had heard that if the Duke of Bridgwater visited Newmarket or any other place where his wife could not accompany him, Rachel went to stay with her mother, who would not 'suffer her to bring Lady Ann Egerton with her'. Instead, 'this very young creature was left alone at Ashridge', which Sarah thought 'unnatural', and the reason being 'the aversion' of the Duchess of Bedford 'to that match'.[37]

At thirteen Diana may have been oblivious to her grandmother's hopes for her. Charles wrote home from Geneva that he was pleased to hear 'Sister Die is so well and handsome' and that 'brother John is so good'. He was perfecting his French at an academy, and pretended shock when his grandmother suggested he was gambling. He found 'play so poor a diversion', he protested, 'that if I had ever so much money to fling away it should be the last thing I would employ it in'. He was also wearing a wig! Diana's sister returned to

England with presents for her grandmother and 'Ldy Dye that was proper for her', and there were gifts for Anne Egerton. Cousin Anne called at Marlborough House to welcome Diana's sister home, Sarah taking the opportunity to ask her bluntly if she knew her father designed to marry her to the Duke of Bedford? Knowing nothing of this, Anne was so 'very grieved' that she was given 'Harts horn drops to enable her to go to the coach'.[38]

In June Diana's cousin wrote to say she would very soon be coming 'to Town with Papa', and hoped for the satisfaction of 'seeing my Dear Grandmama'. Since the letter was accompanied with a claim for her inheritance, Sarah doubted Lady Anne's sincerity. In the event she failed to turn up. That summer the Duke of Bedford's mother died of smallpox, Bridgwater using his position as head of the family to claim guardianship of the duke. Nothing now stood in the way of his marrying his daughter to Bedford, except the duke's own refusal, or Anne's, or the delay of her inheritance.[39]

In September Lady Burlington informed Sarah that 'the Duke of Bridgwater told my Lord Cheyney, that the match between Lady Anne Egerton and the Duke of Bedford was concluded; and that they only waited till the parliament met to have an act to enable him to make settlements'. Sarah was forced at Christmas to part with the money owed her granddaughter from her grandfather's will, and happening to 'have a pen in [her] hand', sent a letter of complaint with it:

[You say] you were very sorry that you did not stay long enough in town to come to me, but as I know you had been with several people to whom you never had the least obligation and that you are but four or five miles from the town, and as you did protest to me that your father never restrained you from expressing your affection to me by letter so long a goe when you were taken away in so strange a manner I can impute this last neglect of me to nobody but yourself & certainly it would have been better in you not to have sent me any message at all than one that was plainly insincere to one who has been so good a friend to you, as well as a parent . . .

She added that Anne 'could not possibly apprehend that I should not be very well pleased that you were to marry the Duke of Bedford', and reminded her that always, 'from a child' she had taught her never to 'depart from the truth upon any account what so ever'.[40]

The letter was sent with two servants, together with a bill for money, and delivered at Bridgwater House. When the duke read the letter he fell into a paroxysm of fury, calling up one of Sarah's servants to him, as well as a servant of his own, telling them 'to witness what he said to the Duchess of Marlborough':

> . . .tell her that I have commanded my daughter never to go to her nor to write or to send her any message nor to receive any from her and desire that she never will send any servant to my house and tell her that I understand the dutty to a mother better than she does her dutty to her children.

When Sarah's servants informed her that 'his Grace was in a great agony', and seemed 'very much out of breath', it may have amused her, but she now knew that she was defeated in her wish to marry Diana to Bedford. To console herself, she added £17,000 to the child's marriage portion, bequeathing her £100,000 in her will should she live longer than herself. This way she hoped to attract to her the best match in England.[41]

Weymouth had meanwhile married the fourteen-year-old daughter of the Earl of Dorset. Shaftsbury may never have been a serious proposition, but there was still Charles Wyndham, and it may have been in some panic that Sarah wrote to his grandfather reminding him of their thoughts of a match. Somerset received the letter just as 'I was slipping into my charriott', and returned at once to his room to read it. Finding some 'expressions in answer to mine to be softened', he had allowed himself to hope for some response to his ardour, but found a 'Refusal was a Refusal'. But 'if my grandson should have hopes I shall be overjoyed', he wrote generously, promising to do anything he could to prevent the boy's father 'treating with any other person than for Dear Lady Di'. For 'shee is my inclination and the only person I doe wishe to have an allience'.[42]

It turned out that Somerset had less influence with the boy's father than he had hoped, and there may even have been some revenge in the next letter he wrote to Sarah. He explained that as she had contracted with 'other persons more agreeable to her mind' than Wyndham, and was at that time 'not pleased to approve him', he and the boy's father had 'taken it to bee as it is always customery in other peoples offers of the like nature, that when a person is refused, he or she are at liberty to treat & to marry with any other person they please without the ceremony of asking leave to do it'. In other words, 'a refusal was a refusal'.[43]

As his own suit for Sarah was now 'thread Bare, Torne, Shattered, and in a manner Thrown off', Somerset married elsewhere. This was Lady Charlotte Finch, put forward in fact by Sarah, a woman she knew would bear him children. Even so, eight months into his marriage, the Proud Duke lamented on how he had 'lost the woman I loved, and I doe still love . . .' Young Wyndham, who grew to be 'a capable and likable man', was to inherit Petworth as Lord Egremont, marry a beautiful wife and have several children, succeeding Pitt as Secretary of State. Somerset in the meantime hoped Sarah would live long, enjoy perfect health, and see 'charming Lady Di – most happily marryed', and that her 'present treaty to that end might proceed'.[44]

With whom this 'treaty' was made is not yet clear, but writing to Lady Cairnes (her daughter Mary, now Lady Blayney of Castle Blayney), Sarah said she was thankful that most of her granddaughters were 'off her hands' and she had 'nobody to marry but Dye'. Nor did she 'doubt of disposing of her with a prospect at least of happyness'. On 10 October, the fourteen-year-old Diana wrote to 'The Best of Grand-mothers', saying:

It is not easy to be expressed how much I love my Dear Mama Duchess, who has always been so extremly good to me, and it is impossible to show my love and gratitude enough to so good a grandmother (or rather mother to me) but I do assure you it shall be my utmost endevour as long as I live (and would do it if it were possible after death) to repay all the favours I have received from you, who am with all the duty and affection imaginable my Dear Mama Duchess forever yours. Diana Spencer.[45]

CHAPTER SEVEN

Secretary of State

'Lady Dye, too perfect to be described'

Diana and her brother Johnny were together at Marlborough House when a letter arrived from the sixteen-year-old Wriothesley, Duke of Bedford informing their grandmother that he and Lady Anne Egerton were to marry in a week's time. The letter was dated 12 April 1725, and read:

> The sincere respect I have for Your Grace would not have permitted me to have been so long near Town without waiting upon you had not living with ye Duke of Bridgwater unfortunately prevented it. His Grace's treatment of me as well as his daughter, convinces me more and more that it is impossible to live with him, with any tolerable degree of satisfaction, to iether of us. Yr Grace who are so well acquainted with his temper, may easily imagine abundance of reasons which make us desirous to be away from him as soon as we can. We are therfore determined, ye first minute after we are marry'd to go away to Woburn, but to keep it from his Grace till we are gone, by reason the violence of his passion ...[1]

This letter must have caused quite a stir in the Marlborough household, and Diana was bidden to take up her pen to write her grandmother's reply – though not to the duke himself, but to cousin Anne. That the dowager discouraged Anne from showing any disrespect to her father is evident from Anne's reply:

> It was no small satisfaction to me to find my dear Grandmama so willing to give us your advice in our present circumstance which you must imagine gives us a great deal of uneasiness, and I long as much as is possible to have all the bustle over. I can't but think with the Duke of Bedford that we shall live in a much freer & easier manner when departed from my papa, but still (as my dear Grandmama advises) I would leave him if possible in the most quiet and decent manner

showing him all the duty and respect that is due, and therefore after long consideration we have determined to go down to Ashridge for two or three days & then to set out for Woburn Abbey ...[2]

Although the now nineteen-year-old Anne was two years and four months older than her betrothed, as Sarah had said, she was young for her age, and was the duke's own choice. All his life the duke had been surrounded by women who adored him, but within the last two years had lost mother and grandmother, as well as his elder sister to a husband who had taken over his household, leaving him no longer king of his castle. While Anne vouched that her stepmother Rachel had 'allways been extreamly kind and obliging to me', with her wedding day approaching she felt in need of her grandmother's advice. Had she married Carnarvon, Diana would certainly have been her bridesmaid, but circumstances demanded it was to be Bedford's younger sister Betty.* Anne was pleased that 'my Dear Grand-mama thinks it right that Lady Betty should be with us', and promised herself 'a great deal of pleasure from her company', feeling her father's ill behaviour towards her would be 'a just plea for the Duke of Bedford leaving him now tho on my account he suppress'd his resentment before'.[3]

The house at Streatham where the Russell family lived when not at Woburn, and from where the couple planned to marry, had been brought to the family by Bedford's mother (Elizabeth *née* Howland), and was a 'fair old brick mansion' set on a hill surrounded by woods and parkland, convenient for London. The St Leonard's church spire rose invitingly through the trees, but in the event the couple were not to marry here, but at Ashridge. After the religious ceremony in the chapel at Little Gaddesden, returning to the great house under the beech trees, bride and groom should have enjoyed a little merrymaking with family and guests before being put to bed together to consummate the marriage; but instead the duke sent out a servant for fresh horses, and while Bridgwater's guests were drinking and dancing, bundled bride and bridesmaid into a coach, and drove pell-mell for Woburn. Although it was not a long journey from Ashridge, all travel was hazardous at this time, Anne and her sister-in-law Betty jolted and shaken

---

* The term 'bridesmaid' was not in common use at this time, but a (usually) younger sister or cousin was chosen to undress the bride for bed, and accompany the couple on their honeymoon.

when dropped off at the Abbey. Nor was the consummation of the marriage to take place here, the duke taking horse at once for St Albans.[4]

The newly-wed duchess spent her wedding night in a strange four-poster bed with only her bridesmaid for company, but at least Lady Betty knew her way about the house. The situation brightened next day when a letter arrived from the Duchess of Marlborough inviting them to call on her in town. A survey of the stables showed the journey to be impracticable, however, Anne writing to say that it was impossible to comply with 'Dear Grandmama's kind invitation' as the coachman had informed her one of the horses was in so bad a condition as 'not to be able to perform even half the journey', and that the 'glasses of the coach' were broken so that 'if it should rain we should be put to great difficulties'. However, if her grand-mother 'should chuse to come hither yourself & take up with poor enter-tainment that we must give you till things are better settled', she would be delighted; and her grandmother was welcome to bring 'lady Dye & whoever else you have with you'. Anne was sure her husband had given Sarah an account of 'our comeing here from Ashridge', and 'how it was taken by my Papa', so there was no need to repeat it.[5]

The dowager Duchess of Marlborough would have been surprised to find Bedford on the Marlborough House doorstep, especially minus his bride, but was ready with sound advice. First he must approach the Duke of Devonshire (his uncle, having married Bedford's aunt), and ask him to accept the guardianship. Bedford could stay at Marlborough House while she, with Diana and Johnny, visited Woburn, the duchess liking nothing better than to look over a noble house.

Woburn Abbey had much in common with Ashridge in that it had been built by a brotherhood of monks, granted to Bedford's ancestors by Henry VIII at the dissolution. The Bedford earls had originally made their home at Chenies in Buckinghamshire (as well as Southampton House in London) until the 4th Earl moved to Woburn to escape the plague of 1625. The family grew attached to the Abbey, slowly rebuilding it in a more secular style, creating a Jacobean mansion. The 5th Earl and his wife had reared their eight children here, employing a retinue of servants, and added to the prop-erty by buying outlying estates. Their happiness ended, however, when their son Lord William Russell was executed on a charge of High Treason for his implication in the Rye House Plot. Although William was posthu-mously pardoned – to be known as 'the Patriot' and a martyr to the Whig cause – and his father created a duke by way of compensation, the family had never quite shaken off their grief. William's son Wriothesley (Bedford's father) succeeded to the dukedom, becoming a fond father, and spending many months of the year at Woburn. Sadly he died young from smallpox at Streatham, his wife choosing to bring up her children there rather than at the Abbey, visiting it only occasionally. Her son Wriothesley (so named after his father) as 3rd Duke of Bedford appeared ready now to change all that.

Woburn was thought 'spacious and convenient' rather than 'fine', but 'exceedingly pleasantly situated', and surrounded by woods. In the previous year the town had suffered a fire, which the family, being 'particularly eminent as good landlords' were quick to 're-edify', Diana, Johnny and their grandmother being spared the sight of charred cottages as they entered the main gates. Inside they were met with a high medieval wall, through which an archway led to a central court. The new duchess and her sister-in-law would be waiting to escort them to dinner, perhaps after a stroll in the cloister, and afterwards to admire the family portraits in the gallery. Sarah had long revered this staunchly Whig family, and would take special interest in the large family portrait of the late Duchess of Bedford and her young children. Like the one painted of Diana as a three-year-old with her mother, it was by Jervas. The Duke of Bedford's mother is shown seated in widow's weeds, clasping the hand of the infant Wriothesley dressed in the long frock customary for boys not yet 'breeched'. His golden hair is curled to his shoulders, and behind him his chubby infant brother (Lord John Russell) is seated on a refectory table, their sister Rachel protecting him from falling, while a little dog leaps up at the skirts of the youngest sister Betty. Both boys are sturdy, Rachel tall and womanly, mature for her years, while Betty is slim, pert and pretty. Shown in the background is a portrait of the 2nd Duke, once so musical, and now sadly dead. Sometime during their stay the visitors would stroll in the formal gardens, to be astonished by the life-like and life-sized statue of an 'old weeder woman' stooping over her work here, and maybe take tea in the Grotto. The Grotto was created within the cloister by the wife of the 4th Earl, and remains there today. Mother-of-pearl shells and mermaid figures decorate the walls and ceiling, a fountain flowing into a pool in a rustic niche, and as it has a northerly prospect it would be delightfully cool in summer. Sarah may have talked to her newly-wed granddaughter here, while Diana and Johnny looked over the house and park.[6]

A letter arrived for Sarah from the Duke of Bedford while the family was at Woburn, Wriothesley having put pen to paper at '12 a clock at night'. He had asked his uncle the Duke of Devonshire to accept of 'ye Guardianship', and intended to stay in town till the affair was settled in Chancery, confident that this would be accomplished in a 'very short time'. He found his decision was approved by 'every person I have spoken with', and hoped Sarah would 'excuse all faults you met with at Woburn considering nothing is yet settled as it ought to have been', and sent his 'humblest service to Ldy Dia & Mr Spencer'.[7]

Sarah was thrilled to find herself in the role of adviser to the young couple, if disappointed that the duke had married, in her opinion, the wrong granddaughter. When the family returned to Marlborough House they found the duke still here, Sarah informing friends that he had quite 'turn'd Dye out of her place of my secretary', and 'far from being lazy he copys out my papers'. Inevitably, when the Bedfords returned to Woburn for the summer, Diana was restored to her former duties, though at first Sarah wrote to Bedford in her own arthritic hand. The duke begged her to 'make use of a Secretary wch will be a great ease to Yr Grace as you have done in ye super-scription to ye last letter', and believed 'by ye prettyness of ye hand it is Lady Di's writing'.[8]

When Sarah inspected the Bedfords' other property in and near London, the fourteen-year-old Diana almost certainly went with her. One was the house at Streatham, a short drive from town, crossing London Bridge. Her grandmother admired the black and silver cabinet she found here, believing it would look well at the Bedfords' house in Bloomsbury; Wriothesley wrote that he believed it was his brother's. Lord John Russell may have remained at Streatham, studying with his tutor Hetherington. A month younger than Diana, John was preparing himself for the Grand Tour. Diana would take pleasure in mounting the Streatham House staircase with its grotesque carved animals perched upon carved newel posts, running her fingers down the twisted balusters. Sarah would also bid at auctions, taking advantage of the condemned South Sea directors' obligation to sell off their houses, Diana, as her 'secretary', almost certainly at her side.

The Duke of Bedford intended to make the house in Bloomsbury his town house, once having persuaded his uncle the Duke of Rutland to vacate it. Rutland had married the younger of Wriothesley's two aunts, Katherine, who died young in childbirth, while the Duke of Devonshire had married the elder sister Rachel, who was to die this year. Named Southampton House, and afterwards Bedford House, this great building overlooked Bloomsbury Square, and had been brought to the family by Wriothesley's grandmother. Named Rachel, she was the daughter of the 4th Earl of Southampton, and therefore like Diana, a descendant of Shakespeare's patron the 3rd Earl. The house appeared to be a long low building compared to its height, and was believed to have been designed by Inigo Jones, and next to it was the house of Diana's Montagu aunt and uncle. Both houses were set in several acres of land, Southampton House stretching back far enough to envelop the present Russell Square. Diana's cousin called here in the spring of 1726, as the new mistress of the house, reporting to her grandmother that she and her duke were to live in that part where 'Grandmother Russell liv'd'. The disconsolate widow of Lord William Russell had lived here with her children throughout her husband's trial (for complicity in the so-called Rye House Plot to assassinate Charles II and the Duke of York on their way home from Newmarket) and for forty years had commemorated the anniversary of his arrest, sentence and execution, keeping them 'as days of total retirement and private prayer'. Anne described to her own grandmother the rooms Rachel had sat in, saying the main room had '5 window curtings', 'four chairs & 2 easy ones', together with 'two stools', their colour a 'prety deep blue, trimd with gold', and was pleased to find the gold not 'so tarnishd' as expected. The young duchess thought 'it will look very well', her husband thinking the 'Genoa Damask & Mohair good enough to furnish ye room we are to lie in'. Only the 'Indian Damask' curtains and chairs in his grandmother's dressing-room appeared worn, for which it might be 'better to bring new ones'. The duke was pleased to have Sarah purchase furniture for him at 'any auction she must be at', and was careful to stipulate that a room must be furnished for Lady Betty. Anne ended her own letters begging to be reminded to 'Dear Lady Dye', the duke again referring to her as her grandmother's 'pretty Secretary'.[9]

The Duke of Bridgwater, meanwhile, was spluttering with rage at the way his daughter had allowed herself to be driven away from Ashridge, describing her as 'childish perverse undutiful & ungrateful', while accusing her grandmother of encouraging Bedford to be 'rude to him'. Wriothesley assured the dowager duchess 'how far this is from the truth', as also were Bridgwater's adverse comments on what Sarah was doing to Southampton House. He had demanded the return of jewels he had given his daughter, saying the Duchess of Marlborough had enough of her own to give her. Commenting on his 'insolent & mad letter', Bedford said his wife had returned the jewels 'with readiness', though she had always considered them hers, and had sent word by a servant that whereas she esteemed herself 'very happy' in her grandmother's kindness, she expected nothing from her but what had already been given her, and that her husband would supply what 'was proper in that respect'. The jewels she returned were 'the little stay buckles' that had once belonged to her mother, their value under £200, which made 'His Grace's action rather ye meaner'. Anne's legacy from her own mother was still outstanding, Bedford remarking that 'I cannot think even ye Duke of Bridgwater so mad as to dispute the payment of ye £10,000 contrary to ye express words of an Act of Parliament'. Altogether it was 'too much reason thrown away on such a man', the young duke felt, but said that his conscience was clear of all suspicion of 'underhandedness or obstinacy'.[10]

Some attempt was made at a reconciliation, Bedford inviting his father-in-law to dinner – but the invitation remained unanswered. Members of the local gentry were invited along instead, though they proved poor company: they 'went to bowles after dinner and then drunk their bottle till they thought proper to go away'. Bedford had taken the opportunity to drink Sarah's 'and Lady Dye's & many other loyal Healths' before he too retired. The duke appeared to be deeply bored with the country, Sarah attempting to entice him back to London as her 'secretary'. But the duke promptly named Diana her grandmother's 'Secretary of State', declaring her 'much my superior in yt office', and that he despaired of 'entering into competition wth her'. What was more, he was proud to be 'an inferior agent under so able a minister'. When Sarah persisted in comparing him favourably with Diana, he said, 'I cannot call ye preference yr Grace was pleased to give me over my rival secretary by any other name than flattery since everybody acknowledges she is much my superior in every way.' He obviously enjoyed writing to Sarah, a duty he may have performed for his mother and grandmother when they lived, both of whom he sadly missed. And he enjoyed having 'News from London', observing that 'Ye proceedings of ye Regency in ye King's absence must certainly be worth hearing, particularly if Sr Robt Walpole be in Town'.[11]*

Having suffered from the dreaded smallpox and recovered under his grandmother's care, Johnny Spencer had set off on his travels to join brother

---

* The king only grudgingly yielded first place to his son during his absence, and instead of giving him the title of Regent, named him 'Guardian of the Realm and Lieutenant', 'an office unknown in England since the days of the Black Prince.' Wilkins, W. H., *Caroline the Illustrious*.

Charles in Geneva. Diana and her grandmother would be pleased when the Bedfords wrote of their intention to join them at Windsor Lodge for the summer, Wriothesley going so far as to turn down an invitation to the York races. The honeymooners called first on the Duke and Duchess of Manchester at their Kimbolton Castle, the Duke of Bedford writing from there that he looked forward to hunting in 'Ye Forest' at Windsor, and planned to 'employ ye mornings' in that, while Sarah was 'in bed or busy'. Once again he sent 'Service to yr pretty Secretary' Di. Sarah continued to delight in him, thinking him 'just as I should have wished him had hee been my own son', but when he and his bride left for Bath, warned him against 'deep play'.[12]

Bedford wrote from Salisbury to assure Sarah that the friends he hoped to meet at Bath were 'by no means wt your Grace calls swords-men', and 'if I lose any money to them either there or anywhere else, I will venture to forfiet all the esteem & kindness yr Grace has ever had for me'. Like Diana's brother Charles, he had 'ye utmost aversions and detestations to it'. He knew that someone had told Sarah he loved drinking, which was 'as vile & as false as ye other'. His handwriting was an imperfect witness to this protestation, crawling unsteadily towards his signature.[13]

Bedford did meet with 'deep play' at Bath, but told Sarah he was sticking to his 'resolution', and had 'neither won nor lost any thing considerable'. From Bath he and his wife and sister went to Bristol, meeting Bella and the Duke of Manchester here, with Lord Essex. Essex was betrothed to Lady Betty, and there was also a 'Mr Fielding' with them. This may well have been the future novelist, Henry, a contemporary of the young people, and was at Eton with Charles and Johnny. His grandmother and sisters lived in Salisbury, where the Bedfords had lodged on their way to Bath, and later in the year he would be bound over to keep the peace after attempting to abduct a young lady from Lyme Regis. This high-spirited bunch of aristocrats moved on to Longleat, where Lord Weymouth was to marry his young bride.[14]

The year 1725 proved a bumper year for youthful weddings, the fifteen-year-old Louis XV (great-grandson of Marlborough's enemy Louis XIV) having at fifteen married Princess Marie Leszczynska of Poland. This inspired Mary Wortley Montagu to write to her sister in France:

I am in hopes your King of France behaves better than our Duke of Bedford, who by the care of a pious mother certainly preserved his virginity to his marriage bed, where he was so much disappointed in his fair bride (who tho his own inclination could not bestow those expressless raptures he had figur'd for himselfe) that he already pukes at the very name of her and determines to let his estate go to his brother, rather than go through the filthy drudgery of getting an heir to it.

She ended with the postscript:

This is true History and I think the most extraordinary [that] has happen'd in this last age. This comes of living till sixteen without a competent knowledge either of practical or speculative anatomy and literally thinking fine Lady's compos'd of Lillys and Roses.[15]

The young Duchess of Bedford may have been as ignorant of 'practical and speculative anatomy' as her husband was, but this would anyway be expected of a virgin bride. The Bedfords were at Blenheim in the autumn, and afterwards in town, Anne joining Diana and their grandmother at the play. The couple had taken possession of their splendid Bloomsbury mansion, Diana continuing at Marlborough House in her capacity of 'Secretary of State'. She copied down her grandmother's copious correspondence, taking down some from dictation, and played ombre and 'Lanskennet' with her, and perfected her Italian. She was now being taught by an Italian master, Angelo Maria Cori, who was paid an initial fee of one guinea, and another five guineas for three months' lessons, plus one guinea for a dictionary, the bill made out to *des son excellence my lady diana Spencer*. Did Diana hope to visit Italy to study the architecture, or was a better understanding of the opera her aim? Though a rival theatre for the Italian opera had opened in Lincoln's Inn Fields, Sarah and her granddaughter continued to support Handel's opera at the King's Theatre in the Haymarket, as did the king.

Not only was Diana growing in learning, but in height and beauty, and she was fitted with the latest fashions. Willigo's governor Nicholas Mann was sent a list of fabrics to purchase in Paris, possibly given him by brother John as he passed through. A proud scholar who made little effort to hide his dislike for the dowager duchess, Mann found Johnny as 'happy and brisk as a bird in a cage' to be free of his grandmother. In reply to Sarah's request for 'stuffs' Mann wrote to her through Diana, regretting there were:

no such lutestrings as she [Sarah] desires, or indeed any fit for a woman of condition to wear, at less price than 20 livres the French ell, that is near 16 shillings the English yard, the French silks in general being little or nothing cheaper than the English, except only such were workt up with gold or silver. And those to fit the Young Lady [Diana] who is not fifteen for whom I could not but have a particular concern, there were no silks but of the last years manufacture, which they call old fashion'd, but within a month the new ones will come in, and my friend promises to search again for some stuffs that may be Her Grace's satisfaction.[16]

Diana would be fifteen next birthday. She had worn stays from the age of ten, she and cousin Anne supplied with 'black stays and green stays, with green laces and black laces' at the time of her sister's wedding; like the Elizabethan stomacher, these rose stiffly over the bosom from a pinched waist, but the latest stays, though equally narrow at the waist, were cut away in a curve below each breast. At fourteen Diana wore a 'blue & white satten quilted coat' and a quilted 'hoop coat', the quilting lending warmth as she walked the long stone corridors of Marlborough House and Blenheim Palace. She was presented with forty-one pairs of kid gloves over a period of only eight months, each pair costing two shillings: these were white, fitted to the elbow, and appear to have been discarded after one use. As Lady Betty was to marry Lord Essex in February, a grand ball was planned at Southampton House for the occasion – a splendid opportunity for Sarah to show off Diana.[17]

If Diana was dressed to look fine, her brothers dressed up to look finer. Their grandmother complained bitterly of the enormous amounts of money they were spending abroad, declaring it more than she and her duke had spent on themselves and their whole entourage on their travels. Johnny's suit to attend the court at Lorraine (decorated with silver lace and lined with 'blew') had cost £630, his twelve ruffled Holland shirts £276, his scarlet riding coat lined with velvet £91, and a hat with a feather £24. Both boys wore bag wigs, and wigs of natural hair, and their square-heeled, block-toed shoes had high tongues and diamond buckles. The quilting of Diana's satin coat cost only nine shillings, her hoop coat seventeen shillings (though maybe the cost of the 'stuff' purchased in Paris was not included). Johnny played hard and worked hard abroad, writing home from Geneva that he rose 'at eight in the morning' to employ himself at his studies, and went to dinner at three. On

Thursdays and Saturdays he went 'a hunting', and was now learning to play the German flute. Sarah protested about this latter employment, afraid it would spoil his mouth, but Captain Fish (who had accompanied Johnny to Geneva) reassured her this was not so. Both brothers showed concern for their sisters while away, Charles pleased to hear that 'Sister Bateman was arrived safe in Paris, and that Sister Die is so well and handsome'. Johnny asked affectionately after 'Sister Dye', and both corresponded with her, though sadly these letters do not appear to have survived.[18]

Diana's cousin Willigo (Lord Blandford since his mother became duchess) had so far managed to avoid matrimony, having put off his return to England year after year. He kept late hours in Paris, his governor Mann complaining how 'we continue to sup at mid-night' and to 'sit up often to day light', and how Willigo was getting fat. This was in sharp contrast to the hopeful youth who had matriculated at Oxford before setting sail for France at seventeen. His grandmother complained bitterly of his heavy drinking, deep play and keeping ill hours, her admonishments falling on deaf ears, until at one point Willigo ceased writing to her altogether. Mann, despite himself, managed to bring about a reconciliation, regretting it later when Sarah wrote Willigo 'three sheets full' at a time, putting him in mind of an animal that 'stifles her young with too much fondling'. She wrote sheets-full to Johnny and Charles too, warning them against playing at cards with French women who were 'all cheats', and reminding Fish that the Swiss academy was not for wasting time and money, but in place of a university, to 'keep them out of harms way'.[19]

The great ball at Southampton House, celebrating Lady Betty's wedding, took place in February 1726. Sarah had little love for Lady Betty (who may well have found Sarah interfering, coming as she did so soon and so strongly into the Russell lives after the death of her mother). Lady Burlington wrote to Sarah saying she 'always thought that the Duchess of Bedford [Anne] had a great deal of goodness and soundness of temper for it must be owing to that, that she shows so much fondness for Lady Betty Russell, for I never read a less pleasing description than you gave of her'. Diana's old neighbour from Piccadilly, her mother's close friend, was disappointed that Sarah had not 'mentioned one word of Lady Die' in her letter, which reminded her of a story she had read of a painter who had 'drawn the sacrifice of Epheyenia',* vividly expressing the grief and compassion of the spectators,

---

* Saint Euphemia, third-fourth century, an early Christian martyred at Chalcedon.

while drawing a veil over the faces of the sacrificed martyr's parents. When asked his reason for this, the artist replied that while he could represent the passions and grief of the less concerned of the onlookers, it was 'impossible to do it of theirs'. From this Lady Burlington deduced that Sarah must think 'Lady Die too perfect to be described, or else sure she deserv'd a share when you were upon a pleasing subject'.[20]

Diana, floating up the Southampton House steps in her hooped gown, would have been as aware of the building as she was of the glamorous clothes and flashing jewels of the guests. Inside the house she would find the Raphael cartoons copied by Thornhill 'as large as the originals', and many other works of art, but as a young girl approaching sixteen years her first thoughts would have been as much on the music and dancing, to say nothing of the young men. Wriothesley's younger brother John would be here, perhaps the first to ask Diana to dance, though as a 'younger son' he did not feature in her grandmother's list of possible suitors. Short and plump, he was not strikingly attractive, but had a 'merry good-humour'. Gossips at the ball were more interested in the elder brother Wriothesley, one remarking how well the Duke of Bedford did the honours, 'particularly what related to drinking!'[21]

Difficulties in the Bedford marriage had shown themselves from the very beginning, and it had not helped that Wriothesley's aunt, the Duchess of Devonshire, had died in the first year of their honeymoon. Obliged to go into mourning, Anne wrote complaining to Sarah of the unfairness of having to remain at home when such 'relations as the Duke of Rutland & all that family were at Mrs Kemps last night & all public places', and 'my Lord goes everywhere so that I am the only one (who am not a relation) that stays at home for her, which I have done above a week'. As ex-premier lady of a queen, Sarah was strict on protocol, instructing her granddaughter as to correct procedure. Pathetically Anne hoped her grandmother would not think she did 'worse than her whole family in going to the play to night', having been engaged to go with Lady Bristol who had 'places above this week'. If she did stay at home, '(I mean not go to the play) no body will think it is for her when they see all her relations there'. Tearfully Anne signed herself her grandmother's 'Dutiful Daughter'. The shortcomings of the marriage had worsened, becoming the talk of the town, and in a bid to save her from the 'misfortunes which anybody might easily foresee', her grandmother took her aside to warn her. Anne's reaction was to be as 'dumb' as cousin Harriet had been after her wedding, and when 'no reason nor kind expressions could prevail', Sarah suggested that Anne might not care to come to her since she (Sarah) was obliged to tell her 'everything that I heard could hurt you'. Anne's answer was that she did not know whether she should come or not.[22]

From this time on, Anne began to go to places expressly forbidden by her husband, while he turned more and more to drink and dicing. In the November of 1726 Anne took·refuge at Casiobury, home of the newly-wed Betty and Lord Essex. Estranged from both husband and father, Anne was aware she could expect little sympathy from society as a whole, her grand-mother approaching Bedford's guardian the Duke of Devonshire. She begged him to persuade Anne to return to her husband, and being short of money, with no equipage of her own, Anne finally submitted. She wrote in tiny neat writing that she was resolved to return to Woburn since it was the only way she would have the satisfaction of knowing she had done 'every thing that is right', though hardly hoping it would have the effect 'my Dear Grandmama wishes it may'. She regretted the 'differences' she had had with her grandmother, and hoped to be 'esteam'd' by her as she used to be.[23]

All this, as Sarah's 'Secretary of State', Diana must have known. Her grandmother had found the Duke of Devonshire the most 'reasonable and worthy man' she knew 'in the world', who told her 'all that has happened in this affair', for which she was sorry. But she was surprised that Anne had 'so great a difficulty' in acknowledging she had been in the wrong in going to any place that the Duke of Bedford 'desir's you would not', and thought she should have had no scruple in doing and saying just 'what he desired you to' in order 'to save your self from ruin'. At the same time she admitted, 'though I never did before', that the Duke of Bedford was 'extremely in the wrong'.[24]

Such an admission by Sarah meant that Bedford was very much in the wrong indeed. But as divorce could only be brought about by means of a private and costly act of parliament, in which the wife was likely to forfeit her dower rights and most of the money she had brought to the marriage, Anne had little choice but to stay. As her grandmother said, in order to save herself from 'utter ruin' she must otherwise 'throw herself at her father's feet'. The best thing was to 'live well with the Duke of Bedford', and 'in any way that he shall insist on', for her own 'future quiet'. It was Sarah's opinion that 'if you can't make yourself easy at home, you can never have any great happiness abroad', and she hoped Devonshire's endeavours to make her happy would 'not be fruitless'.

Sarah revealed her true opinion of Anne's plight to her friend Mrs Boscawen, believing that Bedford's drinking might not have been so bad had he not had 'a great aversion to his wife'. Alas, if only he had married Diana! When she invited Wriothesley to confide in her he was too embarrassed to speak, the duchess having to accept that although she was the 'Grandmother' she could not know 'the secrets between them'.[25]

The Duke of Devonshire and the Earl of Essex had meanwhile departed for Woburn to sort out Anne's dowry, and arrange a personal allowance for her. Anne took the first opportunity she could to tell her grandmother how 'my Lord Essex came back from Woburn a Sunday Night with the contract signed', and she found it 'rather better than I could expect'. She thanked Sarah for her goodness in speaking to him 'to get me more', and promised that as soon as Lord and Lady Essex returned from a visit they were making to Portsmouth she would have them drive her to Windsor. If only she had 'equipage of my owne', she wrote, 'I should have come myself'. She meanwhile presented her 'Service to Lady Dye'.[26]

Diana had learned much of Marriage *à la Mode* in her sixteenth year, and with £30,000 for her portion, as well as heiress to another £100,000, and being young, beautiful and accomplished, she was likely to learn more. When the king celebrated his sixty-seventh birthday that year, grandmother and granddaughter were within hearing of the guns in St James's Park booming out the number of his years. From the Marlborough House windows they would see the spectacle of brightly adorned courtiers flocking to the court in their 'birthday clothes', and may even have joined with them. But as Sarah was to celebrate her own sixty-seventh year in eight days' time, they were more likely preparing for the country. The king embarked on the Royal Yacht some days later, bound for his beloved Hanover, consuming a vast quantity of melons on his way. One hour into his journey out of Delden he fainted, recovering enough to be driven to his brother's Osnabrück home. George I died on the following morning of 11 June. It was a bad-tempered Prince of Wales that emerged from the royal bedchamber at Richmond Palace, breeches in hand, to find Walpole lowering his great bulk to the ground. When told the news of his father's death, George II commented, 'Dat is one big lie!' But it was true, and meanwhile where and who was the new Prince of Wales?[27]

CHAPTER EIGHT

Lady Rich and the Prince of Wales

'so valuable a young creature as Dye . . .'

Diana's brothers wrote begging to be allowed home for the corona-tion of George II in October, 1727, their grandmother refusing to give her consent. Writing to their governor Fish, she said nothing would be more ridiculous than to 'leave all the improvements that they can have abroad . . . only to see some old & odd people walk in red velvet upon green cloath for hansome figures'. Nor did she consider anyone worth coming so far to look at 'only out of a window'. She was herself numbered among the 'old & odd people', however, taking her place in the procession of peers, as was their twenty-seven-year-old brother Sunderland, who had the honour to be Lord Carver. Johnny and Charles must content themselves with reading the news-prints, and changing the gilt buttons and the scarlet linings of their coats to black, in respect for the late king.[1]

Must Diana stay at home, helping her grandmother into her crimson robes (brushing away signs of moth and dust of the previous reigns), and placing the tiny strawberry coronet onto the honey-washed hair? Must she watch from the window as her grandmother departed in her coach, knowing that her sister as Viscountess Bateman, her cousin Anne as Duchess of Bedford, and her cousin Charlotte as Baroness De la Warr, were among those honoured to attend? Or were 'Ladies' invited too? If so - why not the Honourables Charles and Johnny? With the help of sticks, their grand-mother walked bravely in the procession of peers and peeresses, until exhausted she subsided onto a drum – guards and onlookers raising a cheer. In Westminster Hall after the ceremony the peers and peeresses sat opposite one another at table, the king and queen with their five princesses and one prince seated above them on a dais. It was odd that the youngest prince (the Duke of Cumberland) was here and not his twenty-year-old brother Fred-erick, left behind so long ago in Hanover.* After Diana's brother had carved the first of the succulent meats for their Majesties, the company thrilled to

---

* Frederick had remained in Hanover when his parents and sisters joined George I in England in 1714, when he was only seven years old. He had not seen his parents or siblings since.

see the King's Champion enter on a 'goodly white horse richly caparisoned' and in white armour make his challenge: three times he cast down his gauntlet, and three times it was handed to him again. As no one took up his challenge, the king drank a toast to him, handing him the golden bowl from which he had drunk. In reply the Champion drank the new king's health, then departed, keeping the golden bowl as his fee.

Up in the gallery the twenty-seven-year-old Mrs Pendarves (future Mrs Delaney) was determined to miss nothing. She had set out at half-past four in the morning, 'squeezed nearly flat', and had lost her cloak in the process, but had managed to obtain a good seat. Her chief interest as always was the 'dresses of the ladies', all of them 'becoming', and most of them immensely rich; she had spotted Diana's cousin Lady De la Warr, who 'was one of the best figures'. Charlotte may have surpassed even the newly crowned queen, who, though 'extravagantly fine', did not in Pendarves's opinion 'make show enough for the occasion'. The three older princesses wore stiff bodices of silver tissue, their purple mantles edged with ermine, and held up the tip of the queen's train. There was a wonderful moment when the 1800 candles in the chandeliers, branches and sconces 'were lighted in three minutes by an invention of Mr Heidegger's'. When the peers and peeresses sat eating at the long tables, the ladies in the galleries let down their baskets on strings, drawing them up to find them 'filled with cold meat and bread, sweetmeats, and wine'.[2]

Charles and Johnny had left Geneva and were finishing their education in Paris, studying drawing, painting, architecture and medals. They 'ride well, and don't dance ill', reported Fish, and 'may soon improve themselves in the last as much as one could wish', Paris being almost 'the only place where there are good teachers'. Charles was as bored as his grandmother had been when 'abroad', looking on travel as a very 'insipid entertainment', dreading the thought of journeying into Italy. As Charles had come of age one month after the coronation, Fish warned Sarah that he 'thinks of nothing but England, and pines for it'. Charles and Johnny had not forgotten the women left behind, ordering two 'mantilles' to be made for their grandmother and sister, and 'I believe you will like them,' wrote Fish, for not only were they 'the high mode here', but 'very handsome when they are well put on, & very convenient'.[3]

Named variously the *saque, robe battante, contouche* and 'Watteau flying Gowns', these 'mantilles' had been fashionable in France since the 1720s. Voluminous in shimmering silks and satins and even fine cotton, they proved warm and comfortable as well as elegant, grandmother and granddaughter getting used to wearing them with the 'right air'. Charles arrived in England at about the same time as the mantillas did, and Sarah wrote to thank Johnny for sending them, as well as for his directions on how to wear them. She had 'never lik'd any fashion so well', and 'your sister is so fond of it that I believe she will find some excuse to wear it even when the weather does not require it'! She found Charles less pleasing in himself, complaining that he 'does not look near so well as he did when he went out of England', and had developed 'a little tone in his speaking English' which seemed to her 'affected'. Though others thought he had 'sence', she found 'nothing entertaining' in him at all. Having looked forward to hearing him prattle with Diana in French, she found him as inarticulate in that language as in his own. 'He speaks through his teeth', she complained, and 'like several women I have noticed in this country who don't articulate but think it pretty to make a noise like a bird'. She hoped Johnny had not picked up that way of speaking, she told Fish, 'for if he has I think it is very indifferent what language he talks in'![4]

Diana must have been delighted in having Charles home again, but was soon parted from him as he scuttled away from his grandmother's tongue to be with his brother at Sunderland House. Not that Sarah and Diana were short of company, several visitors calling at Blenheim when they were there, among them the philosopher Voltaire. Sarah had written to the brothers that 'Here is a French man that I believe is about three score, who has learned in a year's time to read all the English authors & both writes and speaks English'. He clearly put the boys to shame, though in fact was only thirty-three. He was introduced to Sarah by Lord Chesterfield, the English ambassador to the Hague, a man whom, as we shall see later, was clearly impressed by Diana.[5]

As Diana's eighteenth birthday approached, her grandmother, still seeking a husband for her, became deeply alarmed when a swelling appeared on her neck. She immediately sought the advice of her doctors and physicians (despite her general disapproval of them), her bank accounts showing payments of up to £190 towards a cure. Sarah let her fears be known to Johnny, who wrote saying he was pleased to hear his grandmother had a remedy that might cure his sister, and mentioned the King of Sardinia's physician, who 'has a great deal of practice in that country for the cure of swelled necks'. Sarah, still anxious to try anything that might do Diana good, replied:

Your sisters neck is certainly better than it was, with the remedies we have got; but there is still a great deal to do. I should be extream glad that you would get me the advice & medicin you mention of the man that has done so much good with it and to send the receipt how to make it (besides the medicin) for I will not give her any thing without knowing what it is.

Anxious not to deter prospective suitors, Sarah was careful to emphasise that 'Your Sister Dye is in mighty good health & looks better than ever she did in her life.'[6]

Johnny was suffering toothache, two of his teeth 'drawn', and must now 'have another'. Concerned for his looks, too, Sarah wrote to say she hoped they were 'out of sight', having observed 'the loss of teeth before [in front] is a great blemish', and advised him to chew tobacco. If chewed 'for half an hour or thereabouts', tobacco was highly beneficial, and 'nothing in the world would preserve them so much'. When Johnny fell sick of a fever, suffering headache and pain in his side, things were more serious. Captain Fish nursed him to health, but then he too fell sick. The Duke of Kingston had taken the two young men into his care, but when Johnny recovered it was to tell his grandmother that Fish was dead. Sarah begged Johnny to return home as soon as he was well enough, for 'no words can express how dear you are to me, & I shall be in torture till I see you'. Johnny, with commendable efficiency, arranged an autopsy on Fish (his lungs were found to be ulcerated and his heart 'full of polypuses'), and arranged for the body to be embalmed. Sarah advised him to bring the captain's gold watch in his pocket, and wear it for his sake – and she would pay his father for it. The body of the faithful captain (who had played Antony so coolly at Blenheim) was shipped home to his father in England.[7]

Johnny was home in November, Sarah settling him into an apartment in the Marlborough House courtyard where she could keep an eye on him. She was deeply fond of him even 'from a little child', for he had 'a great deal of spirit & quickness & has much good nature, which are charming qualities'. She looked for a way to make him 'Lord Churchill' so he might represent the 'Dear Duke of Marlborough' in the world, prepared to support the title through her personal estate, but it was not to be. For all his difficulties abroad, Johnny had not forgotten his sister's sickness, and on 10 February 1729 a receipt for the 'Plaster for Lady Dies neck' arrived at Marlborough

House from Milan, together with medicine. The 'plaster' was a compound of 'Arabian incense' to be laid around the swelling, the patient to adhere to a strict diet of 'little water and only broth'. Since this was all the patient could readily swallow, and was a healthy diet, it made sense, as did the message attached to the medicine, saying that if it did the 'Lady no good', it would 'do her no harm'. The medicine was to be taken in four doses: one every night as the 'patient goes to bed; and must only be taken in ye last quarter of the moon'. It was sweet and not unpleasant to the taste, to be 'left to melt in one's mouth without chewing'. If the medicine contained iodine (an extract from seaweed, or saltpetre) it might well have done her good. [8]*

George II's son Frederick, the uncrowned Prince of Wales, was hosting a ball at the Herrenhausen Palace outside Hanover when a messenger arrived with an order for him to leave for England at once. Frederick was distressed by the death of his grandfather, the only member of his family to have visited him since they left for England thirteen years ago. Public pressure may have been brought to bear, the people naturally longing to see their prince. It was snowing when he left Hanover, he and his companion in so much haste that their carriage slipped from the road and careered into a frozen marsh. Later, in thick fog, the coach plunged into the deep waters of a dyke, and the prince was subjected to a further soaking as the rowing boat carrying him to the packet-boat for England was caught up in ice-floes. His passage over rough winter seas can have been little better, the prince landing at Greenwich to find no one on the shore to meet him. Nor was there a relay of messengers to convey the news of his landing to London. When the prince and his companion finally reached Whitechapel they were obliged to take a common hackney coach to St James's Palace, and if Diana had chanced to glance from the Marlborough House windows at seven thirty on the evening of 7 December 1728, she might have spied a slightly built young man alight from the cab at the Friary (a group of buildings between Marlborough House and the palace proper), and proceed toward the queen's back stairs.

The dowager Duchess of Marlborough had been unwell that winter, but let nothing stand in the way of her attending the court now the prince was here. She took her place at the card-tables although 'forced to be carried to the table

---

* As late as 1927 the Log Book of Rockley School in Wiltshire records that chocolate containing iodine was given as a 'remedy for goitre'. The child concerned was reported 'decidedly better' after only two or three months. Mary Roberts, *Rockley – A Wiltshire Village.*

in a chair, & fixed there before the King & Queen came'. Was Diana with her, her neck tenderly concealed by a scarf? Sarah was effortlessly vivacious, her mind as alert as it had ever been, rising from the card-table the winner of £390. Her spirits were so high, reported Lady Bristol, as to be 'beyond anything I ever saw', and afterwards she 'had company to sup, and sat up between 3 & 4 this morning'. Lady Bristol's son Lord Hervey had befriended the Prince of Wales in Hanover, a friendship that was renewed, and by inviting his mother to supper, Sarah opened up many an opportunity for royal introductions.[9]

Sarah collapsed from these exertions in the end, becoming so ill it was thought she was dying. Her daughter the Duchess of Montagu wrote anxiously to her niece asking after her grandmother's health, beginning 'Dear Lady Dye':

I am sure you will believe that I am in a great deal of concerne to hear that my mother is so ill, & I beg you will have the goodness to let me know how she does to day. I did not care to send but to you, for fear it might be any way uneasy to her. I am dear lady Dye your most humble servant M Montagu.

This was a considerate and tender letter, but Diana's answer was cool, her grandmother having doubtless ordered the tone. Addressing her aunt as 'Madam', Diana informed her:

My Dear Grandmama has suffer'd a great deal, but I hope the remedies she has taken have done her some good, tho' she's far from being as I wish Her.

The letter ended with the 'greatest respect', Diana signing herself her 'Grace's Most obedient and most Humble Servant'.[10]

Diana's own infirmity seemed forgotten as her grandmother (except for a few weeks in the summer) collapsed into total impairment. She was carried about in a chair on poles, a mechanical hoist devised to lift her in and out of her coach, and though Diana's brother Sunderland showed grave concern for her, the dowager saying he had as 'much compassion as his mother', as soon as she showed signs of improvement, took himself off to Paris. Apart from servants, Diana was left to shoulder the burden alone.

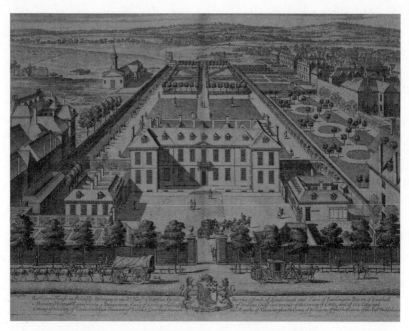

Top: Burlington House, showing the gardens of Clarges House (right) which as Sunderland House became Diana's childhood home in London. By Knyff-Kip. *British Library.*

Above: Althorp, the Spencer's country seat in Northamptonshire. By John Vosterman, 1677. *Courtesy The Collection at Althorp.*

Lady Diana Spencer as an infant with her mother, Anne (Churchill) Spencer, Countess of Sunderland, c 1713. Attributed to Charles Jervas. *Courtesy The Collection at Althorp.*

Left: Diana as a young woman when living at Blenheim Palace. By Charles Jervas. *Photograph by Jeremy Whitaker. Reproduced by kind permission of His Grace the Duke of Marlborough.*

Right: Diana's father Charles Spencer, 3rd Earl of Sunderland. Engraved after Godfrey Kneller. *British Museum, Prints and Drawings.*

Above: Holywell House, St Albans, where Diana first lived with her grand-parents. By John Storer after G. Shepherd. *From The Beauties of England and Wales.*

Below: A north view of Blenheim Palace engraved in the mid-eighteenth century. By John Boydell. *British Library.*

Sarah, Duchess of Marlborough, Diana's maternal grandmother. By Sir Godfrey Kneller. *Photograph by Jeremy Whitaker. Reproduced by kind permission of His Grace the Duke of Marlborough.*

Above: John, Duke of Marlborough, Diana's
maternal grandfather. By John Closterman.
Reproduced by kind permission of His Grace the Duke
of Marlborough.

Right: Diana's brother, Charles Spencer, 5th Earl of
Sunderland and 3rd Duke of Marlborough. By Van Loo.
Photograph by Jeremy Whitaker. Reproduced by kind
permission of His Grace the Duke of Marlborough.

Left: Lady Anne (Spencer) Bateman, Diana's sister. By Enoch Seman. *Courtesy The Collection at Althorp.*

Right: Diana's brother, The Hon. John Spencer, with his son John (the future lst Earl Spencer) on horseback. By George Knapton. *Courtesy The Collection at Althorp.*

Diana's cousins Lady Harriet Godolphin, future Duchess of Newcastle, with her brother William ('Willigo') Godolphin, later Lord Blandford. By Charles Jervas. *Photograph by Jeremy Whitaker. Reproduced by kind permission of His Grace the Duke of Marlborough.*

Diana's cousins, John, Lord Brackley, and his sister Lady Anne Egerton.
By Charles Jervas. *Photograph by Jeremy Whitaker. Reproduced by kind permission of His Grace the Duke of Marlborough.*

Left: Wriothesley, 3rd Duke of Bedford. By Isaac Whood. *By kind permission of the Marquess of Tavistock and the Trustees of the Bedford Estate.*

Right: Anne (Egerton), 3rd Duchess of Bedford. By Isaac Whood. *By kind permission of the Marquess of Tavistock and the Trustees of the Bedford Estate.*

Above: Windsor Lodge, in Windsor Great Park. Engraved after Thomas Sandby. *British Library.*

Below: Frederick, Prince of Wales, and his sisters ('The Music Party'). By Philip Mercier, 1733. *Copyright National Portrait Gallery, London.*

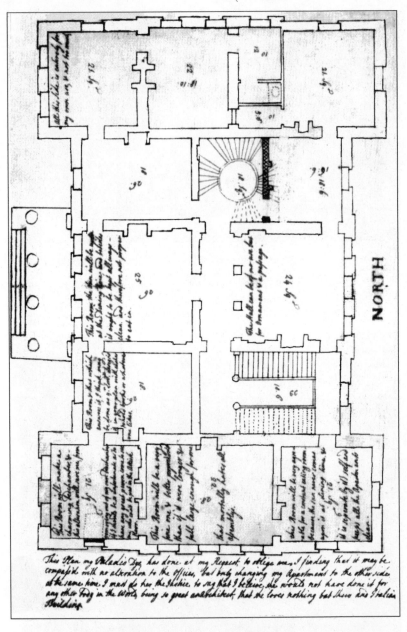

Plan of Wimbledon House drawn by 'Paladio Dye', endorsed by her
grandmother the Duchess of Marlborough.

John, 4th Duke of Bedford. By Thomas Gainsborough. *By kind permission of the Marquess of Tavistock and the Trustees of the Bedford Estate.*

Diana (Spencer), 4th Duchess of Bedford. By Thomas Hudson.
By kind permission of the Marquess of Tavistock and the Trustees of the Bedford Estate.

Woburn Abbey 'in its former state'. Gardens had been planted in Diana's day, but the building was much as shown here. Only the North front, with its grotto, remains as part of Woburn today. *From* Woburn and its Abbey, *by J. D. Parry. Longman, 1831.*

Bedford House, Bloomsbury. By Pieter Rysbrack. *By kind permission of the Marquess of Tavistock and the Trustees of the Bedford Estate.*

The king and queen had vetted Frederick before presenting him to the public, the king remarking that 'I think he is not a son I need be much afraid of'. The queen took him out and about on visits, her face full of smiles, everyone receiving him kindly. Frederick must have dreamed of the day when he would be reunited with his family, meeting for the first time his younger siblings, and gave delightful parties for his elder sisters. He appeared to be knowledgeable, and was fluent in several languages, his appearance neat and dapper. As time went by, his popularity with the people increased; he walked the Mayfair streets among them with no attempt at disguise, while his father called him 'an intruder, an imposter' and a 'changeling'. Eventually the king declared him no son of his. He had 'never liked the puppy', he growled, the queen and his three elder sisters also turning against him. Seeing him cross the courtyard one day, the queen had burst into a fit of passion, crying, '. . . that wretch! . . . the villain! I wish the ground would open at this moment and sink the monster to the lowest hole in hell!'; indeed she wished he had never been born. Princess Caroline thought this too much energy wasted on what was impossible, saying it would be best if the prince simply burst, 'then we may all go about with smiling faces, glad hearts, and crape and hoods for him'. Alas poor Fred! His nose was heavy, his eyes slanting, his complexion sallow, and the only members of the family undisturbed by his presence were his brother the Duke of Cumberland, and his new little sisters, the princesses Mary and Louisa.[11]

When Queen Caroline's birthday was celebrated on the first day of March in 1729, Frederick, who was now officially Prince of Wales, appeared at court looking delightful in 'mouse coloured velvet turned up with scarlet and very richly embroidered with silver'. Mrs Pendarves was here, busily making notes, saying he danced very well, especially country dances, and at the magic moment when:

The clocke struck twelve, the French dances were just over, and every man took the woman he liked best to dance country-dances, the Prince set the example by choosing the Duchess of Bedford who is the queen of his fancy at present . . .

Diana's cousin had blossomed into a beauty despite her intolerable marriage, and the prince felt more comfortable with married women since they gave rise to less speculation. Lady Bristol described the prince as 'the most agreeable young man it is possible to imagine without being the least handsome', his person 'little but well-made and genteel', and he had a 'liveliness in his eyes that is indescribable'. His manner of winking at the servants while gobbling up jelly would certainly have beggared description.[12]

Later in the year the new King George set off for Hanover, as his father had done so often before him. He had delegated the Regency to the queen in his absence, rather than to his heir, which, with few duties to occupy him, and a niggardly allowance, assisted in the pile-up of Frederick's debts. His night life included whore-mongering, deep play, drinking and smashing windows, the last landing him in trouble with the neighbours. After attacking Buckingham House (the future Buckingham Palace) he received a discharge of grape-shot for his trouble, and Lord and Lady Berkshire demanded an apology for other breakages, refusing to appear at the St James's court till one was received. Frederick seldom drank himself under the table, however, and if he did play recklessly, it was only in an attempt to top up his allowance.

Sarah took Diana to Tunbridge Wells for the summer, where the waters might improve both their healths, and on their return news reached them that Robert Lord Spencer was struck down with a fever in Paris. Sarah at once sent medicine by express, and despite her disabilities, followed after them in her coach, believing there was no such thing as 'a good doctor in France, nor medicine'. Diana was doubtless with her, and both would be brought up short by the news of Diana's brother's death. He had been bled and purged, which Sarah believed was 'always thought prejudicial to fever'. The apothecary's bill came to £1379, together with the *necessarie de porcelaine* at £144, and £200 for the coffin. The cost of bringing Robert home was £600, his body carried to Althorp to lie beside his parents at the church at Great Brington. At least he had done 'little mischief to the estate', and Diana's brother Charles became 5th Earl of Sunderland. Willigo, the Marlborough heir, was in trouble with his family, having at the age of thirty taken a 'low odd woman' to wife, Maria Catherina (de Jonge), a mere burgomaster's daughter, from Holland![13]

Another visit to Tunbridge Wells was planned for the following summer, Sarah as anxious about Diana's health as her own. Now rising twenty, with no husband on the horizon, everything must be done to keep Diana's sickness at bay, her beauty maintained. Fortunately Sarah believed in the importance of fresh air and exercise, and this was her reason for encouraging a friendship with Lady Rich. This lively redhead, Elizabeth, had organised Diana's equestrian lessons when she was a child, and at the time of Diana's birth had married Sir Robert Rich, a much respected military man. Twice wounded fighting under Marlborough, and descended from the elder branch of the Earls of Warwick, he was now Groom-of-the-Bedchamber to George II. The Rich couple had two sons and a daughter, and while Sir Robert was away on military duties, his wife frequented literary circles. A derisory poem concerning her 'immorality' was written by Pope, which appears to have escaped Sarah's notice, and Lady Mary Wortley Montagu spoke of her 'giddy vanity'. An illicit relationship with 'the polite Mr Holt', though 'bound in a treaty of marriage with one of the prittyest Girls in Town', was suggested, this gentleman appearing 'better with [Lady Rich] than ever'. Lord Hervey was aware of her existance, and when complaining of a dearth of company at Bath, remarked that 'the only people whose faces I know, whose names I have ever heard, or who I believe have names belonging to them' were 'the Duchess of Marlborough [Henrietta], Congreve, and Lady Rich'. It seems incredible that Sarah should not have known these things, encouraging the thirty-eight-year-old Elizabeth's friendship with Diana.[14]

Sarah allowed Lady Rich to spend a great deal of time with Diana, the two delighting in each other's company, attending the play, and afterwards supping at Marlborough House. Having grown up so closely with her grandmother, Diana would appreciate older company, and Lady Rich considered herself young. With her auburn hair and 'unsully'd complexion', she made up to Diana for the loss of mother, cousins and sister. They would canter together along the St James's bridle-way, and take a carriage through Hyde Park, talking poetry, plays and opera from sun-up to sun-down. Lady Rich was a bubbly and incurable romantic, as well as girlish in her ways, and a strong attachment grew between them. If parted for as much as an hour, notes flew between the pair.

Suddenly, for no apparent reason, the Duchess of Marlborough cooled toward Lady Rich. Perhaps she had at last heard hints of the gossip surrounding her, and this sudden coldness rendered Elizabeth uneasy. She dared not ask the cause, and as the summer grew warmer, and the streets of London stuffier, Sarah let it be known that she and Diana were to depart for Tunbridge Wells without her. Elizabeth, having obviously expected to go with them, was hurt, consoling herself that Sarah began at least to be pleasant towards her, inviting her to call on Diana as often as she wished before their departure. Relieved to find herself reasonably in favour again,

Lady Rich faced up stoically to the separation, the two friends planning to write often.

On the jolting journey to Tunbridge Wells Sarah advised Diana to let some time lapse before writing to her friend. Diana would agree to do as her grandmother advised, waiting two days after they reached their lodgings before doing so. A letter soon winged its way to her by way of reply, Lady Rich pleased to have had her letter, but complaining pettishly that she 'did expect one sooner as the post goes out every day it comes in every day, & as you got there a Saterday I might without being very unreasonable have hoped you would not have passd Sunday and Monday without writing.' Diana's letter had been so kind, however, it had made amends.[15]

Writing from her house in Grosvenor Street, the heat of the summer having driven friends and neighbours to the country, Lady Rich was desolate. 'Nothing here is worth repeating,' she cried, and 'next tuesday carrys away 6 people out of eight or ten that I am acquainted with'. Having expected to spend the summer at Tunbridge, she had failed to make plans of her own, but was relieved by an invitation to a wedding. On 'Tuesday night Lady Mary was married', she wrote Diana, in reference to Diana's younger Montagu cousin, 'and all the people that are in town with them, I amongst the rest.' Since Mary was three years Diana's junior, and apart from herself the last of Sarah's granddaughters to wed, her own single state would be highlighted. Was this why Sarah had rushed her off to Tunbridge Wells? Lady Rich informed Diana that the bride looked 'most miserably', and thought 'she wou'd have swooned every time there came in a new body'. Her mother the Duchess of Montagu looked 'mighty well', however, wearing 'as fine a manto as is proper for the time of the year, white and gold striped', the bride's gown being of 'white and silver mosaeick'.[16]

Mary had married George Brudenell, the future 4th Earl of Cardigan, a young man Sarah had tentatively marked out for Diana, during that happy, long ago, summer at Blenheim. It must have seemed to Sarah that all the eligible young men had been swept up, an extraordinary situation considering Diana's acknowledged beauty and riches. Her cousin Bella was at her sister's wedding, and as friend and neighbour of Lady Rich, was invited to dine. As Bella was to join Diana and their grandmother at Tunbridge Wells on the following day, there was much to discuss.

Lady Rich would be delighted to learn later that Diana was riding at Tunbridge Wells, believing it both 'pleasant and healthy', and when Bella joined the party, asked if Lady Fane was there too. Lady Fane was to act as go-between for a match between Diana and Lord Middlesex, heir to the Duke of Dorset, whose country seat was at nearby Knole. Before negotiations could begin, however, Sarah made an appointment for Diana to meet the nephew of the Irish Lord Justice, William Conolly, who had died in the previous year, leaving his nephew a fortune of £17,000 a year. But despite his 'sense and a good person', Diana was singularly unimpressed, her grandmother declaring she would not marry her 'to His Royal Highness the Prince of Wales nor to any King in the World, if she did not like it, which is the present case'.[17]

Lord Middlesex, otherwise Charles Sackville, was the brother of Lord Weymouth's youthful bride, six months younger than Diana, and had matriculated at Oxford when he was eighteen. This year he would receive his MA. Sarah was determined that Diana, 'a treasure in herself as well as what I shall give her', should marry someone with a lively mind; and as a friend of the Prince of Wales, Middlesex would later become his Master of the Horse. Since Lady Fane was acquainted with the young man's father, fresh plans were put forward over the card-tables at Tunbridge Wells for negotiating a match.

Diana was happy meanwhile to have cousin Bella in the party, since she brought news of Lady Rich; and as they crossed the Pantiles on their way to the waters, they would have much to talk about. The town existed expressly for the amusement of the rich, with raffles, dancing, ninepins, cards and bowls, a nearby avenue devoted to riding. Beau Nash made a visit to the town this year, but finding the forceful 'Bell Causey' installed as general factotum, put off his 'Kingship' until later. With Bella, Duchess of Manchester, and Lady Fane to accompany her, Diana was able to take regular exercise, the young women cantering on splendid horses, drawing glances from the soldiers in the town. Mindful of Lady Rich left in London, and learning from Bella she was unwell, Diana wrote begging to hear from her friend. A plaintive if histrionic reply came fluttering through the post:

> I obey you my dear Lady Di: tho the whole purport of my letter will amount to no more than what you are quite convinced of; that I feel your absence painfully . . .

And would winter restore to her 'what I Greive for', that was the question! Lady Rich had been 'mighty ill humoured' since Diana had left her on the

Friday, and believed 'it will continue for, I look upon the three following months as so much lost time.' She had read her 'eyes out', she wrote, and grown weary of it, for there was no falling at once from Lady Di 'to the people she had left behind'. She had been 'this three days quite blind,' she complained, and the pain in her head had 'fallen' into her eye, so she could not have 'writt to save my life', and was 'very bad now'. She begged Diana to give her 'service to the Dear D[uchess] of Man[chester] – with a thousand thanks for her goodness to me and excuse me till Tuesday next by w[hi]ch time I intend to be well. Adieu my dearest Lady Di.'[18]

The Duchess of Manchester and her grandmother, meanwhile, were not getting on at all well, Sarah saying to Bella, 'You are a good creature and I love you mightily – but you have a mother!' Bella, whom Horace Walpole observed as 'all spirit, justice and honour', and like her grandmother 'could not suppress sudden truth', replied, 'And she has a mother!' Sarah complained how Bella would 'snap her up', Bella recapping with 'I had my ill humours from my mother, and she had them from you!' Lord Hervey described Bella as 'ferocious', 'infinitely proud', who 'shrugs and barks' and bites the tips off people's noses, and the only reason 'she never deprived her dear Duke of his [nose] is that she hopes one time or other to lead him by it!' Yet Hervey's long-suffering wife Mary Lepel described Bella as very sweet-tempered. Bella was unhappy in her marriage and had no children, Mary Wortley Montagu putting her misfortunes down to 'the want of instruction in her youth'. As Sarah had said, Bella had been like a bird out of a cage when she married, and despite their many disagreements, was fond of her, furnishing a house for her, and singing as she sewed.[19]

Lady Rich had meanwhile visited Windsor 'in broiling heat and dust' which made her eyes 'considerably worse'. There she dined with Lady Burlington which gave her 'the pleasure of talking' of Diana, whom they both loved and admired. Afterwards Lady Rich came 'home by moonlight', which was 'charming', building 'the delightfull'st castles', but the 'grief' she felt when she 'came upon the stones to think they were impracticable set me a moralising for the rest of the night', and which ended in the confirmation of two lines in Prior,

That all our wars are sad extreams
  & all our pleasures floating dreams . . .

She wrote to Diana on the tiny sheets of notepaper then fashionable among ladies, Diana noticing her grandmother's disapproval when yet another of these delicate missives was delivered. When Diana advised Lady Rich to use larger sheets in future, such as her grandmother used, Lady Rich promised she would 'when these detestable eyes are better, for I hate the fashion and find it will in time be gentile to write upon a card'. Meanwhile she was more Diana's than words could express.[20]

Lady Rich had only just sent off this last letter when her husband Sir Robert Rich arrived home, asking her to use her influence with the Duchess of Marlborough in requesting a warrant for a buck out of Windsor Park. Thus it was that Lady Rich was obliged to send a second missive on the self-same day, begging Diana to act as an intermediary for her, for 'I am greatly ashamed to trouble her but if dear Lady Di did think it proper, I shoud be obliged to her'. She explained that the buck was to be distributed to friends of her husband 'that live at Windsor', but 'Dont do it if you judge it wrong,' she begged, 'but write me word.' As she had just 'writt' to her she said she would trouble her 'no more but with Sr Robts humble service', and was ever hers . . .[21]

Tactful though this letter was, since it arrived on the very same day as her previous letter it struck Sarah as extravagant and ridiculous. Having already intimated to Diana that her correspondence with Lady Rich should 'drop by degrees', she now made it clear that there was 'a great noise in the town' concerning their exchange of letters, and she had been told sometimes in London that Diana wrote 'three times a Day' and had as many letters by return. Was Sarah troubled by memories of Queen Anne's daily correspondence with herself, which had often proved irksome, and when related to the queen's later passion for Abigail Hill, embarrassing? While she believed Lady Rich had many good qualities, she told Diana she had not 'a character good enough' for her to have 'such a violent friendship with', and rather than make 'comedies for the world', Diana's friendship with Lady Rich must draw gradually to a close, although she intended to be civil to her herself.[22]

Diana was now in her twentieth year, at a time when many women were married as early as fourteen, not for passion, but for money and status; and when married to their husbands their whole life was generally taken up with creating a home, and producing heirs. Protected from sexual encounters till at least the time the marriage contract was signed, such needs were often sublimated through passionate same-sex friendships. Sarah had experienced this in the hothouse atmosphere at the court at Richmond Palace, when Princess Mary and Princess Anne had intense friendships with their female courtiers, Anne ardently adoring Sarah herself. Sarah spoke of all this as 'pretty amusements to pass away the time'. While she understood the depth of feeling between Lady Rich and Diana, she disapproved of the lady herself, and disliked the kind of gossip their friendship might arouse. All this, she insisted, Diana must convey to her friend. Since no copies of Diana's early letters to Lady Rich have survived, her expressions can only be assumed from the recipient's replies. Lady Rich's answer to Diana's last letter reached her on her way home to Windsor Lodge, and was handed to her in her grandmother's presence. Sarah had asked 'to see it', that being 'natural', and it was 'impossible for her to refuse to shew it me'.[23]

Having acknowledged 'dear Lady Di's kind letter', Lady Rich expressed her deep hurt regarding the Duchess of Marlborough's attitude to her, saying angrily, 'as you say she resolves to be very civil to me <u>it will oblige her to some sort of forme to deceive me as she imagins, and I promise you I will distress her, that way.</u>' She would, however, 'in every thing' follow Diana's 'advice'. Just now she was suffering 'a violent fitt of head ack from cold', and must defer a fuller answer till the next post, begging Diana to never '<u>believe any body can love you more than I do</u>', and promising her 'Never whilst you breath shall anyone creature know any thing you say to me', not even 'Sir Robt.', and that Diana could safely 'believe it dead'.[24]

Elizabeth's expressions, and the tone of her letter, suggested Diana and she were in collusion, and Sarah concluded that Diana had simply not put her position strongly enough. In her next letter Diana must be more explicit. This time, dating her letter 'Monday, August 30', and a copy of this letter was kept, Diana wrote:

> I must now explain to you the reason that my Grandmama disliked my writing to you so often was upon something that she had been told occasioned by your self, but perhaps it might be aggravated [exaggerated] in the relation of it to her. However your manner of expressing your self upon her subject to me that you will distress her & etc: is so shocking to me that it must needs take off the uneasiness I might otherwise have had upon what I have told you in my former letter, for as no mortall ever had so many obligations of all kinds as I have to my Dear Grandmama, I should be the most ungratefull wretch upon Earth

if I held a correspondence with any body that had not a regard for her, & the greatest Idiott in the World if I could believe that any body can love me or wish my happiness so much as she does & I must be quite void both of principle and sense if I could suffer anybody to say the least awry word of her, to me, who I know to be the kindest parent that ever was as well as the most valuable friend. & after what has happen'd I am certain you can not reasonably blame me that I can never say more to you then that I am Madam

Yr Ladyshps most humble Servant[25]

This was a cold letter, and Lady Rich was certainly surprised by it. Now at Barn Elms (where hopefully she found the weather cooler) she took up her pen: 'The surprise and concern I've been in since I received your letter is easier conceived than expressed,' she wrote, and 'I assure you I find no word that will come near it my dear Lady Di as I know you just & that you know me and all I think.' Lady Rich was persuaded that she did not 'deserve one word thats in that letter' and was 'in a maze about it & can account for it but one way, that some way or other its occasiond by the Duchess of Marlborough'. For one thing the 'stile is not yours', she protested, besides which 'you are too sensible I never ment to offend her in anything, and wou'd not lay hold of an unguarded expression writt in the first minute of my concern at finding your writing to me so seldom was occasioned by the Duchess of Marlboroughs disliking you shoud'.[26]

That Lady Rich had known another Diana, one not to be found in any of her other letters among the Blenheim papers, appears certain. Lady Rich continued to justify herself at length, saying she always wrote 'with rapidity', would 'seldome think twice', would 'never study for fresh phrases' nor 'correct things'. Her explanation of the one remark that might justifiably give Sarah cause for alarm, and which had doubtless upset Diana, i.e.: ('I promise you I will distresse her that way'), was to do with her need to discover how she had displeased the Duchess of Marlborough, and by endeavouring to be with Diana 'eternally', both at home and abroad, which if her Grace disliked it, 'would distresse her & oblige her to give me some reason for that dislike by wch I might know how I came under her dis-pleasure, without betraying that you had hinted it to me which I gave you my word to conceal'. She appealed to Diana to believe her meaning by her 'words', and to 'let heaven witness' that she was not 'proffligate enough' to have meant any other. She was fully aware that the Duchess of Marlborough was 'all' to Lady Diana, and that in all the 'many happy days' she had passed with her, she, Lady Rich, had never suggested one thing that was 'not exactly according to her liking in the most trifling perticulars'. All this confirmed her in her belief that the letter was not Diana's at all, and she, Elizabeth, would 'everlastingly regret the happiness Ive lost, rigidly innocent of any cause by wch I have merited it'.

But there was to be no whitening of Lady Rich in the eyes of the Duchess of Marlborough. Lady Rich finally protested, in her letter, that 'As for the things that may have been told her Grace of me, I can say nothing to them, being entirely ignorant what they related [to her]', and 'all I know is that no one single body ever was or ever will be proof against lyes'.[27]

The last was a truth Sarah could not deny. Sometime during Diana's stay at Tunbridge Wells, perhaps riding along the bridle path with Bella outside the town, or purchasing raffle tickets in the 'toy' shops, or dancing in the Assembly Hall, Diana appears to have struck up a liaison with Lieutenant Thomas Bloodworth. Once Captain of the Royal Irish Fusiliers, now Lieutenant Colonel of the Coldstream Guards, Bloodworth appears to have been a thoroughly macho male – fit to light a flame in any unattached heiress's heart. Their brief acquaintanceship was certainly enough to cause the fans to flutter at the Wells, and send a ripple of speculation through the company at the Assembly Hall. We find no mention of this affair among the family papers of Blenheim Palace, only elsewhere in a letter to the Countess of Strafford by her friend the Countess of Huntingdon. It was written after the Duchess of Marlborough and Diana had left the watering place for London, Lady Huntingdon writing:

The Duchess of Marlborough left Tunbridge in a great hurry upon receiving a letter from an unknown hand that Lady Die would marry Bloodworth, and 'tis said this intelligence came just in time enough to prevent it. 'Tis said Lady Drogedy was the confidant, but I beg you'll never name my sending you this account . . .

Sarah and Diana had certainly departed the Wells in a hurry, those left behind left to make of it what they would. That Diana's health was improved appears certain, however, confirmed by her cousin Harriet, Duchess of Newcastle, who wrote in the following January:

> Lady Die is as handsome as an angell, & her neck so well, that I'me sure if it had allways been just as it is now, nobody would have thought it any thing: for it can only be perciev'd with looking narrowly for it, & it is no more cover'd than any body's else is.

Harriet added that there was 'a very strict eye over her', but dared not write 'all the particulars I could tell you!'[28]

Following their return from Tunbridge Wells, Diana and her grandmother spent four months at Windsor Lodge, and during their time here (in September) the Prince of Wales was visiting the castle. Lord Hervey was seeing a lot of Diana's sister and brother-in-law, the Batemans, who had a house here, saying, 'I dine there, they dine here; they hunt with us in the morning, play with us at night, and seem to take very kindly to the Court.' He noted that the Prince of Wales was 'particularly civil to them', and 'Old Marlborough is come to the Lodge and lets Lady Di sometimes be of the party.'[29]

It would be natural for the Prince of Wales to pay attention to Lady Bateman's pretty younger sister, and that such attention should encourage speculation. Horace Walpole, the fourteen-year-old son of Sir Robert Walpole, was ever receptive to scandalous titbits that dropped from his father's table, one of them concerning Diana and the Prince of Wales. He would tell in old age how the prince, 'even early after his arrival had listened to a high act of disobedience', and that 'Money he soon wanted', and:

> old Sarah, duchess of Marlborough, ever proud and ever malignant, was persuaded to offer her favourite granddaughter lady Diana Spencer . . . to the prince of Wales, with a fortune of a hundred thousand pounds. He accepted the proposal, and the day was fixed for their being secretly married at the duchess's lodge in the great park at Windsor.

The summer had been a disturbing one for Sarah, what with her granddaughter developing a swelling on her neck, and moreover having nursed an unsuitable passion for a woman, while eligible young men were made forfeit. The prince on his part was in debt, and one way to improve his finances would be to marry a rich heiress. If Sarah had allowed herself to cover her disappointments by marrying Diana to a prince, perhaps she could not altogether be condemned. Certainly when out hunting with his sisters (all dressed in identical suits of 'blue trimmed with gold, and faced and lined with red') the prince became acquainted with Diana, dressed equally well, a lace cravat tied neatly at her neck. Nothing would appear extraordinary in Sarah's inviting the prince to dine after a hard morning's hunt, her beautiful house in the forest a stately and elegant stop. During hearty eating and drinking she might well tap the Prince of Wales on his wrist with her fan, point out her granddaughter's beauty, and hint at the great fortune she would have if she married the right young man. Sarah had always loved to flirt with young men, and £100,000 would do much to solve the prince's present problems. Indeed such a marriage was perfectly valid, there being no Royal Marriage Act at this time. Horace Walpole reported how 'Youth, folly, and indiscretion, the beauty of the young lady, and the large sum of ready money might have offered something like a plea for so rash a marriage, had it taken place.' Unfortunately 'Sir Robert Walpole got intelligence of the project, prevented it, and the secret was buried in silence.'[30]

This was a romantic story, with some foundation of truth in it, but against which we must place Sarah's intense dislike of the royal court. Would she really have jeopardised her favourite's chance of happiness in allowing her to go against her future in-laws' wishes? And would Diana herself have agreed to such a proposal? There may have been some joshing with the idea, but Sarah's earlier remark to Lady Evelyn must also be remembered: 'I would not dispose of [Diana] to His Royal Highness the Prince of Wales nor to any King in the World; if she did not like it, which is the present case.'[31]

And Sarah had other fish to fry. Lady Fane had put forward the proposal for Diana to marry Dorset's heir, Lord Middlesex, Sarah driving a hard bargain. She expected the Duke of Dorset to match Diana's portion of (now) £50,000 (and £100,000 should she outlive her grandmother) with a settlement for her 'to live as she aught to'. Upon examining Sarah's proposal, Dorset remarked that he had not quite thought of a 'Smithfield bargain'. This allusion to a London cattle market was not lost on Sarah, who decided to take it humorously, agreeing that money and estates did not always give the best prospect of happiness, but 'as to a Smithfield bargain', she would 'not insist quite upon that'. Why, if she expected a 'Smithfield bargain' she would have wanted 'five thousand pounds a year jointure for fifty thousand pounds down & such an allowance as is fit for the Duke of Dorset's eldest son, to support him and his children during his life'. The duke replied:

> Lady Di may very shortly expect much better offers than it is possible for me to make her & when I say I not only wish her the greatest match in England, but that she may be the happyest woman in it, I dont think I wish her anything more than she deserves . . .

Lord Middlesex, with his Master's degree under his belt, departed on the Grand Tour, his father soon to leave also, to 'King it' as Lord Lieutenant in Ireland. So another proposal of marriage hit the dust.[32]

At Windsor Sarah took it upon herself to write a long letter to Lady Rich telling her in no uncertain terms that she was in the wrong in her dealings with Diana. She 'ought upon the receipt of Dy's letter of excuse for not having written so often' to have told her that whatever trouble it might occasion her that she 'lov'd her too sincerely ever so much as to wish that she shou'd write or do the least thing contrary to what I approv'd of'. No one could blame her (Sarah) for 'being very nice and carefull that no sort of handle should be given to the World that could possibly prejudice in the least, so valuable a young creature as Dye is, & who is under my care, & so dearly belov'd as she is by me'. As her grandmother, she must 'guard what I love more than all the World put together' from all things that 'may but look foolish in the World . . .'[33]

As Sarah and Diana set out for London, their coach passed that of Sir Robert Rich, both drawing to a halt. Lord Rich sent his servant across to the duchess, to deliver his wife's answer to the letter the dowager had sent her. Addressing the duchess as 'Madam', Lady Rich wrote:

> I had the honour of your Grace's letter, and if all I've say'd allready, and Lady Dis wittnessing of it, w[hi]ch (as she knows it to be true) I am sure she will; cant convince your Grace; it wou'd be needless to trouble you any more. Therefore I will only say that I think it hard

usage, and that tho I might not have merit sufficient to deserve the goodness you have had for me, I've never deserved to forfit it; and shall continue to expresse my self always with the respect due to your Grace; on all ocations . . .

And she added:

I must take the liberty to say there never was so false a story as has been told yr Grace of our corrispondence in London, that is except, by way of message, to know whether I shoud dine with you, or sup with her, or what time I shoud come, such sort of things, wch were writ on bits of paper & never seald. I dont know I either writt or received a letter, when we were both in the same town.

London. Sept ye 10th.[34]

It was a dignified, if sad, letter, and for the time being there were to be no more meetings between Lady Rich and Diana. Lady Rich, who was 'converted to everything by slow steps', may have been unhappy for a time, but had a life of her own to pursue. Her husband had made it clear he supported his wife by delivering her letter to the duchess, and they had a son and daughter of their own to rear. The daughter Elizabeth would marry Sir George Lyttleton, Fielding's beloved patron to whom he dedicated *Tom Jones*, and although the Lyttleton couple eventually separated (Mary Wortley Montagu believing it caused by Elizabeth being 'ill educated'), it was a feather in her mother's cap for a time. Lady Rich would read a report of her son's death after the battle of Culloden, only to learn later that he was wounded, but alive. Her last letter to Diana read:

Whilst Ive life to love you as I have done, nothing on earth shall alter me.

She had been careful to keep the letter three days to 'overlook it' before sending it, having never read it 'without tears'.[35]

CHAPTER NINE

A Quiet Wedding

'. . . the charmingest thing in the world'

A painting at Althorp shows the seventeen-year-old Willigo Lord Rialton together with his two Egerton cousins, Lady Anne and Lord John Brackley, for all the world like a holiday snap. Willigo is dressed in dark blue velvet trimmed with gold, his brown hair curling to his shoulders, eyes dark blue like his Marlborough grandfather's. His black, gold-buckled shoes boast high fronts and heels of scarlet. Soon, having obtained his degree from Clare College, Cambridge he will leave for the Grand Tour in the company of his cousin Robert Lord Spencer, both in their mid-teens. His grandmother the Duchess of Marlborough will send enough medicine with the two young men to sink a ship.

As Marquis of Blandford, Willigo had been absent from England for thirteen years, and grown indolent and fat. Worse in the eyes of his grand-mother and his parents, he had engaged himself, as noted, to marry the daughter of a burgomaster of Utrecht. To marry 'a woman unknown to all the world but low people' was shocking to Sarah, as if 'a daughter were run away with and had lost her reputation'! When Willigo insisted that his betrothed was a highly respectable and very beautiful woman, her sister no other than the Countess of Denbigh, his grandmother answered that all the time she was in Holland she 'never saw but one woman that looked like a human creature', and if this person 'was no more tempting than Lady Denbigh, you must allow that people will wonder at your choice'! About to turn thirty, and in possession of a generous allowance from the Marlborough Trust, Willigo was free to do as he pleased, but for once his grandmother was united with his parents in their disapproval. The marriage went ahead on 25 July 1729, Sarah being obliged to make the best of what could not be avoided. She begged Willigo to return to England, and to make up with his mother from whom he had been long estranged, Willigo replying, 'When you reflect how good a daughter she has made you', and 'a wife to my father & mother to me, you will see what reason she can have to complain of my want of duty'. His mother's 'long ill conduct' towards his father and himself, he said, had led him to make a 'resolution never to see her', but he was 'willing to have my father's consent to return upon that condition'.

Willigo was as embarrassed as any son might be at his mother's scandalous affair with the playwright Congreve, while his father, aware of his own sexual inadequacies regarding women, and his understanding of his wife's strong emotional needs, upbraided his son for 'indecent omissons' towards her. He told his daughter Harriet that her brother's proposal to see himself and not his mother was one he could 'never come to'. He insisted that Willigo should 'live well' with his mother as a condition of 'living well' with himself, upon which Willigo quit himself of the obligation of 'seeing either of them'.[1]

As he was heir to the Marlborough dukedom after his mother, and Blenheim Palace, to say nothing of the massive fortune that went with them, Sarah could hardly ignore her first grandson, and it was the generous allowance she had squeezed for him from the Trust that had made him independent of his parents. Once married, Blandford consented to come to England, bringing his wife with him, and settling in a house in Grosvenor Square. His sister Harriet, Duchess of Newcastle (who referred to him as 'Lord Worthless'), invited him and his wife to dinner at Claremont, while dreading the occásion: 'You may be sure I satt in a good deal of pain til t'was over,' she told her aunt Boscawen, but 'nothing extraordinary happened' except for his 'agreeable laughs, which dispos'd me much more to cry, than to join with him in his mirth . . .'[2]

Diana and her grandmother were to meet the bride at Willigo's Grosvenor Square house, their fellow guests being Sir John and Lady Evelyn (grandson of the diarist, and his wife), together with the Earl and Countess of Winchilsea, the bride's sister Lady Denbigh, and her husband. Lady Denbigh was indeed beautiful, her younger sister Lady Blandford no less so, if somewhat less intelligent and more easily led. They gathered for dinner at a little after three o'clock, during which time the Duchess of Marlborough was able to observe the bride whom she had chosen to despise. A stranger to England, and new to her marriage, it must have been a gruelling occasion for the young woman, especially when four o'clock came, then five o'clock, and still no Lord Blandford. At last she thought fit to call for dinner, and they were half-way through the meal when Willigo made his entrance, his grandmother greeting him with 'all the good humour in the world', saying, 'Oh my Lord, I conclude you have been at the house of commons?' To this Blandford replied, 'I have not.' Sarah continued to talk to him playfully, saying, 'Then I wish I was nearer to you, that I might beat you!' Willigo answered, 'Then I am very glad you are not.' He was gracious enough to add that 'I did not think that you would have come before five, nor did I think you would have stayed for me', and at six o'clock he went out to the play, leaving his guests to play quadrille the whole evening.[3]

When Blandford did come home 'he came into the room again for a minute', then went away before the Duchess of Marlborough and Diana had left. Lord Winchilsea put Sarah 'into her chair', she and Diana being thus carried through the torch-lit streets to Marlborough House. To 'compleat the history', as Harriet told it to her aunt, 'the occasion of Willigo's being so late was, that he went and dined at Lady Meadows's, and so came to his company at his own house between 5 and 6 o'clock that he knew was waiting for him all that time. Sure there never was such a crea-ture born.' She fancied, however, 't'would be entertaining to hear the D of M give an account of it!' As for 'Lord Worthless', Harriet did not doubt that he deserved that name 'more than ever . . .'[4]

Sarah was still anxious to dispose of Diana in marriage, since she was now rising twenty, and on 5 February gave her a ball at Marlborough House. There were thirteen couples invited, and unlike the ball given for Lady Anne Egerton on a similar occasion, the Montagu cousins were included, being now married and released from their mother. Anne was here, in her role as Duchess of Bedford, together with Willigo's wife Lady Blandford, and Diana's sister Lady Bateman. Female friends included 'Lady Bab North, Lady Anne Wentworth, Lady Fanny Montague, Miss Masham, Miss Montague, Lady Bishope, Miss Lutwitch, Miss Boscowan' – the name 'Masham' being the most surprising. Could this possibly be a daughter of the despised Abigail? The men were 'the Duke of Manchester, Lord Brudnell (Mary Montagu's husband, the future Earl of Cardigan), Lord Bateman, Mr Fielding, the two Mr Foxes [Stephen and Henry], Mr Evelyn, Sir William Yonge, Mr Meadows, and Mr Gordon'. Among the three missing names must have been the Duke of Bedford and Willigo. As most of the men were married, the most eligible suitors were Henry and Stephen Fox, who would often ask after Diana in their letters to Lord Hervey. The 'Mr Fielding' may again have been the future novelist, currently enjoying success with his comedy *Tom Thumb* in the Haymarket. His anti-Walpole stance and devotion to Marlborough would endear him to Sarah, and being related to the Earl of

Denbigh, he had connections with Lady Blandford's sister. Henry Fielding was a brilliant dancer, and would liven up any party.[5]

Meanwhile proposals of marriage were coming through the post for Lady Diana. One letter from Lady Gertrude Hotham, whom Diana had met at Tunbridge Wells, proposed her brother Lord Chesterfield as a possible suitor. Gertrude's letter was followed by a proposal from the earl himself, the Duchess of Marlborough deeply flattered on her granddaughter's behalf. Phillip Dormer Stanhope, 4th Earl of Chesterfield, who had called at Blenheim with Voltaire, was in his thirty-seventh year, his single aim in life being to make 'every man he met like him and every woman love him'. With this in mind he had honed his manners to perfection, sharpening his innate wit to a rapier-like brilliance. Sarah had been impressed with his good sense when she met him as a young man at Antwerp, and since then he had modelled his manners on Louis XIV. His service as Gentleman-of-the-Bedchamber to the Prince of Wales (now George II) had led to his becoming Ambassador at the Hague. He now hoped to return to England to regain his health and recoup his finances (he was an incurable gambler), in the time-honoured way of taking a rich and beautiful bride. From the Hague he put forward his suit, dated 14 August 1731:

The person, the merit, and the family, of Lady Diana Spencer, are objects so valuable that they must necessarily have already caused many applications of this nature to your Grace as they oblige me to add to the number of them, and though they may be all so much better founded than mine, as to leave me very little hopes of success, yet I could never forgive myself, If I omitted even the least possibility of being so happy.

There was something of the Duke of Somerset's old fashioned gallantry in Chesterfield's request, asking to be permitted to 'throw my self at Lady Diana's feet', and 'to offer her the absolute disposal of myself, and fortune', that may well have appealed to a Restoration lady, but less to one of the Age of Enlightenment. Sensible of how unworthy both he and his fortune were, and how 'small a chance I have of their being accepted', Chesterfield felt he could only hope for it 'from an error, in both Your Grace's judgement and hers'. But if he could obtain permission to make court to Diana in person, his short stay in Holland would allow that. He concluded by assuring Sarah 'that the honour I should have of being so nearly related to you, is not one of my least temptations'.[6]

The dowager replied that she was 'sure nothing could have contributed so much to my happiness as such an alliance', but regretted that she was 'too far engaged in a treaty, to break off', and only wished that his Lordship would be so good as 'to let me see you sometimes'.[7]

The fact that Chesterfield's mistress Mme Du Bouchet was to bear him a son in nine months' time (to whom he would write his famous *Letters to a Son*), appears in no way to have deterred Chesterfield from his gallant suit, nor two years later from marrying Melusina de Schulenberg, daughter of George I and his mistress the Duchess of Kendal. But what of this 'treaty' the Duchess of Marlborough was engaged in? Soon after the ball at Marlborough House she wrote to her granddaughter the Duchess of Bedford, proposing a match between Diana and Anne's brother-in-law Lord Russell.

Lord John Russell had been away on the Grand Tour for three years, and like Diana was approaching his twenty-first birthday. Anne replied to her grandmother saying her husband the Duke of Bedford 'knows & likes Lady Dye so well he can wish Lord John no better than to desire he may have her', and would 'do all in his power for it'. Both she and her husband wished the couple so well as 'to hope this will succeed'.[8]

Anne, still in her loveless marriage, would genuinely welcome the prospect of having her cousin become part of her family, and her duke appeared pleased too, thanking Sarah for having so much confidence in him as a go-between, and for the happiness she intended his brother with 'Lady Dye'. Nor could he think his brother 'so bad a judge of his own interest & happiness in this World as to suppose he can have any doubts in accepting so advantageous an offer'. Unfortunately he believed his own influence with John less than Sarah imagined, for there was 'a certain suspiciousness' in his temper 'that makes it difficult for his best friends to persuade him to what is most to his advantage'. It would be his 'chief endeavour to get over this', however, and he agreed to keep the proposal a secret as Sarah had requested, not mentioning it to his brother-in-law the Earl of Essex, nor anyone, 'unless it be as I may have done before, accidentally'.[9]

Although Bedford's letter did not require an answer, Sarah replied at once. Not only were the duke's expressions extremely obliging to herself, but 'so kind to Dye, that I can't defer longer giving you a great many thanks for them', she wrote. She believed her commendation of Diana would be 'rediculous from a grandmother' had not the duke known her so well, for 'she is a favourite of allmost everybody, which makes me think I am not partial to her, because if there were any room for it, there are a great many that would be malicious for her, purely from their envious temper'. Taking her circumstances altogether, Diana must be 'the greatest match at this time in England, or that ever can be, by all the young people that I have seen growing up', and as 'every true friend to Lord John must wish that he may be secur'd by such a wife from any ill accident . . . and since your Grace is of the same opinion . . . I can see . . . nothing that can prevent it, if they happen to like one another when he comes into England'.[10]

Diana's cousin the Duchess of Bedford had been fond of Lord John, keeping up a correspondence with him when he was in Paris, telling him of her loneliness – how she welcomed visitors at Woburn, even if they sometimes fell asleep at backgammon, and how 'All wish you was here to put new life into us'. It may have been his lively sense of humour that attracted Diana to him, enough for her to allow her grandmother to pursue the match.

Sarah meanwhile made a thorough search into Lord Russell's character, discovering that he had been romantically attached to another before leaving England, and bringing his brother's attention to this matter:

> I believe your Grace may have heard that there was a great deal of discourse of his liking my Lady Fanny Shirley; but perhaps that was only Town-talk without any foundation, but if he did like her when he was so very young, & his passion was not strong enough to be drawn in when the Lady had the advantage of being so much older than himself, I think that it is not likely that he should be hook'd in now that he knows more of the world than he did.[11]

Lady Frances Shirley was four years older than Lord Russell, twenty-two when he left England, and now twenty-five. The fourth daughter of Earl Ferrer's large family, she was a 'lady whose great merit Mr Pope took a ready pleasure in celebrating', and who, on receiving from her 'A Standish and Two Pens' [an ink-well stand and pens] during a bout of writer's block, wrote a minor poem in her honour:

> What well? What weapons? Flavia cries,
> A standish, steel and golden pen;

It came from Bertrand's, not the skies;
I gave to you to write again.*

Judging from a letter Lady Frances sent the Duchess of Marlborough some years after all this, like Lady Rich, she was inclined to be giddy, writing a lively description of a day she spent in town when she had failed to call on the duchess:

> The last time I was in London my two sisters dragg'd me to a play I did not like; assuring me it would be done early, and that I might waite upon you after, which I endeavour'd to do, but did not succeed. I am not vain of my understanding in general, but really am so in one particular, which I intended to have owned to you, and have laught a little about, had I been so lucky to have seen you. I think of being again in town next tuesday and will then try, if you should not be engag'd in business (as I hope you won't) to dine with you. Forgive this, tho' you think it long and remember you gave me leave to write whenever I pleased . . .[12]

That Sarah should give Frances leave to write, let alone call, seems odd in the circumstances. On receipt of a letter from a 'Lady Cheshyre' (writing of a house in Dover Street that Lady Fanny hoped to buy if only 'she had a surplus of that which would help her'), Sarah suspected an attempt at extortion, writing on the reverse:

> This letter from Lady Cheshyre about Lady f. Shirleys having a mind to buy a house which Lady f. contrived in that cunning way to make me buy the house for her . . .

Had Sarah hinted at paying some kind of compensation should Lady Fanny lay off John Russell, only conveniently to forget her debt later? From her love of Lord Russell, Fanny turned to 'a long flirtation with Lord Chesterfield', after which she took up with George Whitefield and the Methodists. She was to die unmarried.[13]

Sarah's dismissal of Russell's boyhood passion as mere calf's love appears, however, to have been well founded, but as to his 'Suspicious

* Bertrand's was a 'toy [or gift] shop' in Bath.

Temper', Sarah thought that proceeded from his 'being so very young' when Bedford last saw him, and he must now be better able to 'judge for himselfe'. Indeed she thought 'what people call suspicious in a young man, will be of great advantage to him with the generality of the world, which is now grown so very bad that it is prudence not to believe too easily'.[14]

Sarah suggested Woburn would be the most natural place for the young people to meet, where they might 'easily see whether this alliance can be, without giving any occasion for Town-talk in case it can not be effected'. She hoped the warm weather they were enjoying just now would give her strength to come to Woburn, 'which will always give me a great satisfaction, whatever may happen in this affair . . .' It would be nothing out of the way for Diana to meet the newly returned traveller at her cousin's home, since they were related through marriage, and even if she had not been made aware of her grandmother's intentions, she would almost certainly guess. It was customary for the proposed bride to be kept ignorant of proposals at this stage of the proceedings, if only to spare her blushes should she herself be rejected, but the young man was informed from the start. Lord Russell had every reason to observe his prospective bride very keenly, and Sarah, if not Diana, was delighted with him. Though known to be 'little', and plump, the dowager described him as tall. Since he hunted, and had travelled far, his flesh may have been kept in reasonable check at this time, his skin golden from months spent travelling on horseback in the open air, eyes bright with youth and mirth. As Diana was not slow in turning down men she disliked, Lord John's personality, if not his looks must have gone far to recommend him. As the couple walked together in the pleasant gardens, the company careful to leave them alone, they might discuss painting and architecture, Diana having a special interest in buildings – Lord John able to commend those he had seen abroad. As the weather was warm they might shelter from the sun in the pearly Grotto, seated together on the sea-shell chairs, the fountain playing beside them. It was either here at Woburn, or on his later visit to Blenheim, that Lord John proposed marriage.[15]

In September, after an 'unexpected journey into ye Fens', the Duke of Bedford wrote to Sarah saying he was pleased to see an affair concluded which he 'knew to be so agreeable to your inclination', while Lord Hervey wrote to Stephen Fox:

> I do not know whether I sent you word of Lady Di's match with Lord
> John Russell being quite agreed. He is at this moment lisping love in
> her flippant ladyship's ear at Blenheim . . .

To this Hervey added that it had been 'kept secret from Lord Sunderland
and the Bateman's, till three days ago'.[16]

Sarah's reason for not telling Diana's brother and sister of the wedding
until all was in writing was that she believed Anne Bateman might interfere
with her plans. The original plan may have been for the marriage to take
place at Blenheim, Sarah arranging for the chapel to be consecrated, but on
24 August something happened to throw her plans awry. Word came from
nearby Oxford that Lord Blandford had collapsed at (of all things) a Tory
meeting at Balliol College. Sarah took coach for the town at once, Diana
accompanying her, as well as the heavy basket they took with them on the
shortest of journeys. Sarah had a clear premonition of her grandson's condition, saying as soon as she arrived, 'I suppose he's dead!' Willigo had
indeed died of a 'drunken fit or fever' apparently in the company of hard-
drinking Jacobite friends. Sarah declared she would have given half her
estate to have saved him, and hoped 'the Devil is picking his bones who
taught him to drink!' She turned to her granddaughter to ask, 'Where is my
basket, Di? Did I not charge you to bring it?' Upon this Diana ran to the
coach. As well as the silver her grandmother carried with her to mollify the
swarms of beggars that inevitably crowded at her coach steps, she carried
medicines and cordials in case of accident or sickness. Though too late to
save Willigo now, Diana was able to offer sympathy to his widow Lady
Blandford, while Sarah tidied up the corpse, discussing the case with the
doctors.[17]

Blandford's body was laid in a 'decent Chappel belonging to Baliol
College' until the Blenheim chapel was consecrated, then embalmed and
put into a leaden box, and a wooden case 'handsomely carv'd [and lined]
with velvet so it will be preserv'd with delicacy'. On 4 August 1731 Willigo
was the first of the Marlborough family to be laid in the Blenheim crypt.[18]

Sarah must now consider her granddaughter's wedding. The sad
circumstances leading up to the wedding may well have caused it to be
moved to a later date than planned, Sarah consulting with the Duke of
Bedford as to the place. With his usual impeccable politeness, Wriothesley
wrote:

As to ye place where they are to be marry'd, your Grace may be assured I shall always desire to attend your conveniency, and never with greater pleasure, than upon this occasion. But as you are so good as to say, it is indifferent to you, & to leave ye properest place [to me], both on yr Graces Account, who may be in danger of catching cold by being so late at Blenheim, & on my own having a little business may call me up to Town, about that time. I am with greatest respect . . .[19]

From his ambiguous ending we can assume that Marlborough House was the chosen venue, being in town and not so cold as Blenheim might be. Certainly Diana and her grandmother were in town in September, Lord Hervey reporting to Stephen Fox that 'Mount Aetna [the name he gave Sarah] and Lady Di are come to town', and the 'latter is to be married as soon as the writings can be finished'. A special licence of the Archbishop of Canterbury was issued through the Vicar-General's office on 6 October, proclaiming that 'the said Marriage shall be solemnised according to the Tenor of the special Licence' and 'according to the Form of the Book of Common Prayer now by Law established'. Diana and John were free to marry at any place they chose, so long as a man of the Church officiated.[20]

Charles gave away the bride, Johnny present, sister Bateman bristling at not having been told till it was 'in every mouth and Gazette within a hundred miles of London'. The *Gentleman's Magazine* reported that the couple were married from 'Marlborough House, St James's', on 11 October 1731, the bride's fortune being £30,000, with £100,000 at the 'Death of the Dutchess Dowager of Marlborough, her Grandmother'. Just yards from where her collateral niece and namesake, the future Princess of Wales, would spend the eve of her wedding at Clarence House 250 years later, so Lady Diana married Lord John Russell. The wedding was a much quieter affair than the other would be, however, Hervey reporting to Stephen Fox:

Lady Di. was married yesterday, and nobody present but her two brothers, Lady Bateman, D and Duchess of Bedford, and Lady Essex.

Lord Blandford's death and the dowager's disabilities were sufficient excuse for so quiet a wedding, and there being 'a great court and a ball at night' at Hampton Court Palace, the wedding party repaired there after-wards. A week later Lord Hervey wrote to Stephen Fox:

Lord John Russell and his bride came here from Windsor Lodge last Sunday. She was as fine as lace and brocade and jewels could make her. I asked her if she liked being married as well as she fancied she should; and she said she thought it was the charmingest thing in the world.

Lord John was just as happy, having 'a very conjugal languor about him'. Hervey had something to say about 'Old Marlborough' too, who 'talks and thought so much bawdy upon this occasion that she is as coquette as she was at eighteen, and as rampant as if she were drunk'.[21]

The bride and groom and their guests would drop Sarah off at Windsor Lodge after the ball, afterwards driving the twelve miles to the Russells' new home at number 51 Grosvenor Street in London. It was a slightly tearful Diana who wrote to her grandmother next morning:

I believe it is quite unnecessary to say how sorry I was to part with my Dear Grandmama since I am sure you must see how much I felt & if I had not been so much concern'd I must have been the most ungrateful-creature in the World, which I am sure I am not capeable of being to anybody, & much less to my Dear Grandmama. My heart was so full yesterday to say half what I thought or indeed am I capeable of doing it at any time but I must beg leave to return you ten thousand thanks for all the kindness you have ever shown me and to assure you that it shall be the study of my life to deserve & return it, with all Imaginable Duty & Affection.

The young woman who had scarcely been parted from her grandmother since she was six years old, expressed herself sincerely. She went on:

We came here in three hours all very well, & found the house in extream good order, & very clean, & I think it a much better place than when I first saw it; we went immediately to the Duchess of Manchester's who looks vastly in beauty. We found Lady Fanny Shirley with her who was extreamly civill.

Diana reacted in a mature way to her meeting with her husband's ex-love just days after her wedding, even if her description of Fanny's reception of her is cool. She did not mention the presence of Lady Rich, but Lord Hervey wrote to Henry Fox:

> Lady Russell, whom you inquire after, is at present very happy. She lives in Grosvenor Street, and with the same people she used to do. My Lady Rich's restoration was the first act of her new reign; it immediately succeeded her coronation.[22]

All the company that had come with the bride and groom supped with them that evening, Diana hoping they would give her grandmother a 'good account of my housekeeping'. The tall, red-brick terraced house on the south side of Grosvenor Street may have been smaller than Diana was used to, but was a desirable property nonetheless, previously owned by the Duke of St Albans.* At the close of her letter Diana wished for 'rainy weather' in hopes it might bring her grandmother to town, which would be 'the greatest pleasure to your most Duty full & obliged Daughter'.[23]

During the first week of their honeymoon the newly weds received calls at their Grosvenor Street house from friends, and attended the performance of a play. Afterwards there was the 'tedious work of returning visits'. This Diana would do in her 'new coach which is extream handsome', and 'the chariott' she hoped to 'make a figure in on the Birthday'. She promised she would give her grandmother an exact account of all she saw and heard, and only wished 'there may happen anything to give you entertainment'.[24]

The King's Birthday would be a great occasion to dress up and celebrate in style. But Diana, feeling unwell after her many exertions, drove straight after the birthday to Windsor Lodge. Although her stay was short, it was refreshing, and after her return she wrote from Grosvenor Street to her grandmother to say she was almost 'quite well, which I am persuaded is partly owing to my having seen you, since I am sure being pleas'd contributes more to health than anything else in the world'. Her husband's sister Lady Essex dined with them that day, Diana thanking her grandmother for the venison she sent with her, which was 'the best I ever tasted', and afterwards they 'all drank your health when it was eaten'. They were

* 51 Grosvenor Street now houses Lloyds Private Bank.

to travel to Totteridge on the day she wrote her letter, 'where we shall lie tonight', and from there on to Woburn. Sister Bateman was to accompany them, from 'whence we shall go to Althrop'.[25]

A round of visits to country estates was all part of the eighteenth-century 'honey-year' enjoyed by the rich aristocracy, and Diana looked forward to meeting brother Charles. As the new Lord Sunderland since their brother Robert's death he was now in possession of Althorp, the happy country house of Diana's childhood. Woburn, her husband's brother's estate, was a convenient port of call on the way, as well as presenting an occasion to socialise. Diana was delighted to find her horse waiting for her when she arrived, writing a letter for the groom to take back to her grandmother. As well as her thanks she had some disturbing news:

> I return many thanks for your goodness in sending my horse as I desired it, who arrived here yesterday in perfect health. We set out from Totteridge yesterday morning & came here to dinner, & found the Duke of Bedford in much better humour than expected, for I suppose you have heard of his loss, which till you have it confirm'd I fancy you will scarce give credit to, but it is most certain that he has lost Thirty Thousand pounds at Newmarket, at one Sitting, from ten o'clock one Saterday night till eight on Sunday night . . .

Two card-sharpers, 'Janssen and Bladine', had played with the duke at Newmarket, and so that no time might be lost a 'Mr Menill' kept the scores for both sides. This man was 'such a blackguard', Diana said, she wondered the duke did not 'lose his whole Estate'. Wriothesley, she continued:

> was quite drunk when he first began, & one would think he continued so for the whole two & twenty hours, for 'tis incredible that a man in his sences, should suffer such a villain as Menill is known to be, to keep account of so vast a sum of money without once asking any question about it till he rose from the table.[26]

All this made it appear as Lady Mary Wortley Montagu had predicted, that having no desire to make heirs, the duke was determined to throw away his estate. Diana went on:

These four were lock'd up in a room together, & had candles & the shutters shut all Sunday, because they were afraid, (being very scrupulous people) of giving offence by being seen to play on Sundays.

All this information must have been given Diana by her cousin Anne, for during her stay the Duke of Bedford had 'not once name'd it to anybody here & seems even afraid to hear so much as the name of Newmarkitt'![27]

On Sunday bride and groom appeared at Woburn church, all the town here 'to make me their compliment & gave me a prodigious ring of bells'. Here, fifteen years earlier, a bell had tolled the passing of Diana's mother. Meanwhile Diana reported that 'Lord & Mr Bateman [William's brother Richard] are just come here in order to set out with us to-morrow for Althorp, where I believe we shall not stay above a fortnight.'[28]

The party arrived safely at Althorp in time for dinner, Diana writing to say they had 'company enough to make out a sort of a Ball every night, with a couple of men; we like very well to make a shift that way to pass these terrible long evenings. Lord Harry Beauclerk, is my sister Bateman's Partner, & Mr Fielding mine . . . ' Diana found them 'all very good humoured people, & we live very agreeably', and when 'all the hunting company are abroad the rest play at Billiards, & we have once play'd at Hooper's hide . . . '[29]

Again we may ask whether Diana's partner was Henry Fielding the writer. She would later mention a 'Mr Charles Fielding' who was reported to have shot his servant (it turned out not to be true), which suggests the Christian name was used to differentiate him from that other Mr Fielding at Althorp. It was also usual to call the eldest son of a family (which Henry was) 'Mr', followed by his surname, unless of course he had some other, superior, title. Henry's enormous success in the previous year with his burlesque *Tom Thumb* (played to packed houses including members of the Royal Family) had come to an ignominious end when an earlier play which had ridiculed Sir Robert Walpole led to warrants being issued to apprehend any player who acted in it; Fielding was consequently compelled to suppress his latest play, a musical, *The Welsh Opera*. His association with the Haymarket now at an end, nothing would have been more convenient for the writer than to hole up at a grand house such as Althorp for the summer. Fielding was to dedicate his next play but one, *The Universal Gallant*, to Diana's brother Lord Sunderland, which suggests gratitude of some special kind; and Diana's husband would also become Fielding's benefactor as acknowledged in his novel *Tom Jones*. Although somewhat grotesque in appearance with his hooked nose and prominent chin, Fielding's extraordinary strength of mind, his physical vitality and charm, inspired many a young woman to admire him; and being six feet tall, he would make a splendid partner for the tall and slender Diana.[30]

Lord Hervey, writing to Henry Fox after the company had returned to London, reported:

I saw Lord Sunderland, Sunday, Monday and Tuesday, which is every day he has been in town since his sister was married. He is grown so confirmed a fox-hunter, that he has two packs of hounds, in order not to lose one day in the week besides the Sabbath. Lord John and Lady Russell, Lord and Lady Bateman, and Dicky [Richard Bateman], *one* Mr Maudaunt, and *one* Mr something else, and three or four more anonymous misters, have been with him at Althrop, where I hear their recreations all day were galloping and hollowing, and their pleasures all night stale beer and tobacco . . . [31]

The Russells called at Woburn again on their way home to London, where talk was still of the 'big Debt'. Diana did not see how the duke could avoid paying it, even if the people he had played with were (as she believed them) a 'Gang of Villains'. He did not 'even imagine that he did lose it unfairly', she told her grandmother, 'but on the contrary says he believes them to be all very honest!' Three thousand pounds of it was owed to his brother-in-law Lord Essex, who the year before had given Bedford fifty pounds 'to pay him that sum if ever he lost above £10,000 at a sitting'. Another £10,000 was owed Beau Nash upon the same account. Diana was hoping she would find her grandmother in town when she arrived, for 'I long to see you', and believed Marlborough House warmer than the Lodge in winter. She feared the Duke of Bedford must sell land in order to discharge his debt, which till now he did not know he could do, his chaplain informing her that since he had come of age he had lost above 'two hundred and twenty thousand pounds'.[32]

Diana was pleased to find her grandmother at Marlborough House, but the dowager soon returned to Windsor. Diana's consolation was that she and her cousin the Duchess of Manchester planned to stay with her there when Lord John went to visit his Hampshire estate. But first she and her

husband were to visit Cheam, their small manor house in Surrey. Convenient for town, this had belonged to Dr Lumley Lloyd, rector at St Paul's
Church, Covent Garden, who, having no relations living at the time, had
bequeathed it to the Duke of Bedford. Bedford had made it over to his
brother. The weather being very pleasant for the time of year, Diana and her
husband visited it in November, crossing London Bridge to get there,
calling at the Bedfords' Streatham house on their way. Here Lord John was
'to fetch away what belongs to him', including no doubt the black and
silver cabinet Sarah had so admired when she was here, Diana promising
to send her grandmother a full 'account of my Country House'.[33]

They went to the opera before leaving, Handel having revived *Rinaldo*
with new sets and costumes, and afterwards to Lady Anne Hervey's house
where Diana found herself ignored by her aunt the Duchess of Marlborough (who was refusing to mourn her son, and only pleased he could not
now disgrace the Marlborough title), and who sat talking to Lady Mary
Wortley Montagu all evening. Diana found kind Lady Burlington here, who
asked 'mightily' after Sarah, and on Monday night Diana and John
attended the court. Here Diana met 'with more honour from his Majesty
than ever I did in my life', reporting it all to her grandmother, and they then
went on to Cheam, from where Diana wrote:

> We came here on Thursday last, intending to stay no longer than to day,
> but finding a great deal of business we shall not return to London till
> Monday. But as I promised to give you an account of my Castle, I send
> a man to London on purpose with this letter to you my Dear
> Grand-mama. The house is full large enough for a place so near Town,
> & tho' in a small town is not at all a disagreeable situation. The house
> is extream clean, & one large room in it, fill'd with all sorts of enter-
> taining books. There is scarce any furniture but beds, which I am not
> sorry for, since I shall have the pleasure of doing that my self, & making
> a thousand little alterations, which will give me a great deal of pleasure
> & employment, for alltogether I think it a charming little place.

They had 'no company at all', but the weather was so fine they went out 'in
a chaise upon the Banstead Downs in the morning, which is the finest turf
in the world, and just by us'. In the evening they read or played at cards, '&
now we are employ'd in making a catalogue of the books & putting them

in great order'. She told how at Streatham she found 'a vast deal of china, & a considerable part of it extream fine, & a prodigous quantity of the best Japan that ever I saw, besides a great deal of useful furniture'.[34]

Here was a picture of delightful domestic bliss which might easily have been spoiled by the Duke of Bedford's request to borrow £18,000 from his brother, Lord Russell lending it at four per cent without complaint. 'This shows,' wrote Diana, 'that [the duke] himself does not know that he has it in his power to part with land, and his Steward has told him this is the last money he can take up.' She was of the opinion all would be well if it rested there, and that 'the same Rogues who have got so much of him don't find out that they shall get more, which if they do, to be sure he won't be long ignorant of it'.[35]

Prior to Diana's wedding, the memorial to her grandfather the Duke of Marlborough (designed in the end by Lord Herbert) had been set up in the Blenheim Palace park, both Diana's youthful attempts and Hawksmoor's plans having finally been dropped. The 'Column of Victory' as it would be known, with Bolingbroke's heartfelt panegyric, stands on the spot today. Herbert was to be numbered among the Palladian architects of his day, along with Lord Burlington, and Sarah was impressed enough with his work to ask him to design her a house at Wimbledon. It was to be built on the site of the splendid castle-like Tudor house once occupied by Charles I and his Queen Henrietta, on land confiscated from a South Sea Bubble director, Sir Theodore Janssen; and when alterations were wanted on the ground floor, Sarah had called on Diana to redraw the plan. Sending the altered design to Lord Herbert, Sarah added the note:

This plan my Paladio Dye has done at my request, to oblige me, I finding that it may be compassed with no alteration to the offices, but only changing my apartment to the other side. At the same time I must do her justice to say that I believe she would not have done it for any other body in the world, being so great an Architect that she loves nothing but shew and Italian Buildings.

'Paladio Dye' was obviously taking architecture seriously, and her drawing of the ground-floor plan is still kept at the Herberts' Wilton House.* When

---

* A reproduction of Diana's plan can be seen in the illustration section.

returning to London from Cheam, Diana made a point of passing close by Wimbledon to see how the building progressed, writing to her grandmother:

> When I came from Cheam we pass'd near enough to Wimbledon to see the house, which looks extreamly fine. I did intend to have got out of the coach but it was so cold & the snow so much upon the Ground that I could not.

The house stood close to Wimbledon's St Mary's Church, in grounds with an orchard, vineyard and orange garden. When Diana peered at the building through her coach windows she saw it as it would be later pictured in *Vitruvius Britannicus*, resplendent with a four-columned portico.[36]

Diana meanwhile looked forward to her trip to Windsor with Bella, writing to her grandmother:

> You can't imagine how happy I am to think that I shall see you soon, for Lord John goes into Hampshire Monday or Tuesday next, & which ever of the days it is, the Duchess of Manchester & I will come to the Dear Lodge.

She expected her husband to stay at Stratton 'two or three days, & then he will come to Windsor to wait upon you, & carry us to Town the next day'. She hoped her grandmother would come to town with them, believing the weather much too cold to be in so 'thin a house'. The social whirl of the winter season was to continue, Diana sending news of the Prince of Wales's 'Route' with his mistress Anne Vane, and how 'Lord John carried me to the Masquerade'. Here she had conversed with Lady Wortley Montagu (who looked 'extreamly fine, & well Dress'd') for 'above half an hour, before she knew me'. Diana's fancy dress and mask were apparently a great disguise, but she does not describe it. Nor did she mention the Prince of Wales, though he was very much in evidence, dressed 'like a shepherd, an Adonis, or an Apollo', attended by a band of eighteen huntsmen 'in green waistcoats, leopard-skins and quivers at their backs'. Diana was 'not much entertained by the ball', but admitted that 'the room and so many different dresses when first one comes in, is an extream fine sight'.[37]

Diana had paid a courtesy call on her stepmother the remarried Lady Sunderland while in town, and also the widowed Lady Blandford, finding the latter sad and pale. It was not to last long, however, Lady Blandford marrying Sir William Wyndham, Somerset's son-in-law, and father of Diana's erstwhile suitor, Charles. A more pleasing visit was when she and her husband dined with her brother Charles at Sunderland House, a happy re-experience of her early childhood, and 'we had the best dinner that could be'. Sarah had complained of Charles keeping a mistress, a 'Mrs Smith', fearing he might marry her, and of Johnny having a liaison with an old love whose name was unmentioned, but Diana assured her grandmother that he had never seen her since he came home from abroad. Diana was deeply loyal to both her brothers, and pleased to find her grandmother 'so pleased with Brother John. I think he has as much good nature as any mortal can have', she enthused, 'and a better understanding allmost than any person', which were 'two very good ingredients towards his doing right in every thing'.[38]

Cousin Bella (whose marriage was far from happy still) spent much of her time with the newly wed Russells, and with Christmas on the way accompanied them to Cheam. Here the new Lord and Lady of the manor were 'to Entertain the Tenants & their wives', Diana writing to her grandmother on Boxing Day:

The weather is so excessive fine that the country is extreamly pleasant. We walk two hours upon the Downs in a morning, which gives us all exceeding good stomachs, & in the evening we read, & play a little every day. To-morrow all the tenants are to be entertain'd here. I own I wish that day over.[39]

The business of entertaining her tenants, however much she might like them, or not, would be a nerve-wracking operation for a young and inexperienced bride. Diana was helped considerably by having Bella with her, hoping she would stay the whole time, and the gift of a 'doe' sent by her grandmother was very welcome. It was 'more acceptable today than it could be at any other time', she wrote, and 'Luckily our feast is deferr'd till to-morrow, & to be sure Venison is the greatest Rarity that can be to these people, & they will like it the better for being yours'. She was delighted to find her grandmother of such 'great interest in this Part of the World', and that 'All the Surrey people are extream happy that a Grand Daughter of yours is come amongst them'![40]

Her grandmother continued to guide both her granddaughters in their reading, Diana promising to read *Don Quixote* again, 'though I own it did not suit my tast at all', while the Duchess of Manchester had read it so long ago she had entirely forgotten it: but as soon as she was in town would read it again, for 'she is very sure you know what will please her'. Meanwhile they 'danc'd with the Tenants & their Wives . . . which made them extream happy', and drank the duchess's health 'over the Venison several times & to the memory of the Duke of Marlborough'.[41]

Among the good people of Cheam the year 1731 drew to a happy close, Cousin Bella returning ahead of the Russells to town. John and Diana continued there until 'Twelfth Day', her grandmother having promised to be in town when they returned. Learning she had won money from Mrs Kingdon (with whom she was reunited), Diana was 'sure you aught not to neglect that', and was 'in great hopes of meeting her at the hazard table'.[42]

CHAPTER TEN

Life in Death

'I beg of you to make the coachman go very slow . . .'

On 2 April 1732 the house at Cheam was full of workmen employed to make it larger and more stylish, the owners having left for Woburn. Lady Russell, in the sixth month of her marriage, had left a letter for her grandmother to find when she called to look over the house, for which pleasure the dowager was making a special journey from London.

The Duchess of Marlborough travelled by coach, first crossing London Bridge, then travelling part-way along the road to Ewell before crossing the common on the way to Cheam, partaking of an elaborate picnic lunch on her way. The Cheam house stood in the centre of the village, an old rambling house dating from the sixteenth century, and as Sarah loved poking about old houses she meant to enjoy herself. Finding the house full of workmen, she hobbled out on her crutches into the garden, which was stocked 'full of flowers', and thought them a 'very innocent pleasure'. But there were too many of them, she commented, and she did not at all like the new-fangled 'cradles' they were in. She believed such a garden should have 'the borders stuffed thick with everything that is sweet, useful or that makes a show by the rarity of fine colours, and beds as broad as they are sown in, and little walks to go between that one might go round everything'.[1]

In other words, Sarah would have liked the flower garden to be the same as her own. In the courtyard she found a splendid dovecote and a pillar with a lion on the top, 'a strange tongue hanging out of its mouth', displaying the Lloyd arms. Although she thought the house had 'no great beauty in the situation', considering it was 'within half a mile of the finest downs and best air in England', she noted it was built with as good bricks as those from which Marlborough House was built. After struggling back into the house again, 'too weary to go upstairs', she went into the dining-room to be served with the 'best pigeons that ever I eat in my life', making her 'sorry she had eaten her own dinner first'. It was not 'near so good as what your housekeeper got me', she confessed to Diana, and a 'gentleman there would force me to open two bottles of your wine, one of which was champagne, so very good that I was frail enough to drink three glasses, though I feared it would hurt me'. The dowager had always had a weakness for food, and now found it hard to refuse the housekeeper who 'flew about and everything came so quick, as if it had been an enchantment'.[2]

Diana had taken care to see her grandmother was well looked after, the 'fat man' who served the champagne insisting on showing her the stables before she left. Sarah remarked to him that 'his taking so much pains to please me I took . . . as a mark that he loved my Lady Russell'. Upon this the large man replied that 'there was nobody that did not love her'. 'Paladio Dye' must have been pleased with her grandmother's verdict on the house, saying 'there is sense and reason in this place'.[3]

Diana's taste in architecture was not always thought by her grandmother to have 'sense and reason', however, for Diana had once commended a riverside house built by Lord Herbert at Greenwich which her brother Johnny thought to buy. One of the rooms, Sarah said when she saw it, which was 'not much bigger than one of the Duke of Bedford's tables' when he had company, had four great stone pillars such as 'the Ancients had' to support magnificent rooms that appeared to 'want support', but in Herbert's case took away what little room there was, and were 'plainly to support nothing'. These were the sort of observations Sarah must have made to Diana over the years since she was a small child, and now that grandmother and granddaughter were parted, she continued through their correspondence to advise her. In the coming months Sarah would again ridicule the current craze for pillars, including those in the Assembly Rooms at York built by the Duke of Burlington. This building exceeded 'all the nonsense and madness that I ever saw of that kind,' she wrote to Diana when visiting it, the pillars 'as close as nine pins' so that 'nobody with a hoop petticoat can pass through them', and the gallery for people to see the dancers 'so very high that they can see nothing but the tops of heads!' Later she would relate the Prince of Wales's disgust at finding pillars cramping the newly built stables in the Royal Mews, the prince asking, 'What the devil are these?' For once Sarah was in agreement with the prince, believing that 'the beauty of a stable is to see a great many horses, but in this you can only see two or three as you go up between the pillars'. Indeed she was pleasantly 'surprised at his Royal Highness saying what appeared to me so very rational'.[4]

At Woburn Diana and her husband found the young Duke of Bedford falling into more and more debt, which overshadowed the fact that he was also suffering a decline in his health. The Russells were at Cheam again in

May, their house at last completed, Diana pregnant with her first child. Returning from a day at the local races, she found a messenger awaiting her, a note from her grandmother saying she had received a 'very melancholy letter from the poor Duchess of Bedford'. Anne had been 'dreadfully frightened with the thoughts of being forced out of England, her Lord having declared that he will take her with him, and that he will go in a ship all the way to Lisbon'. The fact that the Portugal climate was recommended for those suffering a 'consumption' was discounted, on account of the duke's previous brutality towards his wife. Sarah spoke of Anne's constitution being 'extremely worn, and God only knows what may be the consequence of distresses which she may be in when in foreign countries where she can have no advice'. Her own advice to Anne was 'that if I were in her circumstances I am very sure I would not go'.[5]

Diana wrote back that she wished 'to God it were in my power in any way to be instrumental to the poor Duchess of Bedford being hindered from this dreadful voyage', but considering 'the obstinacy of the Duke of Bedford's temper, it will be very hardly compass'd without coming to extremities'. Rather than 'hazzard her life', Diana suggested:

> Were I in her place (after she has try'd all the ways that can be thought of to persuade him to let her stay at home by fair means) & if he can then be so cruel as to refuse her, sure it will be very justifiable (in the manner they live together) to see if any man has it in his power by law, to force his wife abroad to the prejudice of her health, & more probably the loss of her life. But I am sure my Dear Grandmama you are much better able to judge what is the most likely way to succeed in this case than I can . . . [6]

Diana's cousin was now living apart from her husband in the Streatham house where she had been courted by the duke in happier days and which, like Cheam, was on the south side of the Thames. She lived in terror of having to leave England and all those she knew, her nerves in shreds, complaining also of 'great pains in her chest from a bite she had with a horse'. Sarah, having once persuaded her to submit to 'everything in the world' for the sake of her marriage, now admitted that she knew 'of no instance of any woman who has so much gentleness in their nature to submit to everything, as she has done under such terrible usage'; and like

Diana, she felt that under no circumstances should she hazard her life to go with 'so great a brute'. The old duchess proposed that Anne should tell her father how apprehensive she was 'of going abroad', and how she believed it would kill her; and surely, considering the way her husband had always lived with her, 'he can't possibly have any pleasure in taking her with him'.[7]

Diana's husband, who appeared to be as solid in his ways as his brother was shiftless, had nonetheless managed to get himself involved in a duel. With whom, and for what reason, is unknown, but his Stratton neighbour in Hampshire, Dr Alured Clarke, wrote to Sarah's friend Mrs Clayton:

Last week Lord John Russell wrote Lord Lymington a particular account of his duel, out of great inclination he has to stand well with his Hampshire friends: but I am very sorry to hear from another Lord that the quarrel is not healed yet. One would think the ways of destruction are but few, and that men were hard put to it to find them, before they could think of sacrificing themselves to the shadow of honour and the silly tyranny of custom: and I question whether in many cases that might be mentioned, duelling is not more justifiable than self murder . . . [8]

Lord John's wife being pregnant, he had apparently put all such foolishness aside, now racking his brains to find ways of saving his sister-in-law from having to accompany her brutal brother abroad. While Diana agreed with her grandmother that Anne should approach her father first, if that did not do (which it almost certainly would not) she fancied her grandmother must 'talk the Duke of Bedford into reason'. It would do 'no harm', and her grandmother would have 'the satisfaction of having done all you could to do good, which I am sure will always be a pleasure to you'. In fairness Diana thought, 'Perhaps [the duke] does not care to leave her here to live by herself, & if that is so, his knowing (as you told me) that you would be so good to let her live with you would possibly make him comply more easily.' But as to that, Diana was sure her grandmother 'knew best'.[9]

Diana showed diplomatic skill in dealing with her grandmother, careful not to offend her, while nudging her on to do what she thought was possible and right. The letter concerning her cousin was a long and thoughtful one, and another idea occurred to her before she was through, that a physician or two of note might be approached 'that could say they altogether thought it might put her life in danger to undertake so long a voyage'. Surely after that 'no person who calls themselves a human creature could be so barbarous . . . as to force her away, for I think it would really be murder!' She said she had shown her grandmother's letter to Lord John, '& he thinks as you do, that in the circumstances he positively would not go'.[10]

Lord John would know his brother's temper better than anyone did, and joined with his wife in inviting the long-suffering Anne to stay at Cheam for a few days. Diana had asked her grandmother to dine with them whenever she visited her Wimbledon house, convinced she would be 'more pleas'd with our own dinner, than to have a feast'. She told her how the Duchess of Bedford 'came here last night and will stay with us till Sunday', and was 'extream happy with your saying you will speak to the Duke of Bedford'. She warned her that when she first spoke to him 'his answer will be that she [Anne] has desir'd herself to go with him; but as his Grace does not always stick litterally to the truth, you will easily believe this is far from it, but he has taken it into his head to tell everybody so'. In fact the young duchess 'never thought of desireing it, but that she dare not seem to dislike going'. But if Sarah told the duke it would be 'a great obligation to you if he would leave her in England', she was sure 'he will be very well pleas'd to do it'. Diana ended her letter by saying: 'I hope with all my heart that this & every thing else you desire may succeed as you wish yourself', and told her that Johnny was also with them at Cheam.[11]

Here there were more family matters to discuss. Brother Charles (having tired of 'Miss Smith') declared he was to marry Elizabeth Trevor in five days' time, a fact carefully kept from his grandmother till a short time before the papers were to be signed. Charles had asked Diana to acquaint their grandmother of his intentions, and once she had done so called on Sarah at Windsor Lodge. Finding cousin Bella posted outside their grand-mother's door, he was informed that the old duchess was too ill to see him, the young man (having half expected to be snubbed), leaving a message to say he was to marry a Miss Trevor, and would go to his sister Bateman at Totteridge next day to complete the formalities.

Sarah had claimed she was dying when Charles called on her, but was able to sit up and dictate a letter to be sent to him after he had left. For many months she had been seeking a suitable bride for him, she said, and was prepared to accept a woman with no fortune supposing she was 'pleasing and well bred'. Instead he had chosen a girl whose grandfather was the first Baron Trevor, a 'remarkable Prosecutor of their own Grandfather', and whose name Queen Anne had 'plucked from her pocket' and made him a peer, in order to facilitate the smooth passage of the Peace Treaty of Utrecht through parliament, of which Marlborough was strongly opposed. Members of the whole Trevor family were, in Sarah's opinion, 'sad people'. She described the proposed bride as 'bred very low and dont know how to behave herself upon any occasion', and 'not at all pretty', having a 'mean, ordinary look', and worse, had 'very bad teeth'. She had been told Charles did not even love the woman, which if he had might have been some excuse to marry. As etiquette demanded that a female member of the groom's family should negotiate the formalities with the proposed bride's female representative, instead of his grandmother Charles chose his 'overbearing sister' Lady Bateman. Sarah was beside herself with fury. [12]

Charles's reply to his grandmother was proud and not a little haughty. He refused to be moved by his grandmother's 'Invectives' as he called them, which he supposed were to be looked on as 'Arguments', or to be drawn into any quarrel concerning his sister; and as 'for your putting me out of your will', it was 'some time since I neither expected or desir'd to be in it'. [13]

Brother Johnny was now sent for by his grandmother, 'in so ill a state of health that he could not walk across a room easily' (he was suffering from the after-effects of syphilis), Sarah showing him the will she had drawn up in his favour. By removing his brother from her will she would settle £300,000 on Johnny, asking him, 'was this not mighty kind' of her, but that he must live with her as a son. She observed that by not 'so much as a look' did Johnny fault his brother. Afterwards, wrote Sarah, 'his sister Bateman persuaded him to go a journey, in contempt of all I had said, to celebrate that great wedding', and took pains to make Diana go too, 'but that failed', she triumphed, 'which I was glad of for her sake more than my own . . . for I never spoke a word to my Lady Russell about it'. [14]

Diana must have been unhappy about absenting herself from her brother's wedding, which took place at Totteridge on 23 May, 1732, Lord Bateman congratulating Johnny for going along, saying he deserved a statue of gold for his bravery. His grandmother tore up the will she had made in his favour, and blackened the portrait of Lady Bateman hanging at Marlborough House, writing beneath it that she was 'blacker within'. Lady Bateman's attempt to lure Lady Russell to the wedding was, Sarah said, to make her 'appear to the World as black as herself'. When Johnny attempted to visit his grandmother at Marlborough House, she turned him away. [15]

Sarah concentrated her efforts on the Duchess of Bedford, visiting her at her Streatham house. Anne told her grandmother that her duke was 'Mightily pleased' that Sarah wished her to stay with her while he was away, and as he was not proposing to sail till September, Sarah agreed to collect Anne from Woburn when she returned from a trip she was making to Scarborough. She presumed that Anne's father was 'such a wretch that he does not care to take her for a little time, or, that she does not care to be with him'.[16]

Two days after his brother's wedding Johnny was staying with the Russells at Cheam, Diana tentatively sending his 'duty' to his grandmother. Four days later Sarah wrote to Johnny, blaming sister Bateman for forcing him to attend his brother's wedding, saying, 'Lady Anne Bateman has done more mischief to her family in general than ever any woman did and I don't doubt but my Lady Bateman exerted herself to make you commit that folly.' This sister had also taken 'a great deal of pains to make sister Russell commit the same indecency to me: which cou'd be for no reason but to make her appear as black as herself, who is certainly the worst woman that I ever knew in my life'. The letter was signed, 'your very ill-treated Grandmother'.[17]

The dowager duchess made a call on the Russells at Cheam before leaving for Scarborough, and as Diana's cousin the Duchess of Bedford was with them they were able to discuss future plans. As Diana and Lord John were to spend the summer at their Stratton manor house in Hampshire, Anne (and possibly Johnny), returned with their grandmother to Marlborough House. Diana was four months pregnant, her grandmother anxious that no harm should come to her on the journey, writing: 'I sent you some advice yesterday by the Duchess of Manchester', but having 'no great opinion of her as to anything that is serious . . . I repeat it':

I have a great dread of your driving a chaise, because I know the reaching out your arm to whip the horse is a very improper motion at this time. And I hope my Lord [John] won't be affronted, if I say that I had rather have a sober groom lead the horse than have the greatest lord in the world drive you.

What made Sarah so apprehensive was that 'I miscarried of a son myself from follies which I committed when I was very young, and you have now but a few months to make it necessary to be very careful'.[18]

Lord and Lady Russell reached their country house without mishap on 26 June, Diana eager to share her experience by letter. She sent 'ten thousand thanks' for her grandmother's kindness 'in giving me the pleasure of seeing me at Cheam', and hoped she 'got home well, & in good time', and went on to describe her Hampshire dwelling:

We came in here yesterday by four o'clock in the evening, & had so pleasant a journey that I was not in the least fatigued, but went all over the park as soon as we came home. It is but a small one, (3 miles & a half round) but I really think it the most charming spot of ground that ever I saw, the turf is like green velvet, & there is a vast deal of wood in it, with beautiful walks & views through them, & most delightful lawns that is possible, & when the house is built I do believe it will be the most charming place in the world.[19]

The newlyweds planned to build a new house on the site of the old house, plans already drawn up for them by John Sanderson. Hopefully 'Paladio Dye' was not too discouraged by her grandmother's advice:

I think the best advice I can give you as to finishing any house, is to look upon the buildings of my Lord Herbert's or Burlington's, the last of which I think is yet more ridiculous than the first, because it cost him an immense sum of money and has nothing in them either handsome or of any use.

Burlington's enchanting villa at Chiswick is described today as a 'pioneer work in neoclassical architecture', and was completed a year or two earlier, while Lord Herbert's house at Greenwich had already come under Sarah's damning censure, being 'the most ridiculous thing I ever saw in my life'. With its superfluous pillars and glass partition in place of a wall, it could only have been built 'by someone that is mad!'[20]

The Russells' house stood close to the Stratton village, where each cottage had a bridge crossing a stream before it, and there was a church. As a young wife prior to her husband's cruel execution, Lord John's grandmother Rachel had spent many summers here in a 'life full of sweetness and content'. Writing to her beloved husband from Stratton, she recalled her 'rural occupations', such as 'her care for his hawks and his dogs, pears laid up for him in paper and linen, a red deer pie eaten, and the comic antics of their children. The elder girl [John's aunt] – prattled of Woburn: 'She says papa has sent for her to Wobee, and then she gallops and says she has been there'; and the baby son [John's father] 'winking at me, and striking with his drum stick whatever comes within his reach'. At the end of the day she wrote contentedly: 'boy is sleeping, girls singing a-bed'. Diana must have hoped to continue this tradition of warm domesticity, and was busy creating a nursery for her own coming baby. It may have been for this reason the couple meant to retain some of the old building as part of the new, Diana writing to her grandmother:

We live in one of the wings which are to stand, & the rooms are extream good, & when they are furnish'd will be very handsome, & convenient; at present we make shift with Half Beds & hangings, which when the house is finish'd, will be very good furniture for the Upper servants rooms; there is an extream good Laundry & Brew house, & stables for fifty horses, which are built as strong & well as possible, & not too near the house to make it offensive, but at just a right distance for convenience – in short, I am extreamly pleas'd with the place, & I dare say it would suit your tast[e].

Diana was always careful to make her grandmother feel wanted, saying she hoped 'next summer to be so happy as to prevail with you to come, & give me your opinion, & advice, as to finishing the house, for it is a very easy days journey, not quite thirty miles from Windsor Lodge, & I would have everything I do, be with your approbation'.[21]

Sarah had started out on her journey to Scarborough to take the waters, a tedious one for an old woman suffering gout, and 'a great deal of the way very jolting'. As she was leaving Marlborough House she had caught sight of Johnny Spencer's calash (a light carriage with a folding top, with seating for four passengers), and guessed it would take him to Hampshire. Not only were the Russells staying there, but at Upper Somborne nearby, brother Charles and his new bride were at Rookley. Lady Bateman was with them too, Sarah jealously imagining the young people commuting between Stratton and Rookley. As Diana was vulnerable in her pregnancy, her grandmother said nothing of her disapproval just now, concentrating her concerns on the Duchess of Bedford. After a stop at St Albans, dropping Anne here, she called at Woburn for a meeting with the Duke of Bedford.

Sarah's stay was necessarily short, but she was pleased to find the Duke of Bedford polite and charming. Indeed it was 'not possible for any man to behave better than the Duke of Bedford did in all respects', she wrote to Diana, and if she only had 'time and spirits' could tell a 'thousand pretty things he said'. All the same it amazed her to see a man that 'seems to have so much sense and yet to have made such a havoc of his constitution and of his estate'. She had been told in London that he had 'added £6000 more to Mr Johnson's debt', and what he had done 'for the securing anything' she could not learn, but admitted the duke was far from well:

> I find that the people in his family think he is worse than he was, and I think so myself. But his eyes looked well and he would not own that he was not so. Yet I observed when we went into the Gallery to see the pictures, he sat down very often, which I conclude proceeded from weakness. I made him as easy as I could in everything, for I find he cannot endure to be thought ill, and therefore did not take any notice that I saw it, but contrived to sit down often as we talked over the pictures.[22]

Wriothesley told Sarah that he was expecting the Russells at Woburn when they returned from Stratton, who would stay with him for some days. 'If so', wrote Sarah to Diana, ''tis very probable that I may have the happiness of meeting you there.' The duke was not leaving for Portugal until the beginning of September, and Sarah would go from Woburn 'to St Albans to take possession of the Duchess of Bedford'. To this she added ominously: 'Some people think he won't be able to go the voyage he designs, but as he is young and had certainly a great constitution nobody can be able to say how that will happen.'[23]

When Diana sent Johnny's 'obligations' to his grandmother, Sarah had refused wholly to accept them, saying, 'Surely my endeavour to have educated him well, my manner of living with him, the tenderness I showed him on all essential occasions was in reality a greater obligation, even than an estate'. As to Charles's bride, Sarah had heard from one person how Elizabeth was 'simple, ill-bred and knows nothing of a right behaviour', and from another that she had 'a termagent spirit and is ill natured'. The only good thing she had heard was that she had a 'great deal of sense and will disappoint my Lady Bateman as to her design in this marriage, which was to govern her brother and all his finances'. Another informant, who had sat close to the sisters-in-law when Lord Bateman was presented with the Order of the Bath, observed that Lady Bateman 'took her sister [in-law] by the hand several times in that great assembly like a fond lover; which looks', Sarah said, 'as if she intended to manage her as long as she can'.[24]

The letters Diana wrote to her grandmother on her Scarborough journey have sadly not survived, but their contents can be gleaned from her grandmother's replies. Diana had sent a description of Charles's bride whom she met at Rookley, and clearly liked her, while in deference to her grandmother's disapproval of her admitted to 'awkward motions in the hands and arms'. To this Sarah replied:

> The account I wrote to you of Lady Sunderland was what I was told, but I dare say your judgment of her is more likely to be a right one, than theirs.

At the same time she could only wonder 'how she came to have so easy and right behaviour who has always been used to low and ordinary company'. Contrary to her grandmother's findings, Diana had found that Charles was fond of his wife, to which Sarah responded that she remembered how he was once 'so very fond of Mrs. Smith, that some people fancied he would marry her'! When Diana had refused to speak ill of Charles, her grandmother insisted that though her own 'relation is as near to him as yours, if he were my only son I would not love a simple nor an ungrateful man', both of which he 'certainly is'.[25]

None of this prevented Diana and her husband enjoying their sight-seeing honeymoon, riding out and about with friends and family. They visited Wilton, perhaps hoping for advice on the rebuilding of Stratton, but Lord Herbert was not at home. Sarah remembered the Wiltshire house from her own youth, admitting it was 'a very fine place and might be easily made very agreeable'. Diana had found it stuffed with plaster figures which her grandmother might have described as the sort 'my Lady Delaware [Charlotte] would have been mighty pleased with, because the nose was broke off'. She thought John and Diana had missed the most curious thing at Wilton by 'my lord's being absent', he being 'often mad and always very odd'.[26]

Diana's letters to and from her grandmother were deposited at a butcher's shop in Winchester, from where they were sent on to Stratton or collected. Sarah received six letters from her granddaughter when she reached Scarborough, and although they had been a long time coming, 'after one has received the first letter, if you write regularly, the post comes in three times a week as it does to places near London, and it is a great comfort to hear often from one I love as I do you'. She was glad to learn 'the roads are so good where you go', and believed 'being in the air and on good ground will do you no hurt'. Part of the way she had come was 'so very jolting' it was impossible 'for anybody that is with child to go through such roads without miscarrying', which had often made her think of 'dear Lady Russell, and I should not have given you this account but to beg you would not go in bad roads for five months, and when there does happen to be any rugged way, I beg of you to make the coachman go very slow'.[27]

Separation had made Sarah more devoted to her granddaughter than ever, and with the coming birth in mind she had more advice for the mother-to-be. She had been reading a book by a Dr Wittie on the miraculous effects of the Scarborough waters, in which the 'author says a great deal of the benefit people would have in drinking nothing but good water for the generality of their drink'. It was 'what nature first designed', wrote Sarah, 'and I really believe it is best for one's health, and there can be no doubt that it would be for the advantage of young people to drink very little ale, beer or wine'. She was convinced that 'the less wine or malt drink young people take, it is much the better', and for 'people of my age that have been used to drink wine', they could only 'lesson it by mixing it with water', but spring water was the best, she advised, 'especially where it is upon gravel'.[28]

Remembering how Lord John loved venison, Sarah had ordered a buck to arrive at Stratton on 26 July, and another for the 30th to celebrate Diana's 'dear birthday'. Diana would be twenty-two years old. She wrote to her grandmother asking if she and Lord John might stay at Holywell House on their way home, after which they would visit Woburn as arranged. Sarah said she was sorry they thought it necessary to ask permission 'as it may be some ease to you in making a quiet inn of it, whenever you have occasion to pass that way'. And she went on:

You know there's conveniency's enough for anybody that you care to bring with you, and Mr Carr can furnish you with anything that you want. But if you come from London you may bring something that is just good for yourself to eat in your own coach. I think my bed is the easiest and quietest in that place, for nobody is under or over you, but I doubt it is too small a bed for two, and therefore you had better make use of that room above stairs that looks into the garden, and where there's a little bed in the room before it that will serve Jane.

Jane Patterson, who long ago had come to St Albans with Diana, appeared now to be her waiting woman.[29]

Sarah's Scarborough letters were among the most entertaining she wrote, and though plagued by gout, and infuriated by inns 'worse than Hanover', her words sparkled with news and views. She wrote of the Prince of Wales's mistress, Anne Vane, who 'goes a visiting in her chair with her son in her lap and two nurses in chairs to attend her', and of meeting Diana's cousin Bella, telling her she 'goes into the sea and drinks the waters every day', but herself found the place so 'very dirty and so noisy I am going to lay straw in the street to hinder the intolerable noise of the horses that go by my window'. The place where they took the waters was 'extremely steep and disagreeable' to get to either in a coach or a chair, and the toilet facilities were intolerable:

There is a room for the ladies which you go up a steep pair of stairs into, on the outside of the house, like a ladder. And in that room there is nothing but hard narrow benches, which is rather a punishment to sit upon than an ease. When the waters begin to operate, there is a room within it, where there is above twenty holes with drawers under them to take out and all the ladies go in together and see one another round the room, when they are in that agreeable posture, and at the door, there's a great heap of leaves which the ladies take in with them. This sight I am sure diverted the Duchess of Manchester extremely, but it made me very sad. And I came home as fast as I could for fear of being forced into that assembly.[30]

And now the Russells were coming home, spending a night at St Albans on their way. Diana wrote how much she had liked her bed there, and would have had the pleasure of showing Lord John over the Holywell House gardens her grandfather and great uncle Godolphin had created, and the other delights of her childhood. But this was to be clouded over when she and her husband reached Woburn Abbey. Diana was deeply shocked at her brother-in-law's appearance, and her grandmother wrote:

> I should have been myself just as you describe yourself to have been, at the sight of the poor Duke of Bedford. Though there was no reason to expect that a man should ever act right that for so many years has done so very wrong and that it is really a loss to nobody but the sharpers, [but] it is impossible to see anybody, that might have been made so good a figure in such a condition as he is said to be and not be touched by it.[31]

Sarah had put off the day of her return in order to avoid the crowds returning from the York races, so was unable to meet the Russells at Woburn as planned. When she reached St Albans she found a letter from Diana, sent from Cheam:

> I have receiv'd your kind letter my Dear Grandmama . . . & am extream glad to find by it that you think your self better than you have been. I hope this will find you quite well at St Albans, & that you will let me know as soon as you come to London, that I may make myself happy in dining with you. I have just seen the last of the Duke of Bedford's debts, which ammounts to Seventy one Thousand odd hundred pounds, including the £20,000 which he borrow'd of Lord John, & he has oweing him above eighteen thousand pounds, fifteen of which will be paid certainly, but the other I believe is not likely to be paid, & besides this there is fifteen hundred pounds a year annuities to be paid for the lives of two or three people, for which the D. of Bedford has received near fifteen thousand pounds. Though this is a very black list, it is less than I expected, & I find that Janssen has been paid everything owing to him for his name is not in it. One Fleetwood is the Chief person that is owed to. I long to know the time when I shall see you my Dear Grandmama . . . [32]

Sarah planned to remain at Marlborough House to be near her two grand-daughters, Diana being seven months into her pregnancy, and her cousin

Anne in an advanced state of nervous disorder, having accompanied her husband to Streatham. Sarah wrote to Diana:

> I intend to be at London to-morrow night, and to go to Streatham to see the Duchess of Bedford on Tuesday. For she writes me word she has tremblings upon her, which I apprehend a worse complaint than any she has yet made . . . I can't fix the hour, nor do I intend to ask to see the Duke of Bedford, because I could not be uneasy to him. But if you be there upon the Tuesday, I can have the satisfaction of seeing you and it will not be above half as many miles to come there, as [for you] to come to London.[33]

The duke had apparently taken to his bed at Streatham. Diana, as her grandmother suggested, was able to reach the house with reasonable ease, though her body was rounded and heavy with her unborn child. Sarah claimed possession of the Duchess of Bedford while she was there, taking her home to Marlborough House, and a short time afterwards the Duke of Bedford set out for Portsmouth with friends, prepared to board the ship he had hired for Lisbon. As there had been another falling-out between Sarah and Mrs Kingdon, Diana took the latter home to Cheam. Diana was very fond of Jane Kingdon, and would be glad of an extra woman at the birth. When Sarah planned to visit Cheam later, she said, 'I hope my being there will be no uneasiness to Mrs Kingdon who will be none to me'![34]

Diana was suffering some kind of ailment, possibly bleeding, her grandmother hoping that she was well of that 'little complaint you had when I saw you because you say nothing to the contrary'. At the same time she advised her if anything 'of that kind is moderate, I suppose you know it is a very unsafe thing to stop it'. Was Sarah referring to some unspeakable method of preventing a miscarriage? She was sure the Duchess of Bedford had given her an account of all she had heard from Portsmouth, believing that if the duke 'escapes being sick at sea, I fancy he may get to Lisbon'. She promised to call at Cheam 'as soon and as often as I can', and warned her:

> You have but about a month now to be very careful to avoid any ill accident. And I think you should by no means come to London till you remove for the winter.[35]

The Duke of Bedford had meanwhile boarded his ship, a man-of-war named the *Torrington*, the friends who accompanied him so shocked at his appearance they thought it 'impossible for him to recover, or to live any time'. He seemed to suspect this himself, and 'be sorry that he embarqued', wrote Sarah; and when a fair wind enabled the ship to set sail, the duke asked the captain if it would serve to land him at Bordeaux, the captain answering 'it would not'. He seemed 'to be very impatient at the crossness of the winds', Sarah remarked, 'which I am apt to think proceeds chiefly from his apprehensions that the Duke may die before he has compassed the voyage, which would be a vast loss to the captain who will make great advantages by it in merchandising'. A servant or companion, 'Mr Tough', who was with the duke before the ship sailed, on seeing the duke change his linen, was surprised to see him 'so much thinner than when he saw him stripped at Streatham'.[36]

Careful arrangements were made for the birth of the new baby, which was planned to take place in town, Sarah assuring Diana that 'I will certainly not leave London till I have seen you here', and 'You may be sure I will do in that matter, as you would have me'. It was not easy to believe, she said, how much 'I would give to save you from any pain, if that were in my power'. The house in Grosvenor Street had been redecorated ready for the event, Sarah hobbling along to inspect it. She thought the house 'a very good one', and though 'several people have larger rooms, what you have is as much as is of any real use to anybody'. The white paint 'with so much red damask looks mighty handsome', she reported, and all 'the hangings were up in the four rooms above stairs except some pieces that are to be where the glass don't cover all the wainscot, and I think that will look very well'. What she did fear was that 'the red won't be finished time enough to have the room thoroughly clean and to be rubbed dry before you come to town', adding:

And if you come into a room that is but just washed, you will get a cold which will be very troublesome to you at this time.

She did not doubt that Diana would 'take care not to lie upon a new feather bed and to have all the quilts well aired'.[37]

Sarah's only quarrel with the house was with the bed. Having measured it she found it seven feet long and six feet broad, larger than any of those on her principal floor at Blenheim! And with reference to Diana's pet spaniel, she said there was ample room 'for Duchess to lie between you and Lord

John', but the height of the bed was right, not reaching the ceiling, as was the current fashion, though this would doubtless encourage the carpenter to gratify the prevailing passion for making 'two things to stand upon the feet of the bed which I call Gimmey-Gommenys'. Otherwise, if the bed could be cut smaller, the bedchamber was perfectly agreeable.[38]

October seemed to be a quiet month for the family, but early in November Diana was thrown from her chaise, and shocked into premature labour. A little boy, John, was born, only to die on the same day. Remembering her own insufferable grief at the loss of an infant, her grandmother asked that another baby be laid beside Diana till she was more able to accept her loss, Hervey reporting to his friend Stephen Fox:

> I breakfasted this morning with the Bishop of Salisbury* who would not own he knew any thing of a story I heard last night at lady Albermarle's; which was that they were so afraid telling Lady Russell her son was dead, and so embarrassed how to conceal it, that, after a grand consultation where Old Aetna was Speaker, it was determined a child be brought to represent the defunct, till she is strong enough to hear the truth and be told that it was only a Pretender . . . [39]

Little John was baptised on 6 November, and five days later was laid in the Russell family vault at the Church of St Michael at Chenies in Buckinghamshire. Unaware that he had become Duke of Bedford, Lord John Russell was recorded as the baby's father, a title that should have fallen to the baby himself, had he only lived. John's brother, the 3rd Duke of Bedford, had meanwhile died on 23 October, while his ship was sheltering from a storm at Corunna. His body was carried on to Lisbon, embalmed at the house where he was due to lodge, then returned to England. The news travelled slowly, and when it did arrive, nothing could either lessen or add to Lady Russell's grief.

---

* Benjamin Hoadly, who had written the prologue to the play *All for Love*, performed at Blenheim Palace.

CHAPTER ELEVEN

A Natural Affection

' . . . the d[uke] of Bedford is more kind to me every day'

Twelve days after the birth and death of her baby boy, and one week after his burial, Diana sent 'two Ladies' to her grandmother, begging her to pay her a visit. The bereaved mother was aching for the loss of her child, and doubtless depressed from the after-effects of childbirth unassisted by pain-killers or antibiotics. Yet despite this she had been asked in a letter from her grandmother to choose between the long friendship she had enjoyed with herself, and the friendship she had with her sister. No longer was the dowager able to accept Diana coming to her 'in the same manner she used to do', when she knew she 'came from such a viper'.[1]

Lying in the great bed at number 51 Grosvenor Street, the walls gleaming with fresh paint and new crimson hangings, the cradle empty, Diana had an abundance of time to think over what her grandmother had written to her. She would remember the happy days she had enjoyed in Hampshire visiting her brothers, sister-in-law and sister, at Rookley, and must now weigh against that the fifteen years her grandmother had devoted to her, of the duty she owed her, and the needs of an old widow's declining years.

The 'two Ladies' she had sent to her grandmother may have been those who mopped her brow during the delivery of her child, and provided the much-needed aftercare, anxious for the health of a bereaved mother. At Marlborough House the dowager listened to the 'Ladies'' supplications, and after they were gone, took up her pen and drafted a letter to her grand-daughter. In it she expressed all the bitterness she felt towards Lady Bateman, keeping this as her 'copy', and sent a more concise version to Diana herself. This last letter was dated 'November 18, 1732', and addressed to Diana under her new title:

I will come to you this afternoon, my dear Duchess of Bedford since you desire it of me. But I must at the same time own to you, that I think it would be more for your own satisfaction if you would live with me as I proposed; that is with all the outward appearance that is usual between such near relations who have been so long good friends and that would prevent any new discourses in the world, for whatever you do I shall always wish your happiness and think it more consequence than my own, but I can't do impossibilities. Any person that ever loved another must needs be sensible that there can be no great joy in the conversation of those that come to one from one's greatest enemy's [*sic*] and such as have used me in so shameful a manner. Something of this kind I have intended to say to you ever since the monstrous treatment which I had from the rest of your family, which I do believe you were very sorry for, though I have often observed you were very partial to them, and I was unwilling to give you uneasiness in the condition you were in and therefore deferred it. But now I must tell you that you must choose one of two things: which is to live with me as I proposed, or to distinguish yourself by shewing how far you are from having any of Lady Bateman's principles. I dont mean by this that you should not see your brothers, but she is a disgrace to be anybody's sister.

Sarah did not blame Diana's brothers, for 'they cannot help their weakness', nor did she suspect 'a deep plot' from them, but as 'it has been the custom of all times to put a Mark upon the Person that has been the contriver of any Great Mischief', she held Lady Bateman responsible. She had heard from others that Diana and her 'brothers & sister had met and dined at their houses in Hampshire, and that my Lady Bateman was of the party'.[2]

An anonymous letter by the penny post arrived at Marlborough House soon after Sarah sent her letter to Diana, the dowager in no doubt as to who sent it; the letter read:

I know your Grace is mad, but if you ever have an interval do but consider what you are doing now in a family that you pretend to espouse instead of making them considerable by being united which is of more consequence than all your ill gotten money. You are endevoring to bring them into as many quarrels as you have yourself, brother and sisters and all you will have quarrel. I think there is none of those that are in your power but the Duke of Bedford & the Duchess of Manchester that you have not made infamous by quiting my Lady Bateman's friendship only because you have taken a fancy against her. It is not enough for you to exercise your pretty temper your self & for some atonement to your family intaile your money without your wickedness & dye as soon as you can. I must tell you to incourage you not to indevour at quarrels that you can't make that the Dutchess & Duke of Bedford the Duchess of Manchester my Lady Bateman & my Lord Hervey went to the masquerade together last night . . . [3]

Sarah's conviction that Lady Bateman had written the letter was drawn from the fact that it arrived soon after she 'had writ to the Dear Duchess of Bedford a letter full of all the tenderness I felt in my heart for her', and by observing that the conclusion to the anonymous letter was 'very witty and cunning', to convince her that it did not come from Lady Bateman, which 'was a confirmation if one could have doubted it before'. When the letter was written, 'nobody but herself [Lady Bateman] and the Duchess of Bedford knew what I had desir'd', and when Sarah showed the anonymous letter to Diana she was 'so angry at the lie she had told of her being at the masquerade', that she asked Mr Bateman 'who has but one hand' [possibly Richard, the brother of Lord Bateman] with whom she was 'intimate', and 'spoke to him of it'. This Bateman 'could not disown that my Lady Bateman had writ the letter'. All this was guess-work of course, but when Sarah called on Diana at Grosvenor Street, she 'press'd' her 'extremely to do what would make her most easy in this manner', and Diana 'chose to take leave of her sister, and come to me with the same friendship and openness she was us'd to do'.[4]

Diana had conferred with her husband, Sarah telling her she must, for without 'doing everything that is agreeable to him you cannot be happy'. As the duke had no quarrel with Lady Bateman he may have come to some agreement with her over her friendship with Diana, merely to keep the peace. Diana would make no further mention of her sister to Sarah in her letters.[5]

As soon as Diana was able to rise from childbed and resume her normal life, she and her duke asked the widowed Duchess of Bedford to stay with them at Cheam, and also Johnny Spencer. Johnny had been restored to his grandmother's favour on condition he did not speak to brother Charles or his sister Bateman, and though recovered from syphilis, was in need of quiet. Sarah doubtless approved of his being in Diana's care, away from the temptations of town, and likewise for the young Duchess of Bedford, who was vulnerable in her young widowhood. Johnny was in his twenty-fourth year, cousin Anne having reached twenty-seven. For the first time in her life Anne was financially independent, free from the rule of any dominant male, while mischievous Johnny, known as 'Bad Jack Spencer' by his friends, found his energy slowly return. He and Anne had grown up together like brother and sister, and Diana was happy to leave them to their amusements.

Anne celebrated her birthday at Cheam on 19 December, after which there were the usual Christmas festivities, with the tenants' ball, followed by the New Year. Despite being in mourning for the late Duke of Bedford, the company went for healthy rides on the Banstead downs, and there was occasion for a great deal of eating and drinking, with dinner by candlelight, cards, games and music, Johnny playing his German flute. Anne was in desperate need of kindness, while Johnny grew restless. When one night Anne drew Diana into her room whispering that Johnny had something important to tell her next morning, Diana was scarcely able to imagine what it would be. Her astonishment knew no bounds when confronted by Johnny at breakfast next morning telling her he wished to marry his cousin. Diana wrote at once informing their grandmother.

Sarah, lulled into a sense of false security in the belief that her charges were in safe hands, broke the seal of Diana's letter with expectations of pleasure. It was dated 'Jan: 5th. 1733', and read:

I believe my Dear Grandmama you will be as much surprised at this letter as I was at the occasion of it. The Duchess of Bedford last night just as I was going to bed desir'd me to come into her room and told me that Brother John would speak to me this morning: But would not tell me what it was. Just now he told me he had something to say to me which he thought he believ'd would surprise me & that was that he was determin'd to marry the Duchess of Bedford. I was really much more amaz'd than ever I was in my life, and beg'd him to consider before he took such a resolution. He said he had consider'd long enough and was absolutely determin'd. I ask'd him if he had told you of it, and he said No: But that he would go to London tomorrow or next day on purpose. I said I must write to you immediately for that I thought it my duty to aquaint you with it the instant I knew anything of it myself & I do assure you my dear Grandmama that I did not know one syllable of it till last night when the Duchess of Bedford spoke to me. We have been here so short a time that I did not imagine anything of this kind would have happen'd though I saw plainly that she did not dislike him but I never thought it would have come to this. The Duke of Bedford is as much amaz'd & concern'd as I am, as he has allways wish'd her well & he does not think it will be for either of their advantage. I beg my Dear Grandmama that you will let me know how I shall act in this matter, & what you would have me say to Brother John, for I still hope that if you don't approve of it, he wo'nt be so mad as to do anything contrary to your desire, & I really think there is no prospect of happiness in this for either of them.

Diana concluded by saying: 'I beg my Dear Grandmama you would send me your orders by this messenger, for as I am sure I shall perform them strictly, I can't be easy till I receive them'. And she added in a postscript:

Neither of them have yet mention'd it to the Duke of Bedford, but he as well as my self thought that the best thing that could be done was to aquaint you with it, & to know your inclinations concerning this matter. What makes me more concern'd at this is that I believe it will be disagreable to you.[6]

Sarah's reaction to Diana's letter was to write immediately to Anne herself, the effect so distressing to the young widow that Diana took it on herself to reply on her behalf:

The Duchess of Bedford has shew'd me your letter to her my dear grandmama, which I think extream reasonable. She says the arguments you make use of why her marrying Brother John may hurt her health as he is just come out of salivation, she thinks very just, but she seems to take it ill that you should think the marrying her will be his ruin, for she says she does not know why there should be more objections to her than to any other woman, & that if there is any hurt it is to herself, in venturing to marry a man whose health is not establish'd. She is now writing an answer to your letter. I could not tell what to say to her, but that I would aquaint you with what she said. She talks of going to Town on Wednesday, when she says she is sure she can answer all your objections. I am very glad to have gain'd so much time as that, but I fear we shall not be able to make her stay any longer, for she seems very impatient to speak to you. The servant is not yet come back from my Brother Sunderland, but he certainly will sometime today, & I will be sure to send you word what he says to-morrow morning early. The Duke of Bedford desirs his humble Duty to you, & I beg you to believe my Dear Grandmama, that I am,

> Your most oblig'd
> > and most Dutyful Daughter . . . [7]

With Johnny gone to Marlborough House, and Anne preparing to follow him, Diana waited anxiously for a letter from brother Charles, to whom she had conveyed the news. When his letter arrived from Hampshire she wasted no time in acquainting her grandmother with its contents:

I have recieved the enclos'd letter from my Brother to night my Dear Grandmama, & one for me to send to Brother John, which I send by this Man to him. I don't know what is in it for he sent it seal'd. But it is no matter now as you will see by the Duchess of Bedford's letter who has received one from Brother John tonight, in which he says he is very unhappy but that it is impossible they should ever meet again, without giving any reason for it, but whatever it is, to be sure it is much better to be broke off.

Anne must have been hurt at Johnny's betrayal, and was so anxious 'at the thoughts of my Dear Grandmama's being angry with her that I hope you will forgive her', Diana begged, for 'it will make her easy for she really torments herself to death with thinking you will continue to be angry with her, as she says you have too much reason'. Diana dared hope her grandmother would have the 'goodness to pardon this very foolish proceeding', and ended by saying, 'As this affair is now over I hope Dear Grandmama you will never have any other thing to give you the least uneasyness'.[8]

Diana enclosed a letter to herself from Charles, which read:

My dear sister
I never was so shocked at any thing in my life as the news you writt me. I'll write to my brother now though in the confussion I am I cant write half what I wish, but I shall be in town next Wednesday pray

send a letter to my house to let me know if I shall dine with you at Cheam Thursday. I am Dear Die with the greatest truth yours . . . [9]

This was an affectionate letter from brother Charles, which suggests that neither he nor maybe his sister Bateman had any axe to grind with her. Some agreement must have been made between the brothers and sisters in that Diana should continue her links with their grandmother, valuing her gifts as peacemaker and go-between. If the pressure was great, Diana appears to have thrived on it, and was soon sending a delighted 'ten thousand thanks' to 'Dear Grandmama' for her goodness in agreeing to live with the Duchess of Bedford 'so as to hide what you think of her to the world'. If Sarah 'should abandon her now, it would really be her ruin & this indiscreet foolish thing made publick, which otherwise I hope it won't be'. While Diana believed there was 'no manner of excuse of any kind to be made for all this proceeding', she could not help feeling sorry for her cousin 'to see the distress she is in for fear my Dear Grandmama should not continue to live kindly with her', and hoped she would add to her goodness '& not let even her see that you are so much disatisfy'd as you really are'. Here was a supreme example of Diana's skill at managing her grandmother, which she had studied since a very small child. She also hoped 'Brother John may be forgiven for the mad & silly part he has acted towards you & I hope the breaking of this match was oweing in a great measure to what you said to him which might have more effect upon him when he came to consider, than the remonstrances you made him appear'd to have, whilst he was with you . . . ' That her brother had put up some kind of fight is evident, but faced with the threat of disinheritance had submitted to his grandmother's will. Meanwhile Johnny had left town.[10]

Diana and the Duke of Bedford planned to be in town in the following week, '& I will certainly come to you my Dear Grandmama, the minute I have din'd, & then I can talk to you about this affair much easier than I can write'. It is likely they stayed at the splendid Southampton House, since it was now theirs, making plans to improve it for their own use. The widowed Duchess of Bedford had preceded them to Marlborough House, Diana expressing her delight that her grandmother still thought 'so well of the poor Duchess of Bedford, who's unhappiness I do believe has proceeded more from giddiness & want of thought, than any real guilt'. She continued to hope 'Brother John' would behave to his grandmother as 'he ought after

185

the many obligations he had to you', and was sorry that he 'should have behave'd in the manner you say he has done to you'. Knowing him to be 'a little too hot', she hoped he said 'nothing that did not proceed from a too warm temper, which I dare say often makes him say what (when he is cool) he repents off'. The Duchess of Manchester had joined them at Cheam, and all three looked forward to being in town on Monday, 'when', wrote Diana, 'I shall have the happiness of seeing my Dear Grandmama . . .'[11]

Three duchesses presented themselves at a play at the Drury Lane Theatre on 23 January, the dowager Duchess of Marlborough, Diana, Duchess of Bedford, and Bella, Duchess of Manchester. It was a moment of triumph for Sarah. The actress Mary Porter played Queen Elizabeth 'most excellently (with a cane)' at her own Benefit, having suffered an accident two years before. The king was present in his box, and there was 'the fullest audience' ever seen. Lord Hervey observed the duchess trio from the Royal Box, writing to his friend Henry Fox how 'The Alpha and Omega of these three wept at the moving scenes' (Sarah and Diana), calling them 'Tender creatures', and how in one part of the play where Essex says:

Abhor all Courts, if thou art brave and wise,
For there thou never shalt be sure to rise.
Think not by doing well, a fame to get,
But be a villain, and thou shalt be great . . .

Upon this 'her Grace of Marlborough cried charmingly, and clapt her hands so loud we heard her cross the theatre into the King's box'. Sarah could never let go so splendid an opportunity to ridicule the royal court.[12]

The dowager Duchess of Bedford had meanwhile taken a house in Pall Mall, where, with Sarah's help, she was 'very prettily settled'. But Anne was not made for the single life, and within six months of losing Johnny's love, and 'after about a fortnight's aquaintance', was 'resolved to marry Lord Jersey'. This time Anne kept her desires to herself and her betrothed, her grandmother having 'never heard word of it', but apart from some quibbles over jewels and settlements, appears to have approved the match, writing, 'I believe she makes a very good wife and is happy'. Anne was married to William Villiers, 3rd Earl of Jersey, on 23 June 1733, her uncle the Bishop of Hereford officiating, the couple afterwards departing for Weybridge on their honeymoon. Anne's jewels (part of her marriage settlement from her late husband) were sent to the banker Sir Francis Child, who was negotiating their sale to Lord Weymouth. Neither Sarah nor Diana appear to have attended Anne's wedding, Sarah having turned her mind to settling Johnny.[13]

That summer the new Duke and Duchess of Bedford visited their estate of Tavistock in Devon. The farmhouse called Crowndale (to which the last Abbot of Tavistock had retired at the dissolution), had been used by the Russells since it was made over to them at the abbot's death. The young duke and duchess were warmly received here, as a letter from Sarah confirms, this time using Diana's Christian name:

I have this moment received your letter, my dear Di, from Crowndale ... every part of which was extremely welcome and agreeable to me ... particularly to find you are in such perfect health and so well pleased, which I don't wonder at, for the reception which you find in all places shews the great value they have for the Duke of Bedford. And I had rather be a private man beloved, a thousand times, than anything that is hated.[14]

Diana had mentioned Lord Weymouth in her letter, and the duke and duchess may have attended his second marriage. Weymouth's young wife had died while he was away on the Grand Tour, his new bride being Louisa, second daughter of Lord John Carteret. Carteret was the minister who had placed the seals on the Sunderland House doors at the time of Diana's father's death, and being a strong anti-Walpole Whig, had recently regained favour with Sarah. The old duchess was annoyed to learn that his daughter was to marry Weymouth, however, since she had considered her as a bride for Johnny. 'If you think my Lord Carteret's daughter an agreeable woman as everybody now says she is', she wrote to Diana, 'your brother John might easily have obtained her before they thought of my Lord Weymouth'. And considering his 'debts and the charges on his estate, your brother is not a much worse match in fortune, besides the great differences between the two men'. It was odd, Sarah ended dryly, that she had 'never heard the least word in this lady's commendations till she was disposed of'. Meanwhile, 'whom your brother is destined for, I can't yet see'.[15]

Diana was aware that Lord Carteret had other daughters, one of them Georgina Carteret, still unmarried. As Mrs Pendarves (related to the Carterets, and therefore present at Weymouth's wedding) observed, this eighteen-year-old, if 'not so handsome' as her sister Weymouth, nor so 'genteel' as her sister Dysart, was at least 'as agreeable as either of them'. Sarah looked carefully into Johnny's affairs, hoping to make him into a more attractive proposition, and was shocked to find he had lent money to the wildly extravagant Charles. She suggested that the latter should discharge his debt by making Sunderland House over to Johnny, Charles replying that he was perfectly willing to do so, on condition Sarah would leave him Marlborough House. This silenced the old dowager for a while, but she demanded instead that Charles should return the late Duke of Marlborough's diamond-hilted sword. She had given it him in a weak moment following Blandford's death, fearing now that Lady Bateman would pluck out the diamonds to make buckles for stays. Charles returned the sword with a polite note.[16]

From Crowndale the Bedfords made their way home by way of Stratton, calling on Lady De la Warr and her four children on their way. Charlotte was living at Bolderwood Lodge in the New Forest, surrounded by the finest woodland scenery and deer. One of her little girls was named Diana, which suggests she was Diana's godchild. The Bedfords' stay was short, and once arrived at Stratton Diana was able to view the building in progress, and check the nursery once more. She longed to become pregnant again. She mentioned Johnny to her grandmother, who may have been at Rookley with Charles and his wife, as doubtless was Lady Bateman. But soon Diana and her duke must return to Woburn, where the duke had 'business'.

The 'young' Duchess of Marlborough had been reported ill earlier in the year, her mother commenting that 'if she keeps quiet it is likely she will do well, for her complaint proceeds from what is natural'. When news reached her that the fifty-two-year-old duchess was dying, Sarah sent a message saying 'notwithstanding all that was past she woud come and see her if she likd it'. Henrietta replied curtly that she was in no condition 'to see anybody'. Diana, aware that her grandmother would feel more sorry than she cared to admit, begged to let her and her duke visit her, as they would be 'very unhappy to go into the country without seeing' her. The plan was to arrive at Windsor Lodge on Wednesday, and stay overnight.[17]

Mrs Kingdon appears to have travelled with the Bedfords on their tour to the west country, and as she kept a house at Windsor, the Bedfords dropped her at her home before making their final stop at Windsor Lodge.

The visit to Sarah appears to have gone smoothly, and if there was any undercurrent of discomfort, Diana was unaware of it. Next day the Bedfords left in a hurry, calling on Mrs Kingdon on their way, the visit lengthened by a downpour of rain. Afterwards John and Diana stayed at St Albans for the night, dining there on Saturday, and arrived at Woburn the same evening. On Sunday morning Diana wrote thanking her grandmother for the kind welcome she and her husband had been given at the lodge, telling her some of the St Albans gossip ('the Post house is taken from poor Mrs Carr, which I am extream sorry for, as it mortifies her prodigiously'). Diana was longing for her grandmother to call at Woburn, she said, remembering her 'promising to make me happy in coming to this place', and assuring her she would be received with 'all the Joy Imaginable, and as sincere a welcome as we can express'.[18]

Diana wrote again a week later, saying: 'I was extreamly disappointed when the post came in to day & brought no letter from you', and that if Sarah knew 'how uneasy' it made her, she was sure she would write, if 'just a line or two to give me the satisfaction of knowing how you do, and that you think of me with the same kindness you have always shown me'. She told her how on Friday she and her duke had the 'first public Day we have ever had', with 'a good deal of company', but was 'very glad to have the fatigue of doing the honours over'. It was 'much less troublesome in so large a neighbourhood to keep one particular day, & have the rest of the week entirely to ourselves, which otherwise we should not have one day certain'. When two more days passed without a word from her grandmother, Diana sent another letter by a servant the duke was sending to Enfield to fetch back a horse he left there, again asking after her grandmother's health. She could not imagine 'why my dear Grandmama, you have not once let me have the happiness of hearing since I left the Lodge', and sure she must be aware of 'how happy it makes every person to hear from those they love'. As she had 'both the ties of inclination and gratitude to make me desirous of hearing continually from you, imagine my Dear Grandmama how uneasy it makes me to be so long without knowing . . . that you so much as think of me . . . '[19]

With Bedford's servant hovering expectantly at the Windsor Lodge door, the dowager could hardly refuse to reply, and her letter to Diana was delivered at Woburn on the following day. Sarah thanked Diana for the three letters she had received since she had 'the satisfaction of seeing' her, saying there 'was no need of my giving you proof that I wished to see you after so long an absence', but:

I went a great many miles in the dust to meet you, and had the mortification of finding that you could go by my house to be longer with better company, for you certainly did not know that I was gone to meet you till you came to Mrs Kingdon's.

This Sarah pretended not to wonder at, 'because I know that though you are very reasonable and good, it is not possible for any person that has youth and life to take pleasure in the conversation of one that is extremely old and stupid'. But being pressed to speak the truth 'by your letters, I must confess I can't think Mrs Kingdon shewed much prudence (though her wit I always acknowledge) in carrying you by my door with horses that had been so long a journey to set you down, and which must go back again after they brought you to the lodge to set up'. She thought 'that must proceed from her very ridiculous pride, though there can be no doubt of anybody's loving you'. But when they had 'so very short a time to be with me, I can't but think it odd for her to engage you to come to drink tea with her before you went to Windsor, when she knew how short a time you were with me'. And, a 'great while after you had left me, I went out in my coach to take the air, and saw your coaches standing at her door, in violent rain, though you were in so much haste to leave me'.[20]

Here was the rich old dowager duchess living alone in Windsor forest and feeling so neglected. Diana's feelings of mortification on reading this letter must have been overwhelming, and there was more to come:

I am sorry you have forced me to say all this, which I had rather have kept to myself, for I know it signifies nothing to complain. As to my health it is much as it was and it can't be expected that I should ever be well, but though I can have no great pleasure in life, as long as I do live it is natural and reasonable to make one's self as easy as one can, and I am going to Tunbridge in hopes those waters may do me some good for that great difficulty I have sometimes in breathing. Pray give my humble duties to the Duke of Bedford and believe me always very affectionately yours . . .

Sarah, crippled with gout, ended with the words: 'as you have been so much used to my hand I hope you will read it without much trouble'.[21]

Diana's letter of apology no longer exists, but after a week she was sending her grandmother 'ten thousand thanks' for her kind letter, saying if she could only 'imagine how griev'd I have been for having done anything that could have the least wrong appearance to you, I am sure you could not repent your forgiveness', and 'the study of my life will be to deserve the kindness you show me'. Diana had written just such a letter when she was fourteen years old. As well as her forgiveness Sarah had sent news of the Duchess of Manchester, Diana responding with sympathy:

I really love the Duchess of Manchester so well that I could scarce read the account you give me of what she says, without tears. I wish with all my soul that I knew how to remedy her grief, but I fear that it is not easily done, for the D [uke of Manchester] every body knows to be a fool, & I who am perfectly aquainted with him, know him to be the most obstinate one in the World.[22]

Sarah had invited Bella to accompany her to Tunbridge Wells, which Diana thought 'much the best', for 'at least it will give time to think of what may be more proper, which when you see her & know the particulars of everything you will be better able to judge'. The matrimonial troubles between Bella and her duke appear to have been insurmountable, for 'Knowing the Duke of Manchester so well', it was Diana's opinion that 'when his Grace is in the best temper he loves to be humour'd', but that 'no compliance will do when he is either drunk or at all out of humour, which one or other is generally the case'. Diana pitied her cousin, 'for it is hard to know how to deal with any fool & much more an obstinate one'. It had been her intention to visit the couple at Kimbolton, but hoped now to be 'prevented by her [Bella] going to my Dear Grandmama, for I had much rather be disappointed of seeing her than she should be a minute longer so unhappy'. Thinking of Bella's current unhappiness, and remembering cousin Anne in a similar situation some years ago, Diana quoted almost word for word a line from the letter Sarah had sent her, saying: 'I am sure if one is not happy in one's own house it is not possible to be so easy any where else', and said she was grateful that her grandmother had placed her 'where my greatest happiness is at home', for 'if possible the D of Bedford is more kind to me every day than the other, which happiness I can never forget I owe you . . . '[23]

The Duke and Duchess of Bedford called on 'sister Morpeth', Diana's half-sister Frances, whose lord would become Earl of Carlisle and master of Castle Howard in five years' time. Afterwards they drove to the fen country in Cambridgeshire, having through Wriothesley's death inherited the estate of Thorney in the Isle of Ely. Here was a large manor house dating from the 1660s, built by John's great-great-grandfather, 4th Earl of Bedford, who in common with two generations of Russells before him was involved in draining the fens. Although the 1st Duke had not lived here, the gardens were stocked with fruit and vegetables, and the pastures, fields, marshes and fens surrounding the estate had long supplied meat, birds and fish for the Woburn table. Surprisingly Wriothesley had set up house here, planting nectarines, peaches, plums, cherries, Roman nectarines, Turkey apricots, dwarf pears, apples and vines, to serve alongside the local ruffs and reeves and pike and pickled mushrooms. Twelve gallons of arrack and six gallons of brandy filled the cellars, together with wine and ale. Wriothesley may have thought to entertain his gambling friends here, or was this a last ditch effort to overcome his debts and stave off the ravages of consumption? He had purchased a pleasure boat with fishing nets, and while he was here took his part as lord of the manor seriously, entertaining twenty-seven jurymen and thirty-four gentlemen to dinner, and on several occasions treated his tenants to feasts – one to celebrate George II's accession to the throne. A room was set aside for dancing, and punch laid on. The visit by John and Diana may have brought tears to their eyes in memory of Wriothesley, but they found no reason to make this a regular home, leaving house and gardens in the hands of an agent. Orders were given for the gardens to be kept up, vegetables, fish and birds to be sent to Woburn as usual. Here was a small monument to the memory of the departed duke, for just 'as none of the family had ever contemplated living at Thorney before, so none contemplated it after his time'.[24]

The dowager duchess had promised to stay at Woburn on her return from Tunbridge Wells, but in the event merely called in to drop the Duchess of Manchester off on her way to Holywell House. Diana wrote to thank her grandmother for the 'charming kind agreeable visit you made me today', anxious that she reached St Albans without catching cold. Now the cousins could talk of Bella's marital problems. And was Diana's marriage so perfect? Her grandmother proclaimed later that Bedford was the 'most covetous creature in the World', and Diana was quite 'the reverse of him in everything'. For she 'loved expense very much and was very charitable', and whatever she did of that kind 'was with good judgment'. The dowager believed her granddaughter put her husband 'upon a good foot of living as he aught to do', to live 'like a man of great quality, and fortune', but this did not always lead to harmony. The duke was 'upon many occasions very angry' with his wife for laying out 'so much money in building and furniture', and how she got him to 'do what she would against his will' was a 'sort of magik'. Yet Diana did 'everything she had a mind to do and was always as cheerful, as if she had been marry'd to an agreeable man'.[25]

Just now the couple's lives appeared to be perfectly harmonious, Diana looking forward to Parliament meeting in November, when her husband would take his place in the House of Lords and she would meet her grandmother in town. But on 26 October news reached Woburn that the 'young' Duchess of Marlborough was dead. Aware that this must have an adverse affect on her grandmother, Diana wrote to her at once:

> I have this instant heard the news of the death of the Duchess of Marlborough, & send this servant to Town to enquire after my Dear Grandmama's health, for though the shock of loosing her is not so great to you as if you had liv'd together in as much kindness as you wish'd to do, yet I am sure you feel more upon this subject than you thought you should yourself, therefore I can't be easy till I know how my Dear Grandmama does, which I beg you would let me hear by the return of this messenger . . .

Diana hoped Sarah believed her when she declared her grandmother could 'never suffer any uneasiness' that was not sincerely felt by herself.[26]

William Congreve had died some years earlier, from internal injuries after his chariot overturned on a precipice at Bath. He had left Henrietta his small fortune of £10,000, which she certainly did not need, using the greater part of it to bury him with pomp at Westminster Abbey. She spent the surplus on a superb diamond necklace to wear in the playwright's honour. It was rumoured she had an ivory statue of him placed at her table at dinner, to which she talked, and another placed in her bedroom, the feet blistered and anointed daily by doctors. When her mother read the tribute Henrietta had composed to his memory at Westminster Abbey, she remarked acidly that she did not know what 'pleasure' she had from his company, but it was surely 'no honour!'[27]

While the death of the 'young' duchess shocked everyone who was acquainted with her, it affected even more the happiness of her two daughters Harriet and Mary. The widower had written to Harriet throughout her mother's sickness, addressing the duchess affectionately as his 'dear child'. 'Your poor Mama's present and chief illness may more properly I think be called dropsy in her limbs', he wrote to her, and as she steadily grew weaker said none of her doctors thought 'it possible she can recover'. After the last of Harriet's visits he wrote:

Things here, my dear, continue just the same as when you left this place; your poor Mama seems not to suffer near so much as she did o' Sunday to Monday, not even at such times as she appears fully awake; at those times she makes pertinent and sensible answers to what the Doctors say to her.

She took her cordials and her nourishment when they were proposed to her, 'but has not yet ask'd for any thing herself'. Earl Francis ended with the words: 'God send you a good night My Dear', and within half an hour of his writing Henrietta, Duchess of Marlborough, was dead.[28]

'My right hand is put up in flannel', Sarah wrote to Diana a week later, and 'I can't write to you my dear, without hurting it, though my pain is not much'. Diana had judged right in thinking she should feel 'much more than I imagined formerly I could ever do', and was now convinced 'there is such a thing as natural affection, though I have heard many people laugh at that notion'! Sarah had made several attempts to be reconciled with 'that unfortunate woman' Henrietta, and on hearing she was in great danger, 'did it in a very moving manner', but 'nothing I said or did had the least good effect'. She believed she had done all that was in her power, and 'as to this last shock I do acknowledge it would have been much greater had she lived with me and loved me as she once did'.[29]

Sarah's depression deepened, likening herself to Job, her eyes 'dim with sorrow, and my nerves . . . as shadows'. Diana recognised the signs, writing, 'It has given me a vast deal of concern & uneasiness, to find . . . you are in so meloncholly a way, when I can not be with you', and begged her to come to Woburn, for 'The Duke of Bedford as well as my self desires it –

extreamly, & if you do not care to see any body – I do answer you there shall not be a creature with me, unless the Duchess of Manchester should happen to come again, which I believe would not be disagreable to you'. She had something to say concerning the subject of 'natural affection', believing those people most happy that were 'void' of it, having experienced the effects of it 'in what I suffer'd last year by the loss of my poor little son', and could not 'reasonably ascribe to any other cause, a fondness for what one has only seen one moment, & cant be sure whether it comes into the world for ones happiness or to be the greatest of misfortunes'.[30]

This was the first time Diana had referred to her own sad loss. A day or two later she was cheered by a visit from her brother Charles, who through the death of his aunt had become 3rd Duke of Marlborough. Diana was especially pleased when he showed her a letter he had received from his grandmother offering him forgiveness for his late misdeeds. Whether this was a result of Sarah's new awareness of 'natural affection', or because she realised she must submit to the new head of the family, is uncertain, but 'if my Dearest Grandmama could imagine how happy this reconciliation makes me', wrote Diana, 'I am sure you would be glad to have it in your power to give any body so much true pleasure'.[31]

The Duke of Marlborough called on his grandmother at Marlborough House, where she found him 'extremely good natured' and 'I do really believe, he is very sincere'. She now felt she had 'a prospect for the future of enjoying a great deal of happiness from the three children of your beloved mother', telling Diana that Charles had 'desired his wife might come to me'. Sarah could hardly refuse to acknowledge the new young Duchess of Marlborough, declaring she 'never had anything to say against her', and 'as everybody gives her a good character, I hope she will always behave to him in the manner I wish'.[32]

As Sarah said, 'This is a very surprising turn.' Diana was delighted to have both brothers in favour again, if not her sister Bateman. Convinced that her past suffering could 'not have happened from a man that seems to have good sense, good nature and good temper' as Charles had, Sarah believed 'God for a punishment of some sin of mine, allowed me to be tormented, as he did Job', and she had no need to say 'by whom'![33]

CHAPTER TWELVE

Paladio Dye

'. . . your own Dye, which name I hope I shall always keep.'

A ware of the damp November mists penetrating the thin walls of Windsor Lodge, and the deep depression that had descended on her grandmother since the death of her daughter, Diana wrote saying how sorry she was that she could not prevail with her to come to Woburn, 'where I am sure you will allways be more welcome than at any other place in the world'. Even London, she argued, would be preferable to Windsor, for 'you might find amusements there, to take off some of the melancholly thoughts I am sure you must have when you are quite alone in a cold house'.[1]

The promise of a royal wedding on 12 November did nothing to encourage Sarah to move to Marlborough House, chiefly on account of the expected crowds. The wedding between the Princess Royal (Princess Anne) and the Prince of Orange was to take place in the chapel originally built for Charles I's Roman Catholic queen, Henrietta, and afterwards used by Charles II's queen, and since then used for Protestant worship; it stood, as now, between Marlborough House and St James's Palace. Diana claimed she knew nothing of the wedding preparations apart from what she had read in the news-prints, 'which gives very different accounts every day', but did not doubt 'its being something proud & rediculous as everything is that they ever do'. Her grandmother insisted that she herself would not go to London 'till this bustle of the great wedding is over, and as the gallery is made for the procession to the Chapel, I believe my garden wall will be in danger of being pulled down by the mob . . . '[2]

A large gallery had been erected to enable the wedding party to pass comfortably from the royal apartments into the chapel, and fitted with seats for spectators, and because such a brilliant spectacle would draw crowds of onlookers on the day, Sarah feared the mob might come into her garden and 'do mischief to the house, or rob it'. Diana would be relieved to learn later that her grandmother was to have a guard at her garden wall, 'for it would really be very inconvenient to have it pull'd down as in all likelihood it would be, by so great a mob as there will be upon so very Glorious an occasion!'[3]

Rumour had it that the Prince of Wales was grumbling at his sister being married before himself, and at such expense, Diana remarking that 'I dare say it is very probable for he has been a great while discontented & I fancy they don't take much pains to put him in good humour'. This was an indication that Diana was not altogether averse to the prince, although it was evident she disliked the rest of the Royal Family, going on to say that she thought the Royals' attitude to him was 'very Impolitick', for if he should 'fly out, though the reigning King will allways have the most followers, yet I believe they might make his Party strong enough to give them a good deal of trouble and uneasiness'. She remembered well the occasion in her own childhood when the then Prince of Wales was banished to Leicester House, surrounding himself with a troublesome 'Party'.[4]

'I have heard', Sarah wrote to Diana, 'that the peers and peeresses are to be summoned to walk at this great ceremony, and 'they say that the peeresses are to walk in gowns as they did at the coronation'. This would put them 'to great expense', she said, but that was 'no matter since I think none but simple people and sad wretches will do it', and was pleased to know 'two very considerable peers of my aquaintance will not be there!' By this she meant the Bedfords, of course, commenting that Lord Jersey had been invited. She did not know if Lady Jersey would present herself, since she was pregnant, but said she looked well and had 'not miscarried'.[5]

Diana sent her grandmother a large goose pie, Sarah remarking that it was a 'very great one', and 'I dare say it will be good', for whatever came from her granddaughter was pleasing since 'it shows you think of me'. She had not tasted it yet, having decided to go to London on Tuesday, and had a mind to send 'Mrs Theddy and Con Kingdon [the sisters of Jane Kingdon] some of it'. Tuesday was expected to be the day following the royal wedding, by which time the crowds should have dispersed, but it so happened that the 'glorious occasion' was postponed. The Prince of Orange had arrived in England as expected, but taking ill at church, after placing twenty-five guineas in the poor box, left for a health-giving tour of England. This left the wooden gallery outside Sarah's garden *in situ*, giving rise to her later querulous inquiry: 'When will my neighbour George remove his orange chest?'[6]

Under the terms of his grandfather's will, Diana's brother Charles was obliged to convey the Althorp estate to his brother John, and must do so within three months of his aunt's death. As he had placed heavy mortgages on the estate in order to settle money on his mistress, and to provide for his wife's jointure, his current debts were estimated at £30,000. This meant the transition to his new home in the Windsor Home Park could not be made without the financial help of his grandmother. Diana wrote that she was sorry her grandmother was having so much difficulty settling his affairs, and while admitting he had been 'too extravagant even with so great an estate', was sure he would 'retrench all his unnecessary expenses over the coming year'. As Johnny had gone with his brother to Rookley for a few days, she was sure that as 'my brothers are so good friends, I dare say they will make it quite easy to each other', and make 'a Bargain about Althorp'.[7]

Since the royal wedding had been put off for an indefinite period, Sarah was able to continue her stay in London, sorting out her grandson's finances. When she discovered Charles was playing tennis (as much a gambling activity as a sport), Diana rallied once again to his defence, saying, 'I don't know what he does at present, but if he does play for any considerable sum it is very lately, for I am sure he never us'd to play either to win or lose more than the expense of the house & three or four guineas'. He did it 'merely for exercise, & with people who are no proffess'd gamesters, but play'd only for their diversion'. At the same time her grandmother complained that Johnny was seeing their sister Lady Bateman, Diana begging the liberty to say:

You really wrong my Brother John in thinking he has still a great intimacy with my Lady Bateman, for I can be answerable for him that he neither hears from her nor sees her, except her being once by chance at Althorp when he was there, & I am as sure as I can be of anything that does not relate to myself, that he does not break his word to you in the least, by keeping any sort of correspondence there.

There was a hint of impatience in this letter, causing Sarah to suspect Diana of duplicity and to write on the cover:

This letter is in answer to one I writt complaining of Johnny seeing lady Bateman contrary to the conditions I made with him when I was reconciled to him, but to that she makes no answer, & I believe she sees her, not withstanding all that she said upon that subject. Considering what I said in my letter tis a disagreeable answer taking no notice of my letter in any part of, but what is quite insignificant & that signifys nothing.[8]

Innocent of her grandmother's displeasure, Diana was enjoying an Indian summer at Woburn, the weather being 'so excessive fine that we walk abroad all the morning which is very extraordinary the end of November'. She and her husband entertained Lord Carteret, whose country house Hawnes was not far distant from the abbey. Writing to her grandmother on the morning of her guest's departure, she told her he 'has been with us these three days', and was 'to be sure the most agreeable man than ever was born'. He had 'talked a good deal of my Dear Grandmama', she assured her, and expressed 'the uttmost regard' for her, and they drank her health 'in wine every day'. Sarah was still involved with sorting out her brother's debts, even challenging his Trevor father-in-law regarding the marriage settlement. Diana agreed that 'as to the manner of my brother's match I never did nor shall ever pretend to Justify any part of that proceeding', and without mentioning her sister's involvement in that scandalous business, declared that the 'settlements & shuffling the fortune is so very wrong that it is very sure my brother has not had justice done him'. But since nothing could be changed in all that, Diana really thought Elizabeth 'the best wife' for her brother, 'for I do believe that upon the Earth there is not a creature with a more perfect good nature & such passion for him, that she thinks of nothing all day long but how to please him, which she has found a way to do'. Nor had Diana ever seen a man 'more truly fond of a woman than he is of her'. She hoped 'in God they will allways continue in the happy scene'. Lord Hervey, who had found Elizabeth pleasing at first, now declared her 'tall, fat, course and proud'. Diana also had something to say for Charles's pensioned-off mistress:

> I am pleased extreamly with what you told me of Mrs Smith, for I allways thought her good & she had more temptation & excuse of her wrong step than any body that ever I heard of, for she must actually have starved if her father had dy'd, & she has really behaved herself in the most decent manner that is possible ever since, and I really think is a much better person than several who are Licensed by the custom of the World to be seen in the best company . . . [9]

The visit of Carteret to Woburn was primarily to discuss the coming elections, but must also have touched on matters of marriage. With the approbation of her grandmother, Diana had embarked on a little matchmaking of her own, and by the middle of December, though careful not to mention names, gave her grandmother details of a certain young lady's appearance:

> The Lady that you said was well behav'd and whom you say you have a mind to see, I fancy you may easily compass . . . but after all I am not sure whether you would like her, for I am not so hard to be pleased as you and this Lady I don't think had any great beauty but I think she has a very agreeable well bred manner. She has a good skin, & I think mighty pretty eyes, & fine teeth, but then she has what to be sure is very disagreable, & I have heard you express great dislike to, & that is red Hair tho' from being well dress'd and a good deal powder'd, it is not so very ugly as that colour generally is but I know nothing but her outward appearance, which is the least thing to be consider'd & I don't know who is aquainted with her enough to give any true account of her temper . . . [10]

Having been subjected to 'an unpleasant Remedy' for the gout, Sarah was unable to respond to this letter in person, Diana communicating with her grandmother through her secretary James Stephens. As well as conveying details of the young lady's appearance, Diana made a request regarding the Duke of Bedford's and Lord Carteret's desire to set up Johnny Spencer as Knight of the Shire for Bedfordshire. Sarah agreed, since it might also be of benefit to Johnny's matrimonial interests, the young lady with the 'red Hair' being Carteret's daughter. Diana assured her grandmother that she should not be 'at the least expense or trouble' in the election, and her compliance would make the Duke of Bedford 'very happy'. Very soon Diana was sending her grandmother 'ten thousand thanks' for giving her consent for Johnny to stand for the shire, and for permission for her to speak with Lord Carteret's mother (the girl's grandmother) about a possible union between the two families, and went on:

> As you desir'd me to say to my Lady Granville that I thought you would like to make a proposal for a match between brother John and Miss Carteret, I wrote to her immediately thinking that the best way, as I could not possibly wait on her at this time o' the year. I said that from the knowledge I had of Miss Carteret, it would be a very desirable thing to me, & that I was sure you would make proposals if they

had no preingagement & that it would be acceptable, in answer to which you will see that they are all very well pleas'd with it . . .

Lady Granville (who had a great estate at Bath, and was Viscountess Carteret and Countess Granville in her own right) was delighted with Diana's proposal, and answered her letter at once:

> Your Grace may easily imagine ye great satisfaction yt I have in your Graces friendship to me & my family, by proposing so agreeable a match as your Brother Mr Spencer for my Grand-daughter Miss Carteret. Nothing in ye world can be more acceptable to me, & to my son & daughter Carteret. We have no doubt but my Granddaughter will deserve her good fortune, [for] she has good sence, & good nature, & can never forget ye duty & gratitude she will owe to ye duchess of Marlborough & to your Grace, for having thought her worthy of this alliance with your family. My son will doe himself ye honour to wait on ye duke of Bedford & your Grace . . . [11]

Johnny wrote to his sister to say he hoped he and Miss Carteret 'may like one another', which looked to Sarah as if he was 'inclined to it', and therefore 'under no sort of inclination or engagement' to another. And since Johnny was not 'extreamly nice' (particular in his taste), she thought provided 'that the person be not disagreeable, is healthy, has good sense and good humour', he would be pleased. As to 'great beauties', she did not 'desire one', nor did she ever see one since Diana's 'own dear mother'. The dowager had told Johnny how 'very quick' Diana was, the matchmaker expostulating that 'I have done nothing in the World more than said there was an intention of a proposal if both the Lady & he upon seeing one another approve'd it'.[12]

Diana was soon informing her grandmother that 'My Lord Carteret was here today', who said 'more things than I can repeat of the vast happiness it would be to him if this affair should succeed'. He was to be in town in a fortnight, when 'Miss Carteret shall wait upon me to see if she meets with Mr Spencer's approbation'. Diana had told Carteret that while it was 'impossible to answer for any person's fancy', she 'did really believe [Johnny] could not help liking her', and 'really wished for it'. Lord Carteret had sent 'a thousand compliments' to Sarah, having more obligations 'for this alliance than he should ever know how to return', and saying she should 'always find him full of gratitude'.[13]

The young lady in question was the Honourable Georgina Carteret, third of a family of five sisters and three brothers. As Mrs Pendarves had observed at her sister Louisa's marriage to Lord Weymouth, if 'not so handsome' as Louisa, nor so 'genteel' as her sister Lady Dysart, the eighteen-year-old was 'as agreeable as either of them'. Georgina's mother approved the match, and her father, Carteret, a fiercely anti-Walpole Whig (together with the Duke of Bedford throwing in his lot with the 'Patriots'), was the most likely to take over from Walpole in the coming elections. At the same time his comprehension of German continued to make him a valuable companion to the king, and though Sarah had not forgotten his seizure of Sunderland's papers in 1722, she felt it better to have 'Patriots that have been Courtiers, than to have none at all'.[14]

The Duke and Duchess of Bedford opened up Southampton House after Christmas, the two families to meet there. All went well between the young people, Sarah being impatient to keep things moving once an agreement was reached, for 'when a match is determin'd to be, it is disagreeable & awkward to continue formal visits longer than is absolutely necessary'. She contributed £5000 to the marriage, allocating £200 a year pin money for the bride (no more than was allowed her daughters) to be raised to £400 if there was any increase in fortune, but refused to make Johnny her official heir.[15]

The wedding took place at the fashionable St George's Church in Hanover Square between eight and nine in the evening of 14 February 1734. Lord Hervey sent news of the wedding to Henry Fox, saying, 'Jack Spencer is to be married next week to Lord Carteret's third daughter' and 'The Dss of Bedford made the match'. He added, 'What luck that man [Carteret] has in disposing of his female nursery!' It was a small family occasion, members of both families invited, but with no mention made of the groom's sister Lady Bateman. Mrs Pendarves was here as a cousin of the bride, describing the event to her sister:

After they were married they played a pool at commerce, supped at ten, went to bed between twelve and one, and went to Windsor Lodge the next day at noon. Everybody at the wedding was magnificent. Their clothes are now laid up for the royal wedding, which will be in about three weeks hence.[16]

So it was that Johnny and Georgina, with the help of their speedy match-maker, were married ahead of the Royals. The Prince of Orange and the Princess Royal were married a month later, Mrs Pendarves again making her appearance in a gown covered with 'great romping flowers in purple, green and red'. Neighbour George's 'Orange Box' was wonderfully illuminated with candles, the chapel decked with gold and silver, the royal couple setting eyes on each other for the first time at the altar. The prince was described as incredibly ugly, the princess as short and fat. Mrs Pendarves was so 'crushed and squeezed about', she was forced into the gallery to get out of the way, but Sarah's wall, secured by its guard, remained standing.[17]

The Duke and Duchess of Bedford were in Hampshire in the spring, as were the newly-wed Spencers, and calls were made between Stratton and Rookley. Work had already begun on the Bedford's new building, Paladio Dye's gifts put to good use. Sarah wrote that she was 'extreme glad' Diana and her duke were 'so well satisfied with your building at Stratton, which, you think will please my taste, and therefore I conclude 'tis strong useful and plain'. She hoped it was of brick, for since building the house at Wimbledon she had become 'more averse to Portland stone than ever because I see scales come from it'. John Devall was responsible for the stone portico at Stratton which still remains standing, while John Sanderson built the house. All was going forward hopefully for the young Duke and Duchess of Bedford as they made their way over the little bridges that crossed the stream to gain the acquaintance of their tenants.[18]

Sarah was pleased to hear that Diana continued to like 'Mrs Spencer so much', and 'that Johnny is so very happy in her', believing the young woman had sense, 'and I dare say twill last', Johnny being 'of a humour to make an extreme good husband'. After a short stay, the duke and duchess, and possibly the newlyweds, went on to Bath, and as Georgina's grandmother had extensive lands here, visits could be made to her estate. According to Defoe, Bath was frequented 'more for sport and diversion than a physical prescription of health', but as Diana was longing for a child, and Georgina would hope to get pregnant soon, concern for health was paramount.[19]

This being election year, the spring sojourn was necessarily short, the Bedfords returning for a short stay at Stratton before returning to Woburn. Johnny and his bride set off for Hawnes from Rookley, to find themselves met by a messenger from the dowager Duchess of Marlborough who ordered Johnny to make haste for Woodstock where she had 'opened a great cellar full of strong beer'. This was to soften the electors, but he must just make an appearance, and appoint somebody else to 'ride for him'. He must then drive post-haste to Hawnes where 'the Duke of Bedford, my Lord Carteret and their agents' would be 'managing the whole', and, Johnny being of 'no manner of use', was just to ride about 'as a fine young man in the chair'. She hoped the Duke of Bedford would not take her management 'ill', but felt Woodstock 'more natural for him to stand for' than Bedfordshire. In the event Johnny was to win both seats, his grandmother persuading him to sit for Woodstock, something that would greatly embarrass the Duke of Bedford.[20]

A son was born to Diana's cousin Jersey in March, Sarah writing to inform Diana of the christening. The ceremony, at which Sarah had agreed to be godmother, was to take place on 19 April. The other godparents were the Prince of Wales and the Duke of Bridgwater, so Sarah decided to send a deputy in her own place. This person would tell Sarah how Lord Jersey sat 'the whole time upon the arm of my Lady Jersey's chair, and kissed her and hugged her all the time before the company', and while this must have been pleasing for Anne after her long period of unhappiness, Sarah could not refrain from remarking that she did not wonder at Jersey's demonstrations of affection 'if that would make her live longer, because I am sure he has a sincere passion for the jointure'.[21]

Diana had sent her grandmother a pretty china breakfast cup by Lord Chesterfield from Bath; Sarah was delighted with it, returning her kindness by sending her a china dish of some value to put in her own china cupboard at Southampton House. Sarah meanwhile wanted portraits to adorn the walls of her new house at Wimbledon, begging the duke and duchess to sit for theirs, and thought Isaac Whood should paint them. The artist was a tenant on the Bloomsbury estate, and if 'he can do anything well', she said, 'he can this picture'. But she warned Diana that 'as I believe he sets a greater value upon his own work than others do, I desire that you would make a bargain with him'.[22]

Bedford was to be painted in his coronation robes, Sarah having seen a picture of Lord Chesterfield 'drawn this way that I thought looked very handsome', and as to Diana's portrait, she hoped Mr Whood would 'condescend to copy that picture that was done by Vandyke for that charming Countess of Bedford in the Gallery', and 'the white satin clothes and the posture I would have just the same for you'. She remembered 'that I liked the neck extremely', and 'I am sure, if he copies that, it will be more like yours than any he will draw for you'. Was Sarah worried about a return of the swelling on Diana's neck? The portrait of Lady Anne Carr had been painted almost a hundred years earlier, kiss curls circling her face in the fashion of the times, the costume decidedly of her own era. Charming though the painting was, Sarah agreed that the Van Dyck dress was out of date, saying that if Diana found it 'too old-fashioned for this age', Whood might 'alter the sleeve and waist and make the hair as you like to have it'.[23]

While in town, Sarah visited Southampton House, suggesting to Diana that it should now be called 'Bedford House', a name that the Bedfords subsequently adopted. Sarah had always liked this house (next door to the house of her estranged daughter Montagu), seeing it as 'altogether the most noble and agreeable thing that ever I saw in my life'. It was strongly believed to have been designed by Inigo Jones, and 'Paladio Dye' had thought to improve it, her duke having set John Sanderson to add a new wing, and to stucco the exterior. Sarah admired the work, thinking the appearance of the house 'much mended' with it, and was sure there was 'not so good a house anywhere in the world'. She said she especially admired the 'two courts that are placed on each side of the house for the stables and offices', thinking them 'better placed than ever I saw any in the town or in the country', and that everything 'is done, with good sense which I am sure no architect now living is capable of doing!' Her only quarrel was with the front steps, which she thought 'pinched in the middle', and should be altered to look like those at Marlborough House – but not of marble (as they were), as they were slippery.[24]

Diana's brother Charles had fallen out of favour with his grandmother again, this time for refusing to answer her letters, or just sending cursory notes. Denied the right to live at Blenheim Palace until his grandmother died, and obliged to surrender Althorp to his brother, the young Duke of Marlborough was having to put any money he could raise into improving his lodge in the Windsor Home Park, which had come to him through the death of his aunt. Sarah wrote him sheets of advice, complaining that she was working 'like a packhorse to save him from cheats', and all her efforts were ignored.

Diana appeared to be enjoying her life as the Duchess of Bedford, especially while living quietly at Woburn, writing to her grandmother that 'We are quite alone', but 'I fancy we shan't remain so long'. Not that they were anti-social, seeing 'Mr & Mrs Page almost every day' who were 'extream good humour'd agreeable neighbours, & mighty easy to live with'. Diana was living quietly in the hopes of becoming pregnant, her husband with his 'warm heart and simple boyish gaiety' good company, though it was said he could be stubborn and display a warm temper when roused. He had a good intellect (if 'not of the first order') joined with a capacity for hard work, giving unstinted attention to the estate. After Sarah remarked that part of the house was in danger of falling down, plans had been drawn by Sanderson for a complete new building; but made conscious of a need to stabilise his finances since his brother's extravagance, the duke was holding back. 'Paladio Dye', with no baby to distract her, must have been frustrated by this, desperate to put her 'magik' to work. She appears to have suffered a miscarriage at some unspecified date, causing (according to Sarah) the duke to be 'a good deal peevish lest he should have no posterity', since he had 'set his heart extremely upon Heirs'.[25]

The Bedfords were to call on the Manchesters at Kimbolton before setting off for Althorp that summer, Bella and her duke making a concerted effort for some kind of reconciliation. Kimbolton Castle had been newly rebuilt in golden stone, the interior glowing with fresh wall paintings. Diana wrote extolling the virtues of the house to her grandmother, who replied that she wished 'everything that belongs to the mistress of it were as agreeable as you have described that to be'. Henry Bell, Vanbrugh and Hawksmoor had worked on the building, the interior painted by the Venetian artist Pellegrini. Diana, as painter and lover of architecture, would be filled with inspiration for transforming Woburn.[26]

Diana's mission at Althorp appears to have been to observe her brother's departure from the house, her grandmother being determined that nothing should be taken that rightly belonged to Johnny. This, of course, was not consciously done, Diana sincerely loving brother Charles, but Sarah had asked her to 'draw a few lines of that side of the house next to the park, to show how the water stands, which I am told is at least ten acres'. No sooner were these instructions given than Sarah cancelled them, saying Johnny had explained to her how the water stood, and instead Diana was to make a little sketch:

> that I might see what is built in the first court, where the building for the still house was, and likewise a few lines will show what is done from the gate house up to the front of the house, where the coaches used to go in.

Sarah suspected some wild extravagance on her grandson's part, of which he had failed to inform her, and it was true Charles was responsible for the splendid new stables built here. Designed by Roger Morris, they were to be described by Sir Nikolaus Pevsner as 'the finest piece of architecture at Althorp'.* While Sarah might admire such work when applied to a house to live in, she would consider so much labour and expense for the use of a horse quite thrown away.[27]

While she was here Diana rediscovered a splendid Van Dyck portrait of her Digby ancestor, the 2nd Earl of Bristol, painted together with her husband's grandfather, the 5th Earl of Bedford, when they were young men. The latter earl was the same who later married Lady Anne Carr, whose appearance Sarah wished Diana to assume in her portrait for Wimbledon. This young earl (later 1st Duke of Bedford) was dressed in black with a froth of white lace, Diana suggesting that her own duke might assume this dress, or else the scarlet dress of her Bristol ancestor, since both matched Anne Carr in period. Sarah was delighted with the idea, for 'I believe as you have contrived it, it will be a very pleasing picture', and 'if Mr Whood will take pains may certainly be able to copy' it. She reminded Diana that 'painters, poets and builders have very high flights of fancy' and 'must be kept down', and to be careful to make a bargain with Whood, 'since most people, as well as he, are apt to overvalue their work'.[28]

Whood may well have accompanied the duke and duchess to Althorp, painting them when they were at leisure, and so able to inspect the portrait in question. But there was a note of anxiety in Sarah's letter regarding Diana's appearance, having received a letter from her brother Charles saying she looked very well 'but I had much rather he had told me your shape was not so slender as it was'. Johnny's wife was blooming, Sarah telling Diana that 'Your sister Spencer is bigger a good deal, though she is not quick', and 'looks better than I ever saw her'. She was hoping 'no accident will happen to her, for I do not hear yet that the Duchess of Marlborough is with child'. Nor was Johnny able to do wrong in his grandmother's eyes, and 'appears to me perfectly good and reasonable in everything'. He 'amuses himself with his pheasants, fishing of ponds and riding about the park, and is as busy as a farmer', and 'not much unlike them in his dress'.

* Today the Morris stables accommodate a museum to the memory of the late Diana, Princess of Wales.

These newlyweds may have been staying at Charles's lodge in the Home Park as part of the 'bargain' for his not having yet quitted Althorp. Sarah had visited his Home Park house, pleased to find he had not been at too much expense, and where she discovered 'new charms' in Georgina every day. And 'one thing I will tell you which you will hardly believe, but it is really true, that she looks much better without any powder'. Without it she declared her hair to be 'golden', and her sister Lady Weymouth was as fine a person as Diana described her, and had entertained her by singing to her. If only this lady had been 'married to your brother Marlborough', she sighed, for she 'looks like a woman of quality, and by what I saw I am persuaded she knows what is to be done and said upon every occasion'. She observed that Georgina was 'extremely in love' with Johnny, and both appeared 'equally happy', and she hoped 'it will ever continue'.[29]

Diana's cousin Charlotte had given birth to a child that summer, news coming from London that she was dangerously ill. Laying aside her own physical complaints, Sarah set off to London to visit her, the young woman saying she was 'hurt in her labour' and suffering 'a fever every night'. Sarah, remembering Charlotte's gifts for poetry and rich embroidery, and perhaps even her performance as Cleopatra in the play at Blenheim so long ago, hoped she would recover, for 'she has a great many qualities'. Between caring for her the dowager passed her evenings at Marlborough House reading from the works of Sir William Temple, and copied out an extract for Diana:

> The greatest pleasure of life is love, the greatest treasure contentment, the greatest possession health, the greatest ease is sleep, the greatest medicine is a true friend. Happiness of life depends much on natural temper . . .

'You', Sarah told Diana fondly, 'are luckier in that than most people I ever knew, and I do not doubt but that your good understanding will make you as perfectly happy as I wish you'.[30]

Yet Diana was still without child. One of her cousin's complaints had been something Sarah could not write in a letter, but pimples had appeared on the invalid's 'throat, arms, breasts, feet and head', and Sarah feared smallpox. Her husband Lord De la Warr (a 'thoro' wretch', in Sarah's opinion) had left with Lord Godolphin for his stud in Cambridgeshire, being of the opinion it might 'do him some good'. Diana had meanwhile sent a plan she had made of the Althorp Court to her grandmother, who thanked her for it, saying, 'I think I understand very well'. Charlotte was out of danger, if pale and thin, and ate 'without being sick'. Dr Hollings was of the opinion she had chicken-pox.[31]

By 24 August Diana was at Woburn again, expressing a longing to see her grandmother. While showing concern for Sarah's own health ('tormented as ever with the itching; which I suppose is the scurvy'), she had problems of her own. It was apparent from her brother's remarks that Diana was underweight, and she may have attributed it to an early sign of pregnancy. She wrote to her grandmother:

> I intend making my self happy in coming to you at the Lodge on Monday next in the evening, which I flatter my self you will not dislike, and I beg to be in your house for a day or two, just in the same delightful manner, as when I was your own Dye, which name I shall always keep . . .

The Duke of Bedford was unable to accompany her this time, but 'will give himself the pleasure of paying his duty to you on Tuesday'. Meanwhile she was waiting with 'so great an impatience for the time that I shall see you, that I am sure I shall not be able to sleep before Monday night'.[32]

Chapter Thirteen

King Lear's Good Child

'. . . the charriott stays at the door'

If Sarah found Diana alarmingly lean when she called to see her at Windsor Lodge, Diana in her turn found her grandmother suffering badly from scurvy, and busy sampling a variety of spring waters including those to be obtained from the Dog and Duck at Lambeth, which had done 'a vaste deal of good in the scurvey and sharp humours to several people' she knew. Sarah used these together with an application of deer suet to her swollen, itching, smarting legs, but 'I am sure whatever I do I can never be well', she complained, and 'at my age, as Sir William Temple says, the play is not worth the candles!'[1]

When Diana declared William Temple to be her favourite author, Sarah advised her to read him again, especially with regard to pregnancy:

> You will find that he recommends much to young people drinking a good deal of water and little wine, which certainly does hurt to the blood. And I remember that Queen Anne never brought any children likely to live till she took that method of drinking a good deal of water, and eat a great deal of milk. And after that, the Duke of Gloucester was born.

Diana, anxious not to lose another child, asked if Sarah's Mr Stephens (who was currently studying medicine at Oxford) could be sent to her at Woburn, offering to send some conveyance to fetch him. Sarah replied that 'I cannot say yet when will be easy for me to part with Mr Stephens, but he shall come', and 'I know he likes better to go on horseback than in a coach'. Since the Bedfords had their own physician Dr Carleton, in order not to offend him Sarah took the trouble to ask his views on the use of deer suet for her scurvy, the doctor answering that 'any greasy thing might repel the humour'. Since Diana had known Mr Stephens since she was a young girl, when he taught her brothers, it was reasonable she should ask for him to visit her, if only to have a second opinion about her health. Now her grandmother worried that the exercise Diana was taking was too vigorous, Diana writing back reassuringly:

The kind concern you express for me upon the account of going in a chaise or riding, is more than I know how to acknowledge, but I do assure you my Dear Grandmama that I take as much care as it is possible for anybody to do, & I have got an extream quiet & safe horse, which I ride every day, & not at all madly & when I do go in a chaise I am allways drove by a very safe coach-man but I am so much more fond of riding that I do now very little else except the weather is dry enough to walk.[2]

Whood's portrait of the duke and duchess was now finished, and ready to be hung at Wimbledon House, Diana asking her grandmother if she might keep it a while longer to have a copy made for Bedford House. Sarah agreed readily to this, hoping there might be room in the panelled hall at Bedford House 'to have yours and the Duke's in one piece', as otherwise it must be split into two separate pictures. Brother Charles had not yet begun to sit for his portrait, and Johnny's, 'that was so well begun', had been spoiled by Seeman's painting him with an 'odious periwig full of powder', so must be done again. Sarah hoped that the portraits of Diana and the duke 'is with your own coloured hair'![3]

The year might have slipped peacefully from 1734 into 1735, had the Duke of Bedford not been 'extreamly enraged' with Sarah for insisting that Johnny should turn down the Bedfordshire seat in preference to the one at Woodstock, a place she believed 'he might naturally call his own Town', being next to Blenheim Palace. This had both embarrassed and frustrated the duke, since he was politically involved with Carteret as an anti-Walpole 'Patriot', the two having spent much time and money to promote Johnny Spencer's interest. Sarah thought Bedford 'stubborn against all reason', and declared she 'never saw his grace convinced in anything tho' reason beat ever so strong against him, and there was not one argument of common sense to be made use of on his side'.[4]

Peace was restored through Diana's inherent gift of diplomacy, and the incident allowed to blow over. But in February the young Duchess of Bedford suffered severe 'purgings and feavor', which put an end to any thoughts she might have had of being pregnant; and as no letters between her and her grandmother have survived from this period, it is likely that Sarah stayed with her at Woburn. The dowager had planned such a visit two years earlier, saying she would bring only 'one woman servant' with her 'besides Grace, who may lie anywhere, and one footman'. To have 'my bed things well aired is absolutely necessary to keep me alive', she had warned, but otherwise wanted 'nothing but a room that is quiet from eleven at night till seven or eight in the morning', and if there was a room downstairs 'where a little field bed could stand, that would be better than the finest apartment above stairs'. From there she could 'crawl about sometimes with the help of two sticks'. Lady De la Warr also paid Diana a visit, able to bring comfort to her cousin, though still not completely well herself. Her long exiled father, the Earl of Clancarty, had died in Hamburg in the previous September, which Sarah thought 'happy for him', and 'no loss to anybody'. Charlotte had sent Sarah a thank-you letter after her visit to London so 'prettily and agreeably turned' it caused her to wonder 'mightily that all the women of that family should write so well, and the men so indifferent'![5]

Once returned to Marlborough House, Sarah treated Diana to the latest town gossip, especially with what concerned her deceased daughter Henrietta. Diana replied that:

> the superstition when she was ill confirms what I have heard reported that she was a good deal inclin'd to the Roman Catholic Religion, & I think the late Lord Blandford had a great deal of that way of thinking but I own I can't reconcile the inconsistency of atheism & having at the same time so much faith in a piece of wood . . .

Neither Diana nor Sarah appeared to connect this 'piece of wood' with the currently circulating rumours that figures of Congreve had been set daily at her table, and her bed. Apparently the Duchess of Montagu had failed to call on her sister when she was dying, the two having fallen out, and 'to be sure', wrote Diana, even Henrietta 'could never have been so guilty of any fault towards her that should not be forgott on a death bed'. There was good news of the Duchess of Montagu, however, Sarah informing Diana that this lady and her duke had grown 'excessive fond of one another, which is quite new on one side', and that their daughter Lady Cardigan (Diana's cousin Mary, whose husband had now come into his earldom) was also living 'very well in the country with her husband'. Sarah hoped the last was true, persuaded that Lord Cardigan was 'a very good man'. Even Hervey reported that he 'is fond of his wife, and [is] as tired of his mistress'.[6]

In November Charles's duchess was reported five months pregnant, Hervey observing to Henry Fox that her sister-in-law Georgina Spencer 'says this report is entirely without foundation' and that she 'flirts her fan over her own great belly, with an air of sufficiency & satisfaction, as if she had obtained a grant from heaven of the monopoly of making children for the Marlborough family'. Mrs Spencer believed that 'no body could breed where she came, any more than they can speak'.[7]

Georgina Spencer gave birth to a boy named John on 8 December, and Elizabeth the Duchess of Marlborough to a little girl, Diana, early in the following year. The fact that Elizabeth named her daughter after her aunt suggests strongly that the Duchess of Bedford was godmother to the child, and on 29 May 1735 Diana wrote to her sister-in-law:

> I hope my Dear Duchess, that this will find you as well as when I left you, & Lady Dye in as perfect health and beauty. I have just sent two bottles of Hungary water to your house, & I beg you would let me know when you have us'd them – for I assure you, that I have always enough to send you a fresh supply whenever you want it. I have like-wise bespoke a Hatt for you, & this day given Zinques the Picture to copy, which he says he will take great care to do very exactly & he will make all the haste that is possible – you see I don't forget any of your commands, tho' I can't pretend to any merit in not neglecting the last as it flatters my own vanity at the same time that I am doing what you order me.

Diana obviously had a very positive self-image. Christian Friedrich Zincke was a highly successful enamel painter, painting Diana in miniature, possibly from the portrait by Whood. But Diana had been very unwell, Hervey reporting in February that she was 'very ill and going to the Bath', and was 'thought to be in a bad way'. Her letter to her sister-in-law continued bravely:

> I still grow better every day, & to-morrow shall set out to lye at St Albans in my way to Woburn, where I shall settle the Summer; I will hope that it is possible I may have the pleasure of seeing you there, but in the mean time I hope you will let me hear from you sometimes, and when you are so lazy as not to care to write yourself, I am sure Mrs Trevor will be so good as to take the trouble off your hands. I beg my best complements to her, & tell her I am a very good child & take a

great deal of care of my precious self according to her commands. I am Dearest Duchess ever . . .

Having signed her name, Diana remembered to send compliments to 'my brother', saying that they 'are the last I shall send him for tis troublesome to write a postscript'! This was in response to Charles's own laziness in writing, something that had caused his grandmother so much irritation. 'Mrs [Mistress] Trevor' was Elizabeth's half-sister, her own mother being dead, and her stepmother Lady Trevor a woman of 'strict life and conversation': Hervey described Elizabeth's stepmother as having the 'most virtuous forbidding countenance that natural ugliness, age, and small-pox ever compounded'.[8]

Since Diana's illness her grandmother called her 'my dear angel', and then 'Cordelia', which Sarah said 'was the name of King Lear's good child, and therefore a proper title for you, who have been always good to me'. Diana sent her many thanks for giving her that name, but modestly thought it 'more good to me than I can ever deserve', pointing out:

I cannot think the comparison between her and me at all a just one, for she shew'd her goodness & duty in a surprising manner, to a parent who us'd her in the most cruel way imaginable by which her merit appear'd so strong. If she had been treated as my King Lear has always done me, her being so excessive good to him would have had no other merit, than the doing right, which to be sure is a good deal. But any body must have a very bad heart indeed that does not endevour to make all possible returns to any body who has shown a perpetual kindness to them their whole lives, as my Dear Grandmama has done to me, & which I shall ever study to deserve.[9]

Diana had studied her Shakespeare well. In the summer of 1735 she was once more convinced she was pregnant, and asked Jane Kingdon to be with her again. Cousin Charlotte had died in February, having written to Sarah from Bolderwood Lodge how her cough 'tears me almost to pieces' and how she had terrible fits of illness overcome her, quite sure she would die. The loss of this cousin may have frightened Diana more than she knew, and she spent time at Bath. Now back at Woburn they were having such 'dreadful unseasonable weather' that they were obliged to 'have fires all day long', which Diana found 'very uncomfortable near the middle of

June', and dared not set foot out of doors. Her brother Charles called to see her on his way from visiting Althorp, bringing news that 'Brother John, & Mrs Spencer' were well, and baby John was 'cutting his teeth which makes him a little peevish', but was otherwise 'quite well'. Johnny's family proposed staying with Charles at Windsor in about a month or six weeks' time, and to go from there to Hampshire, giving Diana the hope she might have 'the pleasure of their company here for some days in their way'.[10]

Was it Charles who confided in his sister that his wife was suffering hair loss since the birth of her child? As Diana had experienced the same trouble herself, she was able to send her sister-in-law her recipe for a cure, saying:

> I send you enclos'd the Receipt for the Hair Water, which you will wash your hair with every day when you comb it; it must be made Imediately, for it is now exactly the right time of the year when my hair came off. I made it thick incredibly soon by using this water in a morning, & oiling it at night with oile of small-nuts, which has no sort of smell, you may have it at any Chymists. I buy mine at Godfreys in Covent-Garden. I am as well as I could possibly expect; & have kept house this Week (as it is near the time I have always been ill) & shall do so, as long as ever you or Mrs Trevor would have me, if no Accident happens, which I own I am a good deal apprehensive of. Yesterday I was a good deal out of order, but 'tis gone off today; whatever happens my Dear Duchess you are so good to me, I'll certainly let you know: If care will prevent any thing I am sure I take as much as it is possible.

Diana was convinced she was pregnant, and was building up a warm friendship with her sister-in-law, stronger than she cared to admit to her grandmother, and hoped to see her and Charles at Woburn, saying, 'I long for it, for I assure you it makes me very happy to be with him and you, & I have an extream good Nursery for Dear Lady Dye'. Diana's careful preparation for her much-wanted baby, and her apprehension of losing it, did not prevent her expressing loving kindness to others. Her husband's sister Lady Essex was staying with the Marlboroughs at this time, Diana heartily wishing the duchess joy of being with her, and 'should envy any body but your-self'. Bidding her Marlborough sister-in-law 'Adieu', she signed herself most affectionately hers.[11]

Improvements had been made to the outbuildings at Woburn, which pleased 'Paladio Dye', Sarah hoping the 'house might be made likewise agreeable without pulling down'. She was herself busy at Wimbledon 'making a place pretty that I designed for my dear Cordelia', the furniture being 'extremely handsome and will be almost all new'. From the start she had built the house with her favourite in mind, and had meant all along to leave it to her. 'I am very glad to hear what you say concerning your confinement', she wrote, and 'The method you intend to take is certainly all right and I hope in God it will succeed as I wish.' But by the middle of July Diana was thanking her grandmother for sending her some verses, and only able to add:

> I have been so sick all the morning that I am not able to hold down my head. I am in great hopes of going on; I begin to be very sick & uneasy generally in a morning, but I am much better after dinner, which I eat very heartily. I am forever my Dear Grandmama . . . [12]

This was a very short letter for Diana. Sarah pretended to be pleased with the signs she gave her, saying, 'I hope in God all your care will succeed', and said her servant Grace had told her 'that the whole time from the beginning to the end when she was with child of Nanny, she had violent purgings, which is unusual', but was in 'no doubt of your being with child, but perhaps not so long as you reckon'. She hoped she continued to drink 'but very little wine; for I have reason to think that is a right method from several accounts I have heard of women that miscarried till they tried that way of drinking a great deal of water and sometimes milk'; and it was, she insisted, 'an admirable thing to take every morning as soon as you wake a glass of spring water'.[13]

The Duchess of Manchester, who was always a pleasure to be with, had joined Diana at Woburn, and brother Johnny had called with his wife on their way to Althorp, but had not brought baby John. Diana wrote how they 'are both very well & desire their duty', and that 'the child they tell me is vastly grown, and extream well & strong'. The weather had changed from damp to very warm, the fires dispensed with, but this still left Diana no better in health. Her grandmother wrote anxiously:

> I am extreamly uneasy at the account my dear Cordelia gives of her being so sick – you call it a perpetual sickness at your stomach – because that is something that I never heard of before. It is mighty

common to have people sick in a morning, vomit sometimes, and till they are half gone with child have no inclination to eat anything. But to have a perpetual sickness in the stomach is what I never heard of and therefore hope you will give me a better account in your next. If you have been with child as long as you reckon, I should think you should be a good deal bigger, and it is not common to have people sick at all after they are five months gone with child. I am impatient to hear from you again and hope you will tell me that there is no reason to apprehend your not being as I wish.

Brother John visited Sarah while in town, 'and I have seen his boy', she wrote, 'which is a very strong lusty child'. She could see nothing of 'the resemblance they speak of to his father', but 'I think, as much as one can judge of so little a child, that he is like my Lord Carteret and that family', but 'if he makes a good man and is healthy I do not much care whom he is like'.[14]

Diana wrote her next letter on her birthday, being twenty-five years old, making it the first thing she did that day:

As this is my birthday I am sure I can not begin a new year better than by writing to my Dear Grandmama, & I am sure you will be glad to hear that I have been much better within these two or three days, tho' I can not brag of being extream well, for I don't sleep well at all, & the hot weather is very uneasy to me, & makes me mighty faint, but as my confinement to the one floor will not last I hope above three weeks longer, they tell me I shall grow much easier when I can go out in the air & use a little gentle exercise.

Sarah had not forgotten her favourite's birthday, which she told her was 'kept in my family with great splendour', and 'all my servants had joyful faces & all the women made a much better figure, in my mind, then any of her Majesty's maids of honour upon the great days at court.' But 'I must own I am extreamly uneasy at the account you give me of the way you are in'.[15]

By now Diana had read the verses her grandmother had sent her, which were by George Lyttelton. As a young man leaving Oxford, Lyttelton had written a very complimentary address on the beauties of Blenheim, rapturously extolling the palace and the virtues of its owners, and his recently published *Letters from a Persian in England* may have inspired Sarah to look those verses out. Diana wrote that 'I think Mr Lyttleton's verses extream pretty, and I daresay he must have an honest heart & good principles, he writes so very warmly.' But she could not say that for all 'poets', naming Hervey as 'an instance of the contrary', for 'I think I have seen the finest notions of his writing that was possible for the best men to have, & I am sure not only my Dear Grandmama & I, but all the World agree to the badness of his heart'! Indeed she thought it astonishing 'that people who can think so right, can act so wrong, for they must have some sort of sense to know what is just and right, and then to chuse the contrary appears strange to me'.[16]

Grandmother and granddaughter discussed the possibility of war in Europe in their letters, the dowager saying Charlotte's brother Lord Muskerry had given her 'a dreadful account of the power of France', having seen for himself 'eight thousand of as good troops as ever he saw in his life marching towards Portugal'. Walpole had certainly dispatched a British fleet to Portugal in order to prevent a conflict arising out of a trivial dispute between that country and Spain, an action thought by many to indicate the power he had to enforce his policies, and that England still carried weight as a mediator on the continent. But not so Sarah, who had nothing good to say of the Prime Minister, or his government. And since all correspondence was liable to be opened during time of war, she sent Diana a list of ciphers for her to use when discussing private or public figures, which she proceeded to follow. Diana's description of '7' suggests this represented either the bailiff Mr Theobald (the 'fat man' Sarah had met at Cheam), or even Walpole himself ('The Potent Knight whose Belly goes at least a yard before his nose'), or (more likely) Dr Carleton, saying she thought 'just as my Dear Grandmama does of 7', who was:

near choked I think and grows fatter every day and does not refrain from eating or drinking in the least, for in my whole life I never saw such a stomach, and tho' he does not drink to be out of his senses, he pours down vast quantities of wine, & would allways sit sipping from dinner to supper, if any one will keep him company.

Sarah's own opinion of Dr Carleton was that 'he could not be very skilful, because he pass'd all his time in eating and drinking, sleeping, and going a hunting with his Grace'.[17]

Brother John planned to be in Hampshire on the first day of August, he and his wife to go 'backwards and forwards from Rookley, to Stratton', and 'the child', Diana informed her grandmother, 'is to stay at my house, which I think much the best because of his airing in the park; and besides I believe there is scarce room for a nursery at Rookley'. This was the nursery Diana had prepared for her own baby boy John had he only lived, and now she waited longingly for another child to fill it. If Johnny and Georgina were able to keep their promise to call at Woburn on their way to Hampshire, Diana may this time have dandled her nephew baby John on her lap. Diana wrote that Lord and Lady Jersey were visiting Ashridge, which might bring them to Woburn, but 'I don't know whether they will honour us', since 'they did not last year'. She would look forward to seeing their second baby, named George.[18]

Other people's babies created a desperate longing in Diana for a child of her own. 'I am certainly bigger', she wrote to her grandmother, 'but as I am extream lean 'tis not so much perceive'd as it would otherwise be'. She was carefully counting the days, believing 'at the very farthest reckoning, it is but now just 4 months' since she thought herself pregnant, and 'I don't think people do appear very visibly bigger till five months'. Aware that her grandmother might doubt her pregnancy, she insisted there was:

> no sort of doubt of my being with Child because I must have been more disorder'd by so very long an obstruction, and as for my being faint, it is the most common case in the world for the heat to have that effect upon people that are breeding, & when I am in perfect health, It was allways uneasy to me.

As menstruation had ceased, the only thing Diana could, or wished, to assume was that she was pregnant, though in fact lack of nutrition caused by regular vomiting and 'purging' could have precisely that result. Diana not only believed herself pregnant but felt 'a great deal better even in that respect', hoping 'in God there is not the least reason to apprehend my being otherwise than I should be'. She was sorry to read that her grandmother had made herself 'sick with fruit, for there is none good this year and I am sure when 'tis not ripe, to eat such quantities as I have sometimes seen you do is very unwholesome'. Irritably for Diana, she wished 'in God' her grandmother would 'refrain'.[19]

Reports from those who had called on Diana increased Sarah's fears for her health, and 'as soon as I knew of her illness', she wrote later, 'I went to Woburn to see her'. It appears to have been a sudden visit, for when Sarah greeted her granddaughter, 'to my great surprize and affliction I saw Death in her Face'. Although Diana appeared to eat enough 'to support anybody sufficiently', it was plain that it did 'not turn to nourishment by her falling away so much every day', and when a Mr Garnier told her 'the purgings had never ceased', she could hardly wonder at it. When Jane Pattison observed that Diana 'did cough sometimes', Sarah listened hard, yet did not hear her cough once in the 'six or seven hours' she was with her. She was determined, however, to consult her own physicians in London, stopping off as usual at St Albans on her way. At Holywell House a letter from Diana was already awaiting her, thanking her for her visit. Lifting her pen to reply Sarah found that 'the Tears drop down so fast that I cannot see to write'. It was dismal, she wrote, to have left her Cordelia so 'ill at Woburn to be here alone in a place that makes me reflect upon so many Scenes of Happiness, none of which can ever return'. Arrived at Marlborough House, she found her spirits so low with these 'kind of apprehensions' she wished not to think of her granddaughter at all, but found it impossible, 'for whoever is with me or whatever I am obliged to do, my dear Cordelia is always in my mind'.[20]

Sarah's usual uncompromising approach to what she believed to be the truth was put aside for a time, too painful even for her, and the dowager began to go along with her granddaughter's hopes, agreeing that 'people with child will look extremely ill and pale', and that this 'may proceed in some degree from want of being in the air'. Nor was it usual, she said, for any 'bigness to appear in four months when a person is very tall and very lean'. And Diana must be the best judge as to whether she found 'no alter-ations as to her breasts than when she was with child before at four months', and hoped in a month's time she might be convinced of what she most wished for, and was pleased that Dr Carleton had reported no 'feverish heats'. She believed the best advice she could give her was to take the air, since anything that would 'strengthen the stomach and make a good digestion' must do good. The invalid, determined to be well, wrote to her grandmother on 5 August:

I have but just time before the post goes out to thank you my Dearest Grandmama for your kind letter, & to tell you that upon your advice which will allways have more weight with me than any other bodies, I have sent for my own Chairmen, who are as good & strong as any in the world to come down from London immediately, and I will be sure to go out every day.[21]

Sarah was 'doubly pleased' at this news, seeing there was 'no more reason to apprehend any danger from careful chairmen carrying you up and down broad stairs, than there is to go into a house because there is a possibility that a beam may fall', and fresh air would 'create appetite, and help to make a good digestion and cause good juices'.[22]

After her grandmother's visit Diana had slept well for two nights in succession, and found herself 'refresh'd extreamly' by it, and was glad to read that her grandmother was to visit her again: 'for I am sure being pleas'd is one great ingredient towards health', and 'your being with me is a much better Cordial than any the Doctors can prescribe'. Two days later the chairmen had arrived from London with a chair on poles, and she hoped 'in God it won't be long before I shall be able to Satisfye my Dearest Grandmama entirely; for I can't bear to think you should have the least uneasiness even tho' tis a proofe of your kindness to me'. She believed herself 'bigger a little within these few days, & I think I feel heavyer', and was 'carry'd into the Park yesterday, & will continue it every day', for 'I really thought I felt the Air do me good'. Eager to convince her grandmother she was really with child, Diana went on:

Dr Carleton seems to have no Apprehensions at all of my not being breeding: he thinks me much better within these few days. I tell you my Dear Grandmama what he says because you may think I may be apt to flatter myself, & I do assure you he says he is sincere, & I hope you will believe he is.[23]

Sarah sent for Dr Bloxholme when she reached London, keeping 'it a secret, lest so Wise and Great a Duke [of Bedford] should be offended at my concern and care to save so Charming a Woman'. Sarah was convinced Dr Carleton had 'persuaded' Diana 'she was with child, when it was plainly a consumption', and that they had 'done nothing but what was contrary to the case'. Having thought the duke such a suitable husband for her favourite, she described him now as having the air of a groom or a Hackney coachman, who sat with his elbows on the table, and ate not 'like a human creature'. And whenever the Woburn company went to their 'diversion after dinner to play' he would 'whistle almost the whole time something that tired me to death'. The young duke was doubtless beginning to crumble under the strain of his wife's sickness, and not helped at all by his wife's grand-mother's implied criticism. Diana, so pleased with the results of taking the air, asked her grandmother if she might borrow her grandfather's campaigning tent, so that she might lie out in it as he used to during his illness, Sarah sending her servant to look it out at Windsor Lodge. She wrote:

> I will have it ready packed up with orders to the servants at the lodge to deliver it to your carter when he come for it. He tells me there is some brass thing lost which fastened the tent together, and when he set it up at Windsor Lodge, he fastened it some way or other by tying it with ropes. This, some of your people will find the way of doing till you can get what is lost made; and I hope they will be ingenious enough to find out what I am able to direct. He tells me there is a carpet to put upon a table and a great carpet to lay upon the ground; that I think is very necessary. Some of the chairs he says the rats have made holes in, and as I remember, are whimsical odd things; but you will put in what you like better.[24]

Sarah blamed the Duke of Bedford's carter when the tent arrived a day late at Woburn, having refused to make the journey on a Sunday, but it was delivered at last, Sarah reminding her granddaughter that the chief value of it was that it was 'your dear Grandfather's tent, when he did such wonderful things to secure the nation from being enslaved by the French king', and 'the great provisions he made for his whole family, all which I think should make his memory dear to every one of them and to those who set a right value upon liberty and the laws of their country'. Her attitude to Diana's pregnancy continued to be more positive than it had been, and when Diana complained she had not yet felt her child stir, answered, 'I never did any of my children till twenty weeks after, and I think you cannot be sure that you were with child quite so soon as you reckoned'.[25]

That the Duke of Bedford and Dr Carleton had become anxious for Diana was made evident when they sent for the highly qualified and the highly esteemed Dr Hollings. Sarah was grateful when Diana informed her of their reason for this, for 'if I heard of his going there without knowing the cause of it, I should have been terrified to death'. Hollings may have been called out in only very dire circumstances, replacing 'Dr Hambleton' who had attended Diana's mother in her last sickness, and Diana's symptoms were very like her mother's had been. Sarah was puzzled that Diana should be 'so uneasy after dinner if your stays are not made too long waisted' while remembering, she confessed cheerfully, 'when I was within three months of my reckoning, I could never endure to wear any bodice at all; but wore a warm waistcoat wrapped about me like a man's, and tied my petticoats on the top of it', being so 'prodigious big'![26]

Diana would be much less than 'prodigious big' when Hollings called on her, but sent a hopeful message with him for her grandmother:

I believe my Dear Grandmama will be pleas'd with the account Dr Hollings will give you of me, for he assures me upon his honour that there is not the Least Symptom of any thing but being with Child, and all the Disorders I complain of proceed from that. Mrs Kennon says the same and she has felt the Child Stir several times with her hand.

Diana planned to be in town in a week or ten days time, and to stay at Bedford House two or three days, and then go to Streatham, 'which is so near town that it will be much more easy and convenient to me'. And another thing she proposed 'great joy in', was 'that I shall see my Dearest Grandmama some times', and ended by writing hurriedly:

the Charriot stays at the Door for the Doctor so my Dearest Grandmama I will end with great truth, that I am & ever will be Your most oblig'd & most Dutiful Daughter . . .

On the reverse of this letter her grandmother wrote simply: 'the letter brought me by Dr Hollings'.[27]

CHAPTER FOURTEEN

By All Beloved

'... nothing so silent as true grief.'

What passed between Dr Hollings and the dowager Duchess of Marlborough when he called with Diana's letter can only be guessed at, Sarah having hoped 'in God I shall hear of him that you still grow better'. But her letter to her granddaughter left little doubt of the doctor's prognosis. Sarah begged Diana to not 'miss a day in coming to Town; for I am very sure it is of vast consequence for you to be here'.[1]

Returning from a gentle drive around the Woburn estate, Diana found two letters awaiting her from her grandmother, and wrote thanking her 'ten thousand times' before telling her 'I continue just as I did when Dr Hollings was here, much best in a morning':

I have been 12 miles to day & am not tir'd with it, and the journey to London in two days I dare say will be very easy to mee. I will come as soon as possible to London. I have sent to have the house put in order, and about Sunday or Monday I hope to have the happiness of seeing my Dear Grandmama.

And she added 'as to the purging when Mrs Kennon was here, it was pure by a fit of the Gripes, & I am sure, can't be mistaken in the child's stirring'.[2] This letter was written on 28 August 1735, and was Diana's last letter to her grandmother. The journey to Bedford House in Bloomsbury must have been a testing time for the invalid, despite her limbering-up attempts around the Woburn estate, and once she was settled here, Sarah, 'with a great deal of skill by the means of Mr Heatherington, who was the most sensible man in the family', obtained leave to have Dr Pellett, Dr Bloxholme and Mr Stephens to have a consultation with the Duke of Bedford's own Dr Carleton and Dr Hollings; but, 'to save money I suppose, they had their fees upon the first meeting, and were to come no more'. In two or three days Sarah had them 'sent for again', however, declaring 'it was absolutely necessary that they should attend her as long as there was any hopes of recovery'.[3]

In the great house on the north side of Bloomsbury Square Diana may have been surprised to find so many doctors surrounding her bed, being convinced of her pregnancy, especially when her plan to move to Streatham was curtailed. But her health deteriorated rapidly, and when three weeks passed before 'upon her pressing them to tell her the truth of her condition', and told she would die, she seemed 'dissatisfy'd they had not told her sooner'. Made aware that her short life must come to an end, the young duchess faced up to the truth with courage, and was, Sarah reported, 'very desirous to give away some of her jewells to those she loved', and to see that 'some pensions she had given should be continued'. One was to 'a woman that had lived with her since she was born', a 'most valuable servant', to whom she gave '£500 a year for her life'. This was doubtless Jane Pattison who had accompanied Diana to Holywell House when she was six years old. The Duke of Bedford 'promised he would do all she desired'.[4]

Sarah called at Bedford House every day, but was denied the freedom of the sickroom. Instead she sat in 'outward rooms, bathed in tears', complaining that 'there was no instance of such treatment as I went through, considering the great tenderness I had in my heart for the Duchess of Bedford'. The grandmother who had nursed her 'dear Cordelia' through smallpox as a child, and helped cure her of scrofula, must now sit helplessly in outer rooms knowing she would die. Meanwhile she flattered the Duke of Bedford 'on every occasion that offer'd', out of fear that if she 'did not take that way', he would 'order the porters not to let me in'.[5]

Diana's half-sister Frances was at Bedford House to attend her, as was her cousin the Duchess of Manchester, but no mention was made of cousin Anne, Countess of Jersey, calling, nor of Harriet, Duchess of Newcastle. Harriet was certainly aware of her cousin's sickness, describing it in morbid detail to Lady Evelyn:

> The poor Ds of Bedford is indeed, as you say, going as fast, as 'tis possible. The accounts of her are most melancholy. They say she now directly spitts up her lungs, and her purging is violent. She is nothing but skin and bone, no strength or spirits left, & I believe can last but a very little time longer . . . [6]

Diana was to suffer for another eleven days, Sarah observing how she 'took leave every day of the friends that attended her, and took care every one should know what she had left them'. This, her grandmother could not help concluding, 'look'd as if she was a little suspicious that the Duke might not perform the promises he had made her'. The duke, Sarah declared, 'pretended to be extremely concerned', and 'talked much of his sorrow, and went in perpetually to ask how she did', and woke her 'to be informed'. His duchess 'seemed a little uneasy' at this, and once when she was woken this way, said 'there can be no great alteration in me since I was asked that question so lately'! Sarah thought Bedford's way of expressing his concern 'very different from anybody's that ever I saw'. He 'dined with at least half a dozen people every day when [his wife] was in great extreamety, talked a great deal upon any rediculous subject, and often made speaches like a philosopher, how he would behave when she was dead'. This appeared 'strange' to Sarah, having often observed that 'there is nothing so silent as true grief'.[7]

The dowager concentrated her energy in narrowly observing the Duke of Bedford's movements, recalling how on the day before Diana died he 'had some odd creature, I think an Indian Deer, that he saw, hunted in the garden'. Doubtless distracted by his wife's terrible suffering, the young nobleman found solace in the only way he knew, through the company of friends, and in intense physical activity. This was incomprehensible to Sarah.[8]

If Diana's aunt and neighbour the Duchess of Montagu called to see her niece, her visit was not recorded. Sarah had noted long ago how when 'Di Spencer married, the Duchess of Montagu went to visit her without first sending a letter', to Sarah an unforgivable lapse in etiquette. From childhood Diana had been schooled to be cool toward her aunts, as they would in turn became cool toward her, which was unfortunate, for only they knew her mother as sisters can, and might have filled the many gaps in Diana's knowledge of her. But the person Diana must have most wished to see was her sister Lady Bateman, and this may have been one reason why Bedford kept Sarah from the sickroom. Anne, however, was away in France, Hervey reporting that she had 'been very ill in Paris', having 'lodged in the very room in which her brother [Robert] died, some idiot officiously imparting this circumstance to her'. As her spirits were already 'a good deal depressed by her indisposition', they were now 'so additionally disordered, that she fell into hysteric fits'. When news of her younger sister's sickness reached her she was doubly distressed, she and her husband hurrying home to be with her. On 6 October Hervey reported that 'Lord and Lady Bateman returned to England last Saturday, in hopes of finding her alive', but alas were too late.[9]

Diana had drawn her last breath on 27 September 1735, *The Gentleman's Magazine* reporting her death in the same words that appeared in the *Historical Register*:

Died at Southampton House in Bloomsbury Square, in the twenty-sixth year of her age, of a consumption, the most noble Diana, Duchess of Bedford . . . she was amiable and graceful in her person. In her temper generous and affable, compassionate to the poor, by all beloved; and most tenderly by her grandmother, the Duchess of Marlborough and by her noble Consort the Duke.[10]

Hervey, though ever ready to point out the faults of his friends, believed the Duke of Bedford was genuinely affected by his wife's death. Since the couple were seldom parted during the four short years of their marriage, no intimate letters between them have survived, which makes it difficult to know their true feelings for each other. But if not passionate in display, they appeared to be deeply contented in one other. Their improvements to Bedford House, their rebuilding of Stratton, the start they had made on improving Woburn, and the plans drawn up to do more, were all suggestive of 'nesting'; and if Diana inspired the work through her artistic ambition, her money-conscious husband was charmed into agreement. As Diana said to her grandmother, 'the D[uke] of Bedford is more kind to me every day'. Although much more might have been done for Diana's health in the early stages of her sickness (being cooped up in stuffy rooms must have been considered highly detrimental to her health, even in the seventeenth century) this was partly due to the unusually bad weather, and her fear of inducing a miscarriage. The understanding of tuberculosis in the early eighteenth century was, anyway, abysmally low, and would continue so for the next two centuries. Queen Anne had been the last of the royals to use the 'laying on of hands' as a cure for scrofula, the tubercular disease of the lymphatic glands in the neck to which Diana was subject; and Sarah had been well ahead of her time in eschewing 'bleeding' and 'cupping', and in advocating fresh air and spring water.

Asked to describe Diana's character, Lord Hervey declared that though she 'had a great deal of the *jolie femme* [pretty woman] she had not the least grain of the *honnête homme* [honourable man]', explaining:

She was thoroughly a woman, which I do not mean as a silly sex-reflection; but as I should mean if I said any man was thoroughly human, that is that he had all the passions of humanity unrestrained and all its vices uncorrected. She had beauty enough to make her person likeable, and wit enough to make her conversation entertaining, with coquetry enough to make anybody who liked the one miserable, and insincerity enough to make the other at least as dangerous in its consequences as it was agreeable in its possession. She was vain to a degree that exhausted flattery, more ambitious than any man, as dissatisfied and restless as any Spencer, and as avaricious and uncaring as any Churchill.

These were hard words even from Hervey, but may have had some grain of truth in them. The more positive of the attributes he gave Diana were certainly hers. That she had beauty enough to make her likeable is evident in her portraits, and wit enough to make her entertaining encapsulated in her letters. And one of her letters to her sister-in-law, the Duchess of Marl-borough, admits frankly to vanity, having been praised all her life by her grandmother. Her survival depended on being liked. Although her 'passions of humanity' may have been 'unrestrained', her 'vices' (if they could be called that) were certainly not 'uncorrected', as observed in her obedient withdrawal from Lady Rich; and she could be 'proper' in her social views to the point of priggishness, quick to make her brother Johnny and cousin Anne toe the line. Yet though obliged publicly to forgo her sister's friendship in order to keep her grandmother's affection, she appears to have had no trouble in maintaining both her sister's and her brothers' affections, and even Hervey, who approved of Lady Bateman, made no complaint of Diana's treatment of her.

Diana was honest in that she refused to marry where there was no affection, and if ambitious, this had grown out of living in marble halls that appeared to spring out of the ground around her since she was a small child. Her dabbles in architecture were amateur, but may have appeared highly ambitious in a world dominated by male amateurs. 'Avaricious'? 'Uncaring'? Diana was claimed to be generous, and eager to spend, and had never ceased to love and care for her querulous grandmother despite her increased disabilities and disagreeableness. Asked was Diana 'religious, living or dying?', Hervey replied, 'I think she was so in neither'. He reported that she had asked to see Princess Emily [Amelia] before she died, 'but that happening on the morning that the Sacrament operation was performed she did not see her'. This seems to be a contradiction in terms, which is typical of Hervey's style. There was certainly a touch of arrogance in Diana's attitude toward royalty, imparted by a grandmother who had once practically ruled the country with the queen; but if Hervey's report is properly understood, she expressed no such arrogance towards her Maker. Yet as Diana had remarked to her grandmother regarding Hervey, 'all the World agrees to the badness of his heart'. Hervey's other report that when Diana died her grandmother told the Duke of Bedford 'he had murdered his wife for want of common care', was true however, confirmed by Sarah herself, the bereaved duke being so shocked that he fainted.[11]

The 'moment his wife was dead', the dowager sent to the Duke of Bedford for the jewels she had given her granddaughter at their wedding, 'pretending she had only lent them'. The Duke of Bedford refused to answer her at first, taking himself off to Streatham to mourn his loss, but when Sarah persisted, reminded her that she had said she would never ask for them back until she 'danced at Court'. To this the crippled duchess replied, 'By God then I shall dance at Court tomorrow'! Finally the duke returned the jewels in person, setting them before her and saying, 'Madam wont you see they are right?' Sarah, who kept a list of all her jewels, had made a note that 'I gave the Duke of Bedford the large diamond given me by the Emperor', and 'the diamond given me by Queen Ann I gave to Diana, the Duchess of Bedford'. Whether these priceless gems were among those returned to Sarah is not known, but on the first day of December following Diana's death, the Duchess of Portland wrote to a Mrs Collingwood:

> I am told the Duchess of Manchester has returned the diamond girdle buckle that the Duke of Bedford sent her from the Duchess. Before she died, she desired he would keep it for a George [a jewelled pendant, part of the inignia of the Garter]. He said he had given it to her, [and] he desired she would give it away, and mentioned the Duchess of Manchester.

Upon this Diana had said, 'pray give it her'. The Duchess of Manchester''s response to the gift was that while she 'would have taken it from the Duchess of Bedford if she had left it her', she would not take it 'from him'. The Duchess of Portland concluded that this was just 'to please the *old* granny'.[12]

Another bone of contention had to do with the return of a portrait painted of Sarah, and bought by the Bedfords at a sale, the duke honouring the dowager by refusing to be parted from it.* Upon this Sarah relented, but asked for the Duke of Marlborough's tent to be returned, 'being very certain that your Grace would never make use of it as a soldier'. The bundle of canvas and poles that had once housed the great Duke of Marlborough, and for a time had given hope of a return to health to his granddaughter, was duly returned to the owner.[13]

Diana's slender remains were finally placed in the requisite double casket of lead and wood, lined with delicate fabric, and carried slowly by carriage to the Bedfords' chapel at Chenies in Buckinghamshire. Bells tolled at the various towns through which she passed, and the coffin was laid to rest beside that of her day-old son. Although many quarrels were to be fought over her possessions, Diana had been genuinely loved by those close to her, her memory to live on in the little nieces that were named after her. Deeply saddened by the news of his sister's death, her brother Johnny Spencer wrote to Sarah from Rookley:

> Dear Grandmama,
> I have at last heard the sad news of my poor sister's death. I only wish it was possible for me to hear what I am sure you must suffer on this occasion that is too melancholy to say any more about. But if wishes could be any use she would be alive, & you always happy . . .

And with typical country casualness he added, 'My Wife begs her duty to you. She is breeding.'[14]

This baby was to be named Diana.

---

* This portrait hangs beside that of Diana at Woburn Abbey.

Epilogue

The Duke of Bedford married Gertrude Leveson Gower two years after Diana's death, 'entering on a period of great and lasting personal happiness.' Although not always popular with the public (stones were once thrown at his coach, and part of the wall of Bedford House was pulled down by a rebellious mob), the duke enjoyed a long and distinguished political career. During his lifetime he was First Lord of the Admiralty, Lord Justice of Great Britain, Secretary of State and Lord Lieutenant of Ireland. He was also Ambassador in Paris negotiating the peace treaty following the Seven Years' War.[1]

The dowager Duchess of Marlborough fell into a deep depression after the death of her favourite granddaughter, a visitor to Marlborough House stumbling over her prostrate form as it lay stretched across the floor of a darkened room like a bundle of rags. The dowager explained that 'she was praying', and 'lay thus upon the ground, being too wicked to kneel'. But nothing could keep the dowager duchess low for long; her favourite grandson Johnny and his wife Georgina sent their two children John and Diana to visit her at Windsor Lodge. Afterwards the duchess wrote to their father:

> They are both of 'em charming, and they talk enough. And I find they are mighty fond of coming to me. For I play Drafts with 'em and they both beat me shamefully ... I heard they have been told I intended to give them a present. Upon which they press'd Grace mightily to know what it was? And after she acquainted me with their curiosity I ask'd 'em if they would like a Kiss or Gold and they both cry'd out very eagerly Money.[2]

Little John, whom Diana had hoped to dandle on her knee at Woburn before she died, would be created the 1st Earl Spencer in 1765, and from him the present 9th Earl and his sisters directly descend. Sadly, John's little sister Diana died when she was only eight years old, and no other Spencer girl was named Diana until the present century, when the future Diana, Princess of Wales, was given the name.

The eighteenth-century Diana's cousin Harriet, Duchess of Newcastle, remained childless throughout her marriage, but as her mother had asked in her will that she should care for her sister Lady Mary Godolphin, little 'Minos' was brought into the Newcastle household. The child whom Sarah had once called 'Congreve's moll' married Thomas Osborne, 4th Duke of Leeds, when she was seventeen, Harriet arranging the wedding, and accompanying the couple on their honeymoon to Yorkshire.

Diana's cousin Anne, once Duchess of Bedford and now Countess of Jersey, appeared happy in her second marriage, but having lost her first-born son in infancy, it was her second son George Bussey Villiers who succeeded to his father's title. As Earl of Jersey he was courtly in his manners, a dashing dresser, and dubbed 'Prince of the macaronis' by his contemporaries.

Diana's sister Lady Bateman had never been truly happy in her marriage to her 'morose, homosexual husband', and eventually they separated. On hearing she was in lodgings at Windsor Castle as lady-in-waiting to Princess Amelia, Sarah begged Johnny Spencer to 'take great care the servants who attend your children should not let them go near her; for I am very sure that she is capable of poisoning them in order to bring her nearer to the Estate!' Viscount Bateman died in 1744, his estranged wife surviving him for twenty-five years, dying at Cleveland Row in 1769. Anne was survived by their two sons, John and William.[3]

Two years before her death the dowager Duchess of Marlborough fell so ill that her doctor was overheard to whisper: 'She must be blistered or she must die.' The indomitable duchess sat up in her bed and declared: 'I won't be blistered, and won't die!' It was not until 18 October 1744 that she succumbed at last to the inevitable. By now she had quarrelled with her granddaughter the Duchess of Manchester, who on receiving instructions not to receive Lady Bateman at her house had refused to comply, declaring spiritedly that she would not give up her friends for the sake of inheriting 'twopence halfpenny'from her grandmother. Although the cantankerous old dowager had befriended her Montagu daughter to the extent of leaving her items of personal jewellery, the greater part of her fortune went to Johnny Spencer. This included the Wimbledon House she had originally designed for Diana, together with furniture from both here and Blenheim, some of which is now at Althorp. Johnny died of 'brandy, small beer, and tobacco' two years after his grandmother, aged thirty-nine, his young son John left enormously rich. At their grandmother's death Diana's brother Charles, 3rd Duke of Marlborough, was able at last to take up residence at Blenheim Palace, and to follow the army career also denied him during his grandmother's lifetime. His letters to his duchess Elizabeth and their children were always affectionate, and after his death in 1758 his son George became 4th Duke of Marlborough. George married the 4th Duke of Bedford's daughter Lady Caroline Russell, thus linking the Spencer and Russell families once more, and from whom all subsequent Dukes of Marlborough were to descend.

The first Lady Diana of Althorp had been dead twelve years when the 4th Duke of Bedford decided to rebuild Woburn Abbey, discarding the plans they made together with Sanderson, and employing Henry Flitcroft to carry out the work. The duke insisted that the north side of the building should remain as it was, however, encompassing as it did the seventeenth-century shell-lined grotto. An inventory of 1771 tells of a sedan chair left here, which may well have been the one Diana brought to Woburn to enable her to take her last breaths of fresh country air. If so it was the only possession of hers to remain here, apart from the letters written to her by her grandmother, and her portrait by Thomas Hudson. This hangs here today beside that of her grandmother.

Notes

One: Sunderland House

1 BL Add ms 61442 *f* 40. Anne (*née* Churchill) Countess of Sunderland to Sarah, Duchess of Marlborough, 31 October [1709].

2 Ibid.

3 The house in St James's Square was named after the Earl of St Albans who built it, and had come to the Spencer family through Sunderland's mother Anne (*née* Digby), who was left it by her mother, the dowager Duchess of Bristol. The original house stood back from the present one (no. 31, Norfolk House) and was demolished early this century. *Survey of London*, Vol. 29, p. 189, and *Historical Monuments Commission* 1925, Vol. II, p. 135; Piper, David, *The Companion Guide to London*, pp. 72–3. 'The Queen was very easy in giving my Lord and Lady Sunderland the house where my Lord Nottingham lived in the privy garden'. Godolphin to Marlborough 28.3.1707, Snyder, Henry L. ed., *Marlborough – Godolphin Correspondence*, Vol. 1, p.741.

4 BL Add Ms 61442 *f* 24. Anne, Countess of Sunderland, to Sarah, Duchess of Marlborough, 6 October [1707]; *Letters of a Grandmother*, p. 151;

Survey of London, Vol. 32, p. 381.

5 The first Earl Spencer sold Sunderland House in 1765, building the exquisite Spencer House overlooking Green Park. Sunderland House was then demolished, Melbourne House being built in 1771 on the site, now known as Albany. *Survey of London* 1963, Vol. 32, p. 381.

6 Wheatley, Henry, *Round About Piccadilly*.

7 BL Althorp A 47. (Peter) Flournoy's account book 1705-7.

8 Swift, Jonathan, *Journal to Stella*, 24 November and 30 December 1711, pp. 39, 422 n. The pamphlet, a best-seller, 'discredited the war, and hastened a decline in Marlborough's popularity'.

9 *The New Grove HANDEL*, Dean, Winton, p.14. Knyff Kip's engraving of Burlington House in 1698 shows how the Sunderland House gardens were clearly visible from Burlington House.

10 Green, David, *Sarah Duchess of Marlborough*, p. 30; BL Add Ms 61450 *ff* 22, 29, 55, letters from Mary, Duchess of Montagu, to Sarah.

11 Memorial at Little Gaddesden Church; BL Add Ms 61475 *f* 63, Sarah's 'Directions'; BL Add Ms 61451 *f* 131,

Sarah's dialogue.

12 The Knyff-Kip engraving of Burlington House shows that the rear gardens of Sunderland House might easily give access to the two Spencer families.

13 Green, op.cit., p.171; Margaret, Duchess of Newcastle. This was Arabella's sister, whose husband was created 2nd Duke of Newcastle at the sisters' father's death; BL Add Ms 61442 *f* 1, Anne (*neé* Churchill), Countess of Sunderland, to Sarah, 10 August [1698].

14 BL Add Ms 61442 *f* 90, Anne (*neé* Digby) to [Sarah] Lady Churchill, 2 July [1684?]; Harris, Francis, *A Passion For Government*, p. 82; Plowden, Alison, *Great Families of Britain*, BBC Radio 4; BL Add Ms 61442 *f* 129, Anne (*neé* Digby) to Sarah, 5 September [1698].

15. Walpole, Horace, *Lord Orford's Reminiscences*; Wheatley, op. cit., p 126.

16 *Survey of London* 1963, Vol. 32 p. 382, described by Mackey in 1723. For Handel at Burlington House, see David Nokes, *John Gay*.

17 *The Daily Courant*, 17 April 1716; Holmes, Geoffrey, *The Trial of Dr Sacheverell*, Eyre and Methuen, 1973.

18 Holmes, Geoffrey,*The Trial of Dr Sacheverell.*
19 Ibid.
20 Ibid.
21 BL, *The Speech of Henry Sacheverell, D.D.* upon his IMPEACHMENT at the House of Lords in Westminster-Hall; Holmes, op. cit.
22 Holmes, op. cit.
23 Green, op. cit., 152-4.
24 Ibid.
25 Cumberland Lodge stands on the site of old Windsor Lodge. See Hudson, Helen, *Cumberland Lodge*; BL ADD Ms 61442 *f* 42, letter from Anne, Countess of Sunderland, to Sarah, April 1710.
26 Snyder, op. cit., Marlborough to Sarah, 22 June/3 July 1710; Hamilton, Sir David, *Diary of*, p. 33. The queen was referring to Henrietta, Anne and Mary.
27 BL Althorp A 47, Flournoy's accounts; Register of Births, St James's Church, Piccadilly.
28 Snyder, op. cit., Marlborough to Sarah, 10/21 August 1710. The French dates were 11 days after those in England.
29 Lady Diana de Vere had married Charles, Duke of St Albans, the natural son of Nell Gwyn and Charles II. The duke and duchess were close neighbours of Sarah at Windsor Park, and their sons were friends of the Spencer children.
30 Walpole, op. cit.
31 Hamilton, op. cit., Appendix A.

32 Swift, op. cit., 8 January 1711/12; Curtis, Gilla, *Queen Anne*, p. 191.

Two: Althorp
1 BL Add Ms 61442 *ff* 16, 48, Anne (*née* Churchill), Countess of Sunderland, to Sarah, 'Oct ye 10th' [1704?], 'Sept ye 6th' [1711] Postmark BATH.
2 Fiennes, Celia, *The Illustrated Journeys*, p. 47; BL Ms 61655 *f* 8, Flournoys to Anne (*née* Churchill), Countess of Sunderland.
3 BL Add Ms 61656 *f* 55, Lord Spencer's Expenses.
4 Ibid; Swift, Jonathan, *Journal to Stella*, p. 647.
5 Fiennes, op. cit., p. 229; Evelyn, John, *Diary*, 14 July 1675.
6 Pepys, Samuel, *Diary*, 1 July 1663.
7 Battiscombe, Georgina, *The Spencers of Althorp*, p. 51.
8 BBC, Radio 4: *The Spencers of Althorp*; BL Add Ms 32860, Letters to Henry Sidney from Anne (Digby) Countess of Sunderland.
9 March, Rosemary, *Sherborne Castle*, p. 13.
10 BBC, Radio 4: *The Spencers of Althorp*.
11 BL Althorp Papers, A 9: Chancery suit between Anne, Dowager Countess of Sunderland, and Charles, 3rd Earl of Sunderland; Snyder, Henry, L., *Marlborough-Godolphin Correspondence*, Marlborough to Sarah, 27 June, 8 July 1706.
12 Snyder, op. cit., Marlborough to Sarah, 2/13 June 1709.
13 BL Add Ms 61451 *f* 22, Sarah's dialogue.

14 Ibid.
15 Ibid. *f* 67. Anne (*née* Churchill) to Sarah, 'May ye 26th'.
16 Harris, Frances, *A Passion for Government*, p. 207; BL Althorp papers D 15, Anne (*née* Churchill) to Sarah, 'June ye 12th, 1713'.
17 BL Add Ms 61365 *f* 9, Jervas to the Duke of Marlborough, 21 August 1706; Waterhouse, Ellis, *The Dictionary of 18th Century Painters.*
18 BL Althorp A 47, Flournoys Account Book, 1705-7; BL Add Ms 61442, *ff* 50, 53, Anne (*née* Churchill) to Sarah, 2nd March, 19th October [1713].
19 Swift *Journal*, Sat, Nov. 17 1711; BL Add Ms *f* 56: Anne (*née* Churchill) to Sarah, 'Novr 17th' [1713].
20 BL Add Ms 61442, Anne (*née* Churchill) to Sarah, April 26th, 'May ye 4th' [1714]. Dr David Hamillton was the 2nd physician to Queen Anne, and had acted as 'go-between' for the Duchess of Marlborough during her disputes with the queen.
21 BL Add Ms 61442, *f* 53 Anne (*née* Churchill) to Sarah.

Three: Holywell House
1 Marlowe, Joyce, *George I*, p. 67.
2 BM Add Ms 61656 *f* 104, Althorp Accounts, 1713-14.
3 Ibid., *f* 108.
4 Green, David, *Sarah Duchess of Marlborough*, p. 196,
5 Ibid.
6 *Historical Manuscripts*

Commission, Vol. 1 (1899) p. 361. Lady Sunderland to her sister the Duchess of Montagu.

7 Marlow, op. cit., p 74.

8 The belief that Handel's relationship with the king was cool at this time is exaggerated. Handel's *Te Deum* was performed in the king's presence on 26 September 1714, ten days after his arrival on English soil. Also Handel received a half-year's salary from the Hanover treasury in October 1715, the king doubling the pension he had from Queen Anne. To have an English composer write the Coronation anthem would be a matter of tact and diplomacy at the time. See Dean, Winton, *The New Grove Handel,* p. 19.

9 BL Add Ms 61656 *f* 104, Althorp accounts, *ff* 112-3.

10 BL Add Ms 61442 *f* 20, Anne (*née* Churchill) Countess of Sunderland to Sarah; BL Add Ms 61443 *f* 62, Charles Spencer, 3rd Earl of Sunderland to Sarah, 31 October 1716.

11 BL Add Ms 61442 *f* 64, Anne Churchill, Countess of Sunderland, to Sarah [12 April 1715].

12 Louis XIV had died in the previous September, his grandson no more than a babe in arms, the Regent allied to Britain. When the Pretender arrived at St Germain-en-Laye, he found it no longer his home, and was obliged to set out on his travels.

13 Harris, Frances, *A Passion for Government*, p. 210; BL, Add Ms 701 d. 12 'A miscellany of Divine Poems all written by the late Mr Secretary ADDISON Esq. Viz', including 'Beauty and Virtue, A POEM Sacred to the Memory of ANNE LATE COUNTESS OF SUNDERLAND, Humbly Inscribed to his Grace The Duke of Marlborough By Mr CHUTE. LONDON, Printed for R BURLEIGH.'

14 BL Add Ms 61656 *ff* 124-8, Althorp accounts.

15 BL Add Ms 61442 *f* 76, endorsed by Sarah: 'A copy of what my dear Daughter Sunderland wrote to her Lord not to be given him till after she was dead'.

16 BL Add Ms 61443 *f* 56, letter from the 3rd Earl of Sunderland to Sarah, 13 May [1716]; Green, op. cit., p. 200.

17 Green, op. cit., pp. 200, 260.

18 Ibid., p. 200.

19 Defoe, Daniel, *A Tour Through the Whole Island of Great Britain*, p. 343.

20 Green, op. cit., p. 200; BL Add Ms 61451 *f* 147.

21 Harris, op, cit., p. 10; Harris, *Holywell House, St Albans*.

22 Lynch, Kathleen, *A Congreve Gallery*.

23 HMC, Buccleuch (Montagu House), 30 July 1708. Marlborough to the Duchess of Montagu.

24 BL Add Ms 61448 *f* 1, undated letter from Diana to Sarah [*c*. 1716-17].

Four: Marlborough House and Blenheim Palace

1 Harris, Frances, *A Passion for Government*, p. 214.

2 Green, David, *Sarah Duchess of Marlborough*, pp. 205-6, Vanbrugh to the Duchess of Marlborough, 8 November 1716.

3 Ibid., p. 207.

4 BL Add Ms 61353 *f* 158, Vanbrugh to Sarah, 16 January 1714.

5 Ibid. *f* 209, Vanbrugh to Sarah, 6 November 1716.

6 BL Add Ms 61450, *f* 120, Mary Duchess of Montagu to Sarah; BL Add Ms 61353 *f* 158, Vanbrugh to Sarah, 16 January 1714.

7 Green, op. cit., p. 209.

8 BL 61450 *f* 122, the Duchess of Montagu to Sarah, September [1717-18].

9 Ibid. *f* 125, the Duchess of Montagu to Sarah, 4 November [1717].

10 Snyder, Henry L, *Marlborough Godolphin Correspondence*, p. 281. Swift, *Journal*, p. 651; BL Add Ms 61448 *f* 28, Diana to Sarah, 22 November 1731.

11 BL Add Mss 61466, *f* 177 *passim*, Lady Blayney (*née* Cairnes) to Gen. Cunningham, October 24th 1777.

12 Bl Add Ms 61466 *f* 143, letter to Sarah from Marie La Vie.

13 BL Add Mss 61444 *f* 18, Charles Spencer to Sarah, 24, October, 1718.

14 Add Ms 61446 *f* 177, Lady Mary (*née* Cairnes) Blayney.

15 BL Add Ms 61448 *f* 195, bills for 'teaching the Right Honourable Lady Diana Spencer to dance'.

16 Add Ms 61446 *f* 177, lady Mary (*née* Cairnes) Blayney.

17 BL Add Ms 61443, *f* 75, Sarah to the Bishop of Norwich, 17 Sept, 1717.

18 Delaney, Mary (previously Mrs Pendarves) *Autobiography*, series 1.

19 BL Add Ms 61443, *f* 75, Sarah to the Bishop of Norwich, 17 Sept, 1717; BL Add Ms 61450 *f* 125, the Duchess of Montagu to Sarah.

20 James Craggs ' the younger' (1686-1721). BL Add Ms 61451, Sarah's dialogue.

21 Green, *Sarah*, p.. 215; *Letters to Madresfield Court*, p. 128-135; BL Add Ms 61448 *f* 2, Diana to Sarah, addressed from 'Windsor Lodge, Berkshire' [c. 1717].

22 BL Add Ms 61450 *f* 122, the Duchess of Montagu to Sarah [Sept 1717-18]; BL Add Ms 61449, Earl of Bridgwater to Sarah, '31st Jan. 1718/19; Mrs Carter to Sarah, endorsed by Sarah; BL Add Ms 61443, *f* 118, Sunderland to Sarah, July 2nd 1719.

23 BL Add Mss 61354 *f* 64, 'New making a Quilt for Ye Young Ladies . . .'; BL, Althorp Papers, Inventories, Sarah, Duchess of Marlborough, May 1719; BL Add Ms 61354 *f* 64, Vanbrugh's plan, Blenheim Palace.

24 Green, David, *Sarah*, p. 216; Green, David, pp. 216-7.

25 BL Add Ms 61443 *f* 118, 'July 2nd 1719', and 'Hanover Oct 30 n.s. 1719', Sunderland to Sarah; Green, *Sarah*. p. 217.

26 BL Add Ms 61444 *f* 1, Robert, Lord Spencer, 'Utrecht May ye 2nd N.S.' [1719?].

27 BL Add Ms 61466, Mary Cairnes (Lady Blayney).

28 BL Add Ms 61443 *f* 164; Montagu, Lady Mary Wortley, *Letters*, vol ii, p. 113, vol iii, p. 187, anonymous poem; *An Account of the Death of Mr Hedges*.

29 BL Add Ms 61466, *f* 176, Mary Cairnes; Harris, *Passion for Government*, p. 225.

30 BL Add Ms 61466, *f* 176; Dryden, John, *All For Love*.

31 BL Add Ms 61443, Sunderland to Sarah, 'Hanover Oct 30th n.s. 1719'.

32 BL Add Ms 61448 *f* 4–5, Diana to Sarah [1719-20?].

Five: A Wedding and Two Funerals

1 BL Add Ms 61447 *f* 113, Anne (*née* Spencer) Bateman, 'July ye 10th' [1720].

2 Harris, Frances, *A Passion for Government*, pp. 220, 227.

3 Ibid., pp. 257-8; BL Add Ms 61479 *f* 161, Sarah to Mrs Clayton.

4 BL Add Ms 61443 *f* 144, Sunderland to Sarah, London, 11 August 1720.

5 Harris, op. cit., pp. 227-8; BL Add Ms 61443 *f* 145, Sunderland to Sarah, . London, 16 August 1722.

6 BL Add Ms 61443 *f* 145, Sunderland to Duchess of Marlborough, 'London Aug 16th 1720'.

7 Green, David, *Sarah Duchess of Marlborough*, p. 275.

8 BL Evelyn Mss, Sarah to Boscawen, 2 August 1720.

9 BL Add Mss 61463 *f* 26, the Duke of Chandos to Sarah, 30 May 1721.

10 Green, op. cit., p. 219.

11 BL Add Ms 61466, Mary (*née* Cairnes) Lady Blayney to General Cunningham, 24 October 1777.

12 Green, op. cit., p. 220.

13 Harris, op. cit., p. 224; Marples, Morris, *Poor Fred*, p.123; Wilkins, W. H., *Caroline the Illustrious*, p.447

14 BL Add Ms 61450 *f* 129. Sarah to the Duchess of Montagu, 24 July [no year]; BL Add Ms, Lady Lechmere to Sarah, 'June ye 12 1721'.

15 Nokes, David, *John Gay*, p. 310.

16 BL Add Ms 61443 *f* 148, following, Sarah's dialogue on the 'taking possession of Ld Sunderland's Papers'.

17 Ibid.

18 Ibid.

19 Ibid.; Green, op. cit., p. 225.

20 BL Add Ms 61444 *f* 6, 13 May 1722, Robert, 4th Earl of Sunderland to Sarah.

21 BL Add Ms 61444, notes made by Robert, 4th Earl of Sunderland; Harris, op. cit., p.241.

22 BL Add Ms 61663 *f* 28, Lady Sunderland to her executor Earl Francis Godolphin, 26 July 1723; Mrs Delaney, *Autobiography*.

23 BL Add Ms 61463 *ff* 15-26, correspondence between the Duke of Chandos and Sarah, 1721.

24 BL Add Ms 61451, Sarah's dialogue.

25 Ibid.

26 Ibid.
27 Ibid.
28 Ibid.
29 Add Ms 61466 *f* 177, Mary (*née* Cairnes) Lady Blayney to General Cunningham, 24 October 1777.
30 Ibid.
31 Althorp Papers, funeral list, Marlborough; Harris, op. cit., p. 244; Wilkins, op. cit., pp. 390-1.
32 BL SC 1521, Horace Walpole, 'lot no. 122 on the twentieth day of the Strawberry Hill sale', 1842; Montagu, Lady Mary Wortley, *Correspondence.*
33 BL Add Ms 61446, Sarah to Lady Cairnes, Windsor Lodge, 16 October 1722.

Six: The Best Match in England

1 BL Add Ms 61449 *f* 20, Bridgwater to Lady Anne Egerton, 'friday'; BL Add Ms 61449, Bridgwater to Lady Anne Egerton, 19 August 1722, 'Sonday night'.
2 Ibid., Lady Anne Egerton to the Duke of Bridgwater, 20 August 1722.
3 BL Add Ms 61466, Mary (*née* Cairnes) Lady Blayney, to General Cunningham, 1777.
4 BL Add Ms 61449, Sarah's dialogue.
5 Ibid.
6 BL Add Ms 61446 *f* 172, Windsor Lodge, 21 August 1722, Diana to Mary Cairnes.
7 Ibid, Mary (*née* Cairnes) Lady Blayney, to General Cunningham, 1777; BL Add Ms 61451, Sarah's dialogue; BL Add Ms 61449 *f* 28, Bridgwater to Sarah, Ashridge 23

August 1722.
8 BL Add Ms 61466 *f* 139, Diana to La Vie 'Sept 16 1722'.
9 'I am my dear lady, your humble servant...'
10 BL Add Ms 61449 *f* 30, Bridgwater to Sarah '7th of September'; BL Add Ms 61466, *f* 121 b, La Vie to Diana.
11 BL Add Ms 61451 *f* 121 b, Sarah's dialogue; Harris, Frances, *A Passion for Government*, p. 248.
12 BL Add MS 61449 *f* 34, 25 June 1723, Bridgwater to Lady Anne Egerton. [Endorsed by Sarah.]
13 Ibid., 'An Account of the Duke of Bridgwater proceedings when he took Lady Anne Egerton from the Duchess of Marlborough'. [1723].
14 Ibid., Sarah's dialogue.
15 Ibid., Lady Anne Egerton's letter to Bridgwater, 'June 26 1723'.
16 Ibid., Sarah's dialogue; BL Add Ms 61466, Mary Cairnes as Lady Blayney to General Cunningham.
17 Scott-Thomson, Gladys, *Letters of a Grandmother*, p. 51, Sarah to Diana.
18 Montagu, Lady Mary Wortley, *Letters and Works*, Vol. i, p. 77; Green, David, *Sarah Duchess of Marlborough*, pp. 240, 242.
19 BL Add Ms 61457 *f* 11, Somerset to Sarah, 17 July 1723.
20 Green, op. cit., pp. 242-3.
21 BL Add Ms 61456 *f* 101, Lady Burlington to Sarah, 'London Sep 3rd' [1724?]; Green, op. cit., p. 42.
22 Harris, op. cit., p. 254; John Hervey, First Earl of Bristol, *Letter Books*, Vol.

II, p. 775, Lady Bristol to Lord Bristol, Bath, 16 September 1723.
23 Hervey, op. cit., Vol. II, p. 777, Lady Bristol to Lord Bristol, 18 September 1723; Gadd, David, *Georgian Summer*, p. 74.
24 Devon Record Office, Sarah to Somerset, 'Friday the 20th Sep: 1723 Bristol'.
25 Seymour Mss, Devon Record Office, Somerset to Sarah 'October ye 10 1723'; *Bristol Letters*, Vol. II, Lady Bristol, 21 September 1723; BL Add Ms 61457, 'Petworth October 1st, 1723', 'Oct 3d 1723', Somerset to Sarah.
26 Harris, op. cit., p 258; Add Ms 61441 *f* 141, Mrs Jael Boscawen, August 1722; Wortley Montagu, op. cit, Vol. ii, p. 22, 23 April [1723]; Green, op. cit., p. 257.
27 BL Add Ms 61444 *f* 25, Charles Spencer to Sarah '27 October 1723'; BL Add Ms 61447 *ff* 121-47, Lady Anne Bateman to Sarah.
28 Devon Record Office, 1392 M/L18 23/27, Sarah to Somerset, 20 September 1723; BL Add Ms 61457 *f* 44 'Nov: the 17th 1723', Somerset to 'Ldy Diana Spencer'.
29 BL Add MS 61457 *f* 46, Somerset 'To Ldy Diana Spencer', 'Nov 15th 1723'.
30 Wortley Montagu, op. cit., vol. ii, 20 October 1723; Lever, Sir Tristram, *Godolphin, His Life and Times*, p. 257, Godolphin to Harriet Duchess of Newcastle, '23 Novr. 1723. 11 at night'.

31 Devon Record Office, 1392 M/L18 23/3, Sarah to Somerset: 'friday morning the 7th of Feb' [1724].

32 BL Add Ms 61418 *f* 64, 30 November [1723] Somerset to Sarah; Burnett, David, *Longleat*.

33 Burnett, op. cit; Harris, op. cit., p. 258.

34 Green, op. cit., p. 244, letter from Somerset to Sarah.

35 BL Add Ms 61457 *f* 74, Somerset to Sarah, 'Dec: the 26th 1723'.

36 Ibid. *f* 76, Somerset to Lady Diana Spencer, 'Dec: the 26th 1723'; , Somerset to Sarah, 'Jan the 7th 1723/4'.

37 BL Add Ms 61451 *f* 131, Sarah's dialogue; Harris, op. cit. p. 258.

38 BL Add Ms 61449 *f* 47, Charles Spencer to Sarah; BL Add Ms 61451 *f* 131, Sarah's dialogue. 'Harts horn': an ammonia produced from harts' horns.

39 BL Add Ms 61451, 'June ye 4th 1724', Lady Anne Egerton to Sarah.

40 Ibid., Sarah to Anne Egerton, Christmas 1724.

41 BL Add Ms 61449, Sarah's dialogue.

42 BL Add Ms 61457 *f* 105, Somerset to Sarah, 'friday one a clock afternoon'.

43 Ibid. *f* 109, Somerset to Sarah, 'Petworth Octber [*sic*] the 5th 1725'.

44 Ibid. *f* 109, Somerset to Sarah, 5 October 1725; BL Add Ms 61457 *f* 107, Somerset to Sarah, 'July the 25th 1725'.

45 BL Add Ms 61466 Sarah to Lady Elizabeth Cairnes, 27 August 1724;

BL Add Ms 61454 *f* 6, Diana to Sarah, 'Oct ye 10th 1724'.

Seven: Secretary of State

1 BL Add Ms 61449, Wriothesley, 3rd Duke of Bedford to Sarah, 'Monday April 12 [1725']'.

2 Ibid. *f* 53, Anne Egerton to Sarah, 20 April 1725.

3 Ibid.

4 The Complete Peerage has the couple married at Ashridge, but as there is no record of it here or at Streatham, it is presumed to have been by special licence.

5 BL Add Ms 61449 *f* 55, Anne Duchess of Bedford to Sarah, undated.

6 Defoe, Daniel, *A Tour Through the Whole Island of Great Britain*, p. 427; Blakiston, Georgiana, *Woburn and the Russells*.

7 BL Add Ms 61449 *f* 57, Wriothesley to Sarah, 27 April 1725.

8 Harris, Frances, *A Passion for Government* , p. 260; Green, David, *Blenheim Palace* , p. 275; BL Add Ms 61449 *ff* 62-4, Wriothesley to Sarah, May 1725.

9 Blakiston, op. cit., p. 73; BL Add Ms 61449, Anne Bedford to Sarah, 23 May 1725; BL Add Ms 61449 *f* 72, Wriothesley to Sarah, 10 June 1725.

10 BL Add Ms 61449 *ff* 60-4, Wriothesley to Sarah, May 1725.

11 Ibid. *f* 76, Wriothesley to Sarah, 6 July 1725.

12 Harris, op. cit., p. 260; BL Add Ms 61449, Bedford to Sarah, 3 August 1925.

13 BL Add Ms 61449, Wriothesley to Sarah, 26 August 1725.

14 Ibid., Wriothesley to Sarah, Salisbury, 26 August 1725; BL Add Ms 61449, Wriothesley to Sarah, Bath, 2 October 1725.

15 Lady Mary Wortley Montagu to Lady Mar, August 1725.

16 BL Evelyn Mss, Nicholas Mann to Lady Evelyn, 25 June 1723; BL Add Ms 61440 *f* 81, Mann to Lady Diana Spencer, Paris, 6 March 1725 N.S.

17 Bl Add Ms 61448 *ff* 192-7, Bills for the 'Right Honble Lady Dye Spencer'.

18 BL Mss 61445 *f* 119 Accounts for John Spencer; BL Add Ms 61444, Charles to Sarah, 28 December 1723.

19 BL Evelyn Mss, Mann, Paris 12 September 1725, 'Saturday morning Aug 11 1725'; Harris, op. cit., p. 263; Green, David, *Sarah*, p. 279.

20 BL Add Ms 61456 *f* 108, Lady Burlington to Sarah, 14 September [1724].

21 Ibid. *f* 103, London, 14 September [1724] Lady Burlington to Sarah; Blakiston, op. cit., p. 96; Harris, op. cit., p. 264.

22 BL Add Ms 61449 *f* 104, Anne Duchess of Bedford to Sarah; BL Add Ms 61449 *f* 102, Sarah to Anne Duchess of Bedford, 8 November 1726.

23 BL Add Ms 61449, Anne Bedford to Sarah, 'Chasiobury Monday Night November ye 7th 1726'.

24 Ibid. *f* 102, Anne Duchess of Bedford to Sarah, 7 November 1726; Sarah to

Anne Duchess of Bedford, 8 November 1726.

25 Ibid., Sarah to Anne Duchess of Bedford, 8 November 1726; Harris, op. cit., p. 264.

26 BL Add Mss 61449, Anne Duchess of Bedford to Sarah, 'Chasiobury ye 24th'.

27 Marlow, Joyce, *George I.*

Eight: Lady Rich and the Prince of Wales

1 BL Add Ms 61444 *f* 138, Sarah to Fish at Lorraine [1727].

2 Delaney, Mary, *Mrs Delaney, A Memoir.*

3 BL Add Ms 61445 *f* 2, Fish to Sarah, Paris, January 9, 20, 1728.

4 Ibid. *f* 11; Harris, Frances, *A Passion for Government'*, pp. 272-3; Green, David, *Sarah Duchess of Marlborough*, p. 284.

5 Green, op. cit., p. 284.

6 BL Add Ms 61445 *f* 61, Johnny Spencer to Sarah, 14 July 1728; *f* 67, Sarah to Johnny, London, 16 July 1728.

7 Green, op. cit., p. 284, note; BL Add Ms 61445 *f* 61, Sarah to Fish, 7 July 1728; Green, op. cit., p. 285.

8 Green, op. cit., p. 284; BL Add Ms 61479 *ff* 162-3, 'the Plaster for Lady Dies neck 10th Feb 1728' [/9].

9 Bristol, John Hervey, 1st Earl of, *Letter Books*, Vol. III, p. 891.

10 BL Add Ms 61451, Duchess of Montagu to Lady Diana Spencer [Winter 1728]; ibid. *f* 122, Diana to Duchess of Montagu.

11 Marples, Morris, *Poor Fred and the Butcher*,

pp. 13, 36-8.

12 Delaney, Mary, *Autobiography and Correspondence*, Series ii, Mrs Pendarves to Mrs Anne Granville, 4 March 1728-9; Marples, op. cit. p. 13.

13 Harris, op. cit., p. 275; Green, op. cit., pp. 276-7.

14 Montagu, Lady Mary Wortley, *Letters and Works*, Vol. ii, p. 23, letter to Lady Mary, May 1723, and p. 84, from Ld Hervey to Lady Mary Wortley Montagu, 8 October 1727.

15 BL Add Ms 61454 *f* 172, Lady Rich to Diana, 'Thursday' [1730].

16 Ibid.

17 Harris, op. cit., p. 279; BL Evelyn Ms, Sarah to Lady Evelyn, Tunbridge Wells, 2 July 1730: Lady (Mary) Fane was the heiress of Lord Henry Cavendish, and wife of John Fane, Captain of the Horse. He succeeded to the earldom of Westmorland in 1736.

18 BL Add Ms 61454 *f* 174, Lady Rich to Diana, 'Grosvenor Street, Monday' [1730].

19 Walpole, Horace, *Lord Orford's Reminiscences*; Wortley Montagu, op. cit.; Ilchester, Earl of, ed., *Lord Hervey and His Friends*, p. 121.

20 BL Add Ms 61454 *f* 176, Lady Rich to Diana, 'Tuesday' [1730].

21 Ibid. *f* 178, Lady Rich to Diana.

22 Ibid. *f* 187 *passim*, Sarah to Lady Rich, 7 September 1730; Ibid. *f* 180 b, Lady Rich to Diana, 30 August [1730], Sarah's endorsement.

23 Ibid. *f* 181, Lady Rich to Diana, Sarah's endorsement; ibid. *f* 187, Sarah to

Lady Rich, 7 September 1730.

24 Ibid. *f* 180, Lady Rich to Diana, [30 August 1730].

25 Ibid. *f* 183, Diana to Lady Rich, 'Monday Aug: 30' [1730].

26 Ibid. *f* 184, Lady Rich to Diana.

27 Ibid. *ff* 184, 180, Lady Rich to Diana.

28 *Historical Manuscripts Commission*, Vol. III, 1730, Set 27: 'Lady Drogedy' was Lady Drogheda; BL Add Ms 28,052 *f* 293, Henrietta the Duchess of Newcastle to Mrs Boscawen, Newcastle House, 'Jan ye 7th 1730' [1730/1].

29 Ilchester, op. cit., p. 59, Hervey to Stephen Fox, Windsor, 9 September, 1730.

30 Walpole, op. cit.

31 BL Evelyn Ms, Sarah to Lady Evelyn, Tunbridge Wells, 2 July 1730.

32 BL Add Ms 61447 *f* 18, 'Lady Fane's letter with the Duke of Dorset's proposal for a match with Die', endorsed by Sarah, 'Feb ye 9th 12 Noon'; ibid. *ff* 12, 18, 20, correspondence between Lady Fane, the Duke of Dorset, and Sarah; Ilchester, op. cit., p. 76, Hervey to Stephen Fox, 14 August, 1731.

33 BL Add Ms 61454 *f* 187, Sarah to Lady Rich, 7 September 1730.

34 Ibid. *f* 189, Lady Rich to Sarah.

35 Ibid. *f* 184 *passim* [early September 1730], Lady Rich to Diana.

Nine: A Quiet Wedding

1 Green, David, *Sarah Duchess of Marlborough*,

pp. 280-1; Lever, Sir Tresham, *Godolphin, His Life and Times*, p. 260.

2 Lever, op. cit., pp. 260-1, Harriet to Mrs Henry Boscawen, 'Feb. ye 2nd, 1730'.

3 Lever, op. cit. p. 261, Harriet to Mrs Henry Godolphin, 'Feb. ye 2nd, 1730'.

4 Lever, op. cit., pp. 260-261, Harriet to Mrs Henry Godolphin, 'Feb. ye 2nd 1730', 'Jan ye 7th 1730'.

5 *Historical Manuscripts Commission*, Vol. III, The Countess of Strafford to Selina Countess of Huntingdon, [Feb] 5, 1730-1; Battestin, Martin and Ruth, *A Life of Henry Fielding*.

6 Noy, Michael De la, *The King Who Never Was*, p. 79; BL Add Ms 61447 *f* 24, Chesterfield to Sarah, 14 August 1731.

7 Ibid. *f* 27, Sarah to Chesterfield.

8 BL Add Ms 61449 *f* 108, Anne, Duchess of Bedford, 'Woburn Abbey, April 15 1731'.

9 Ibid. *f* 110, Wriothesley, Duke of Bedford to Sarah, 'April 15, 1731'.

10 Ibid. *ff* 112-13, Sarah to Wriothesley, 'April 19th 1731'.

11 Ibid. *ff* 112-13, Sarah to Wriothesley, 'April 19th 1731'.

12 Pope A. *Minor Poems*. BL Add Ms 61447 f 160, Lady Frances Shirley to Sarah, Twickenham.

13 Ibid. *f* 151, Lady Cheshire to Sarah, 26 September [1732 or 1738?], endorsed by Sarah; Hervey, Lord John, *Memoirs of the Reign of George II*, Vol. III, note 13.

14 BL Add Ms 61449 *ff* 112-13, Sarah to Wriothesley, 19 April 1731.

15 Ibid.

16 Ibid. *f* 114, Wriothesley to Sarah, Woburn Abbey, 12 September 1731; Ilchester, Earl of, *Lord Hervey and His Friends*, p. 85, Hervey to Stephen Fox, 9 September 1731.

17 Harris, Frances, *A Passion for Government*, p. 282; Green, op. cit. p. 281; Willigo received the degree of D.C.L. from Balliol this year. Kathleen Lynch, *A Congreve Gallery*.

18 BL Evelyn Ms, John Sparrow, Oxford, 29 August 1731.

19 BL Add Ms 61449 *ff* 114-15, Wriothesley to Sarah, Woburn Abbey, 12 September 1731.

20 Ilchester, op. cit., p. 100, Hervey to Steven and Henry Fox, 2 October 1731; Lambeth Palace Library, Marriage licence bond, 6 October 1731.

21 Ilchester, op. cit., pp. 101, 104, Hervey to Steven Fox, Hampton Court, 12, 19 October 1731.

22 Ibid., Hervey to Henry Fox, Hampton Court, 13 September, 1731; BL Add Ms 61448, *ff* 8-9, Diana to Sarah, '12 Oct 1731, Grosvenor Street. Tuesday Morning.'; Ilchester, op. cit., pp. 120-1, 'Dec 8/19, 1731'.

23 BL Add Ms 61448 *f* 8, Diana to Sarah, '12 Oct 1731, Grosvenor Street, Tuesday morning'.

24 Ibid. *f* 8, Diana to Sarah, '12 Oct 1731'; BL Add Ms 61448 *ff* 12-13, Diana to Sarah, 10 November, 1731.

25 Ibid. *f* 14, Diana to Sarah [?3 November 1731]

26 Ibid. *ff* 16-17, Diana to Sarah, 5 November [1731].

27 Ibid.

28 Ibid. *f* 18, Diana to Sarah, Woburn, 7 November [1731]

29 Ibid. *f* 20, Diana to Sarah, 'Althorp Novr 9. 1731'.

30 Battestin, Martin and Ruth, *A Life of Henry Fielding*. Fielding, Henry, *Tom Jones* p.35 (Dedication).

31 Ilchester, op. cit., p. 120, Hervey to Henry Fox, St James's 8/19 Nov 1731.

32 BL Add Ms 61448 *ff* 24-5, Diana to Sarah 'Althrop Novr 13 1731'; ibid. *ff* 22-3, Diana to Sarah 'Althrop Novr 13 1731'.

33 Ibid. *f* 30, Diana to Sarah, 24 November 1731.

34 Ibid. *ff* 32-3, Diana to Sarah, 'Cheam Novr 27' [1731].

35 Ibid. *ff* 34-5, Diana to Sarah, 'Grosvenor Street Tuesday Novr. 29. 1731'.

36 Draper, Marie P. G., 'When Marlborough's Duchess Built'. *Country Life*, p. 250, 2 August 1962, Sarah to Lord Herbert, March 1732; Wimbledon House would become home to the Spencers from the time of Sarah's death till it was burned down in 1785, and afterwards rebuilt, this latter building demolished in 1949; Higham, C. C. S., *Wimbledon Manor House under the Cecils*; Bartlett, A., *History of Antiques of Wimbledon*; BL Add Ms 61448 *ff* 34-5, Diana to Sarah, 29 November 1731.

37 BL Add Ms 61448 *f* 34, Diana to Sarah, 29 November 1731, *ff* 36-7, Diana to Sarah, [4 Dec 1731]; Ilchester, op. cit., pp. 115-16.

38 BL Add Mss 61448 *f* 52-3, Diana to Sarah, 22 December 1731, *ff* 44-5, Diana to Sarah, 14 December [1731].

39 Ibid. *ff* 54-5, Diana to Sarah, 'Cheam, Sunday Dec 26th' [1731].

40 Ibid. *ff* 56-7, Diana to Sarah, 27 December [1731].

41 Ibid. *ff* 50, 56-7, Diana to Sarah, 'Grosvenor Street Monday Decr 20', 'Cheam, Sunday Dec 26th', 'Cheam, Monday Dec 27th', [1731].

42 Ibid., *ff* 56-7, Diana to Sarah, 27 December 1731.

Ten: Life in Death

1 Thomson, Gladys Scott, *Letters of a Grandmother*, pp. 17, 19, Sarah to Diana, 'Monday Night April 2nd, 1731': Thomson says the 'cradles' may have been baskets in which the flowers were planted; or a device to protect delicate plants, described by John Evelyn in his recently republished *Kalendarium Hortense* as a 'mattress mounted on a cradle'.

2 Ibid. pp. 17-18.

3 Ibid. p. 18. The Cheam house stood on the site of the present-day War Memorial. Remnants of the brick wall that surrounded the house can still be seen from the car park. The 'fat man' may have been the Woburn bailiff,

Mr Theobald.

4 Ibid., pp. 21-22, Sarah to Diana, 'Monday night, April 2nd, 1732', p. 41, 9 July 1732, pp. 77-8, 25 September 1732. The new stables in the Royal Mews were situated to the north of the present-day Trafalgar Square, where in our own day an early design for the National Gallery's Sainsbury's wing would also come under the disapproval of the Prince of Wales.

5 Ibid., p. 28, Sarah to Diana, May 13th,1732.

6 BL Add Ms 61448 *ff* 60-1, Diana to Sarah, 'Cheam Thursday May 18' [1732].

7 BL Add Ms 61451 *f* 133 b, Sarah's dialogue; Thomson, op. cit. pp. 28-9.

8 Thomson, Katherine, *Memoirs of Viscountess Sundon*, Dr Alured Clarke to Mrs Clayton, Winchester, 6 May 1732.

9 BL Add Ms 61448 *ff* 60-1, Diana to Sarah, 13 May [1732].

10 Ibid.

11 Ibid. *ff* 64-5, Diana to Sarah, 'Cheam Thursday May 18' [1732].

12 Green, David, *Sarah Duchess of Marlborough*, p. 287; Ilchester, Earl of, *Lord Hervey and His Friends*, pp. 288, 135, Sarah to Mrs Stangways Horner, 14 July 1732.

13 Green, op. cit., p. 289; Harris, Frances, *A Passion for Government*, p. 285.

14 Ilchester, op. cit., pp. 292-3, Sarah to Henry Fox, 23 November 1732.

15 Harris, op. cit., p. 286.

16 Thomson, op. cit., p. 30, 24 June, 1732.

17 BL Add Ms 61451 *f* 33, Sarah's letter to John Spencer included in her dialogue.

18 Thomson, op. cit., p. 30, 24 June, 1732.

19 BL Add Ms 61448 *ff* 68-9, Diana to Sarah, Stratton, Tuesday 27 June [1732].

20 Hewlings, Richard, *Chiswick House and Gardens*, English Heritage, London, 1991; Thompson, op. cit., p. 21, 41, Sarah to Diana, 2 April 1732, (Scarborough), 9 July 1732.

21 Blakiston, Georgiana, *Woburn and the Russells*, pp. 70-1; BL Add Ms 61448, Diana to Sarah, Stratton, Tuesday 27 June [1732].

22 Thomson, op. cit., pp. 33-4, Sarah to Diana, Northampton, 'Monday Night July 3rd, 1732'.

23 Ibid., p. 33, Sarah to Diana, 3 July [1732]

24 Ibid., p. 44, Sarah to Diana, Scarborough, 9 July, 1732, Sunday night.

25 Ibid., pp. 50-2, Scarborough, 21 July, 1732.

26 Ibid., pp. 22, 50-2, 54-5, Sarah to Diana, Scarborough, April 2nd, 21 July, 1732.

27 Ibid. pp. 35, 52, 56, Sarah to Diana, Scarborough, 4 July, 21, 25, 1732.

28 Ibid., pp. 61-2, Scarborough, 30 July. 1732.

29 Ibid., pp. 62, 63, Sarah to Diana, 30 July, 8 August, 1732.

30 Ibid., p. 59, 26 July, 1732; p. 64, 8 August, 1732, pp. 44, 45-6, Sarah to Diana, 9 July, Tuesday, 11 July, 1732.

31 Ibid., pp. 66, St Albans, Wednesday, 30 August, 1732.

32 BL Add Ms 61448 *ff* 70-1, Diana to Sarah, 'Cheam, Aug. the 31, 1732'.

33 Thomson, op. cit., p. 68, 3 September, 1732.

34 Ibid., p. 69, Marlborough House, 16 September, 1732.

35 Ibid., pp. 70-1, Sarah to Diana, 22 September, 1732.

36 Ibid., p. 73, 23 September, 1732; p. 78, Monday night, 25 September, 1732.

37 Ibid., pp. 73, 76-7, Monday night, 25 September, 1732.

38 Ibid., p. 77, Monday night, 25 September, 1732.

39 Ilchester, op. cit., Hervey to Stephen Fox, St James's, 11 November 1732.

Eleven: A Natural Affection

1 BL Add Ms 61447 *ff* 80-1, Sarah's dialogue.

2 Thomson, Gladys Scott, *Letters of a Grandmother*, p. 82, Sarah to Diana, 18 November, 1732; BL Add Ms 61448 *ff* 74-9; BL Add Ms 61447 *f* 147, Sarah's dialogue.

3 Thomson, op. cit., p. 83, 18 November, 1732; BL Add Ms 61447 *ff* 78-9, anonymous letter.

4 BL Add Ms 61447 *ff* 78-9, Sarah's endorsement to the anonymous letter.

5 Thomson, op. cit., p. 83, 18 November, 1732.

6 BL Add Ms 61448 *f* 79, Diana to Sarah, 'Cheam fryday, Jan: 5. 1733'.

7 Ibid. *f* 81, Diana to Sarah, 'Jan 7 1733'.

8 Ibid. *f* 83, Diana to Sarah, 'Jan 7 1733'.

9 Ibid. *f* 85 Charles, 5th Earl of Sunderland, to Diana, Somborne, 'Jan 7 1733'.

10 Ibid. *ff* 86-8, Diana to Sarah, 'Cheam Wednesday Jan 10'.

11 Ibid. *ff* 6-7, 'Cheam Wednesday Jan 10' [1733]; *f* 88, Diana to Sarah, [? Jan 1733].

12 Ilchester, Earl of, *Lord Hervey and His Friends*, pp. 156-7, Hervey to Henry Fox, St James's, 25 January 1733.

13 BL Add Ms 61451 *f* 133 b, Sarah's dialogue; Thomson, op. cit., p. 88 [no date].

14 Thomson, op. cit., p. 89, 29 June, 1733.

15 Ibid.

16 Delaney, Mary, *Autobiography and Correspondence*, Series i.

17 Thomson, op. cit., p. 89, Sarah to Diana, 29 June 1733; Harris, Frances, *A Passion for Government*, pp. 292; BL Add Ms 61448 *f* 90, Diana to Sarah, Stratton, 'Tuesday morning July 17, 1733'.

18 BL Add Ms 61448 *f* 92, Diana to Sarah, Woburn Abbey, 'Sunday July 22, 1733'

19 Ibid. *ff* 94, 96, Diana to Sarah, Woburn Abbey, 'Sunday July 29, Aug 1st 1733'.

20 Thomson, op. cit., p. 90, Sarah to Diana, Windsor Lodge 2 August, 1733.

21 Ibid., p. 91-2, Sarah to Diana, Windsor Lodge 2 August, 1733.

22 BL Add Ms 61448 *f* 98, Diana to Sarah, 'Woburn Abbey August ye 9th 1733'.

23 Ibid.

24 Thomson, Gladys Scott: *Family Background*, pp. 145-94.

25 BL Add Ms 61448 *f* 100, Diana to Sarah, Woburn Monday Night [summer 1733]; BL Add Ms 61451 *f* 137 *passim*, Sarah's dialogue.

26 BL Add Ms 61448 *f* 106, Diana to Sarah, 'Woburn Abbey fryday Oct 26th'.

27 The tribute reads: 'Mr William Congreve died Jan. 29, 1728/9, aged fifty-six, and was buried near this place, to whose valuable memory this monument is set up, by Henrietta, Duchess of Marlborough, as a mark of how she remembers the happiness and honour she enjoyed in the sincere friendship of so worthy and honest a man, whose virtue, candour and wit, gained him the love and esteem of the present age, and whose writings will be the admiration of the future'.

28 Lever, Sir Tresham, *Godolphin, His Life and Times* pp. 262-3, 'Harrow, 24th October, 1733. 7 in the evening'.

29 Thomson, op. cit., p. 96, Sarah to Diana, Windsor Lodge October, 1733.

30 BL Add Ms 61448 *f* 108, Diana to Sarah, Woburn Abbey Oct 28 [1733].

31 BL Add Ms 61448 *f* 110, Diana to Sarah, Woburn Abbey Oct 30 1733.

32 Thomson, op. cit., p. 97, Sarah to Diana, Windsor Lodge 1 November [1733].

33 Ibid.

Twelve: Paladio Dye

1 BL Add Ms 61448 *f* 112, Diana to Sarah, 'Woburn Abbey Nov: 1st 1733'.

2 Ibid.; Thomson, Gladys Scott, *Letters of a Grand-mother*, p. 100, Windsor Lodge 5 November, 1733.

3 BL Add Ms 61448 *f* 117, Diana to Sarah, 'Woburn Abbey, Novr 8th 1733'.

4 Ibid.

5 Thomson, op. cit., pp. 103-4, Windsor Lodge Tuesday 6 November, 1733.

6 Ibid., pp. 102, 109, 105-6, Windsor Lodge Thursday 8 November, 1733.

7 Add Ms 61448 *f* 125, Diana to Sarah, 'Woburn Abbey Novr 25. 1733'.

8 Ibid., *ff* 127, 131, Diana to Sarah, 'Woburn Abbey Nov 29 1733' with Sarah's endorsement.

9 Ibid. *f* 127, Diana to Sarah, 'Woburn Abbey Nov 29th 1733', *f* 132, 'Woburn Abbey Decr 4 1733'.

10 Ilchester, Earl of, *Lord Hervey and His Friends*, pp. 192-3; BL Add Ms 61448 *f* 142, Diana to Sarah, 'Woburn Abbey Decre. 18', [1733].

11 Thomson, op. cit., p. 110, December 25th, 1733; BL Add Ms 61448 *f* 146, Diana to Sarah, 'Woburn Abbey Decr. 21' [1733]; Add Ms 61448 *f* 148, Lady Granville to Diana, 'Hawnes December 21st 1733'.

12 BL Add Ms 61448 *f* 150, Diana to Sarah, 'Woburn Abbey Decr 23d. 1733'; Thomson, op. cit., p. 110, December 25th, 1733.

13 BL Add Ms 61448 *f* 150, Diana to Sarah, 'Woburn Abbey Decr 23d 1733'.

14 Harris, Frances, *A Passion for Government*, p. 296.

15 Ibid. p. 296.

16 Ilchester, op. cit., p. 18; Delaney, Mary, *Autobiography and Correspondence*, letter to her sister Anne, 16 February 1733[/4];

17 Thomson, op. cit., pp. 111-12.

18 Ibid., p. 112, April 19th, 1734. Stratton House was subsequently burned down, the portico now standing alone in a meadow, a cross commemorating where the church once stood.

19 Ibid., p. 113, April 19th, 1734; Defoe, Daniel, *A Tour Through the Whole Island of Great Britain*, p. 360.

20 Thomson, op. cit., p. 113, April 19th, 1734.

21 Ibid., p. 116, 19 April, 1734.

22 Ibid., p. 117, 7 June, 1734.

23 Ibid., p. 118, Sarah to Diana, 7 June; pp. 120-1, 13 June, 1734.

24 Ibid., p. 122, 17 June, 1734; p. 123, 21 June, 1734; p. 126, Windsor Lodge Saturday night.

25 BL Add Ms 61448] *f* 150, Diana to Sarah, 'Woburn Abbey Decr 23d. 1733'; Blakiston, Georgiana, *Woburn and the Russells*, p. 105; BL Add Ms 61451 *f* 131, Sarah's dialogue.

26 *Kimbolton Castle*, pub. Kimbolton School; Johnson, op. cit., p. 131, Saturday 29 June, 1734.

27 Thomson, op. cit., pp. 132-3, Windsor Lodge 6 July, 1734; p. 131, Saturday June 29th, 1734; p. 134, Saturday 13th, 1734; Battiscombe, Georgiana, *The Spencers of Althorp*, pp. 68, 73. 'Di's brother [Charles] had allowed him [Morris] to lead him to huge expense at Althorp, with a replica of an Inigo Jones church for stables, an elaborate dwelling for a gardener and a great deal of work in the house itself, leaving it, in [Sarah's] opinion, much worse, when all it needed was sash windows and a plain useful stable of thirty or forty horses.' Charles was also responsible for the splendid Palladian Wootton hall designed by Colin Campbell, and built by Morris at this time. Pevsner calls it the 'noblest Georgian room in the country'. John Wootton painted the series of hunting scenes which gives the hall its name, the riders individually named, and full-length pictures of Charles's favourite mounts. *See* Green, David, *Sarah Duchess of Marlborough*, p. 264; Spencer, Charles, *Althorp: The Story of an English House* p. 13; Althorp Guide 1998.

28 Thomson, op. cit., pp. 134-5, Saturday July 13th, 1734. Van Dyck's portrait of the two earls, known as 'War and Peace', hangs in the Picture Gallery at Althorp.

29 Ibid., p. 128, Windsor Lodge June 23rd, 1734; p. 131, June 29th, 1734; p. 127, Windsor Lodge June 24th, 1734; pp. 129-30, June 26th, 1734; p. 135 'Saturday July 13th, 1734'. Louisa, Lady Weymouth, was to die cruelly in childbirth, 'the most famous of Longleat's ghosts'. *Longleat guide*, and

Delaney, Mary, *A Memoir 1700–1788*.

30 Thomson, op. cit., p. 138, London 20 July, 1734.

31 Ibid., pp. 139-40, Marlborough House 5 August, 1734; pp. 140-1, 2 August, 1734.

32 Ibid., pp. 140-1, Marlborough House 2 August, 1734; BL Add Ms *f* 154, Diana to Sarah 'Saturday Night Aug: 24' [1734].

Thirteen: King Lear's Good Child

1 Thomson, Gladys Scott, *Letters of a Grandmother*, pp. 141-2, Marlborough House 2 August, 1734; 5 August, 1734; p. 145, Windsor Lodge 24 September, 1734.

2 Ibid., p. 145, Windsor Lodge 24 September, 1734; p. 144, Windsor Lodge 21 September, 1734; BL Add Ms 61451 *f* 137, Sarah's dialogue; Thomson, op. cit., p. 145, Windsor Lodge 24 September, 1734; BL Add Ms 61448 *f* 158, Diana to Sarah, 'Sunday' [1735].

3 Thomson, op. cit., p. 146, Windsor Lodge 15 October, 1734. There is a portrait of Diana at Woburn, but attributed to Thomas Hudson. In it she wears white satin, her neck and shoulders displayed much as Anne Carr's are, the dress and hair similar in arrangement to hers, with pearls, but definitely of Diana's own time.

4 BL 61448 *f* 146, Sarah's endorsement to the copy of a letter sent to Diana, 'Marlborough House. 27 Dec 1734'.

5 Thomson, op. cit., pp. 94-

5, Saturday morning September 1733; p. 144, Windsor Lodge 21 September , 1734; p. 146, Windsor Lodge 15 October, 1734.

6 BL Add Ms 61448 *f* 158, Diana to Sarah 'Sunday' 1735; Thomson, op. cit., p. 147, Windsor Lodge 15 October, 1734; Ilchester, Earl of, *Lord Hervey and His Friends*, p. 212, Hervey to Henry Fox, St James's, 2 November 1734.

7 Ilchester, ibid.

8 BL Add Ms 61668 *f* 40, Diana to Elizabeth the Duchess of Marlborough, 'Thursday May 29. 1735'; Hervey, Lord, *Memoirs*, p. 16. Lady Diana Spencer (1734–1808) grew up to be a great credit to her aunt, from whom she inherited her gift for painting, and which she developed into a fine art. She would marry Frederick, 2nd Viscount Bolingbroke in 1757, from whom she was divorced, then Topham Beauclerk in 1768. Her works include illustrations for Dryden's *Fables*. *See* Erskine, E. C., *Lady Diana Beauclerk, Her Life and Works*.

9 Thomson, op. cit., Thursday 5 June, 1735; BL Add Ms 61448 *f* 162, Diana to Sarah, 'Woburn June ye 8. 1735'.

10 Ibid. *f* 164, Diana to Sarah, 'Woburn June ye 12th 1735'.

11 Ibid. *f* 41, Sarah to Elizabeth Duchess of Marlborough, 'Woburn June 15th'.

12 Thomson, op. cit., p. 152, Tuesday 24 June, 1735;

BL Add Ms 61448 *f* 168, Diana to Sarah, Woburn 13 July 1735.

13 Thomson, op. cit., p. 157, Marlborough House 15 July, 1735.

14 Thomson, op. cit., pp. 160-2, Marlborough House July 30th, 1735. Diana's nephew John Spencer would be created 1st Earl Spencer, from whom the present 9th Earl directly descends.

15 BL Add Ms 61448 *f* 31, Diana to Sarah, 'Woburn Abbey July 31 1735'; Green, David, *Sarah Duchess of Marlborough*, pp. 272-3.

16 BL Add Ms 61448 *f* 168, Diana to Sarah, 'Woburn July 13 1735'. Lyttleton was to become the benefactor of Henry Fielding along with the Duke of Bedford, and would take Lady Rich's daughter Elizabeth as his second wife. Mary Wortley Montagu wrote: 'I suppose Miss Rich is now a great Fortune', but felt 'pity and contempt' for her 'considering her education'. The couple married in 1749, and separated in 1759. Rose M. Davis, *The Good Lord Lyttleton*, 1939.

17 Thomson, op. cit., pp. 158-60, Marlborough House 15 July, 1735, and ed.; Montagu, Mary Wortley, *Letters and Works*, vol ii, p. 98; BL Add Ms 61448 *f* 31, Diana to Sarah, 'Woburn Abbey July 31 1735'; BL Add Ms 61448 *f* 137, Sarah's dialogue.

18 Ibid. *f* 169, Diana to Sarah, Woburn 31 July

1735. The Jerseys' first baby boy died young, their second son born in January of that year, 1735. Named George Bussy Villiers, he would become 4th Earl of Jersey and 7th Viscount Grandison.

19 Ibid. *f* 172, Diana to Sarah, 'Woburn Augst. 3. 1735'.

20 BL Add Ms 61451 *f* 137 *passim*, Sarah's dialogue; Thomson, op. cit., p. 164, Thursday 7 August, 1735; Harris, Frances, *A Passion for Government*, p. 311.

21 Thomson, op. cit., p. 164, Thursday 7 August; BL 61448 *f* 176, Diana to Sarah, 'Woburn Augst 5; 1735'.

22 Thomson, op. cit., p.163-4, Thursday 7 August, 1735.

23 BL Add Ms 61448 *f* 178, Diana to Sarah, 'Woburn 7 Aug, 1735', *f* 130, Diana to Sarah, 'Woburn Augst: 10th 1735'.

24 BL 61451 *f* 137 following, Sarah's dialogue; Thomson, op. cit., p. 165, 16 August, 1735.

25 Ibid., pp. 166-7 16 August, 1735.

26 Ibid., p. 172, Monday 25 August , 1735.

27 BL Add Ms *f* 182, Diana to Sarah, 'Tuesday Morn' [Aug 1735], endorsed by Sarah.

Fourteen: By All Beloved

1 Thomson, Gladys Scott,

Letters of a Grandmother, p. 173, Monday 25 August, 1735.

2 BL Add Ms 61448 *f* 184, Diana to Sarah, 'Woburn Aug: 28' [1735].

3 BL Add Ms 61451 *f* 137 *passim*, Sarah's dialogue.

4 Ibid.

5 BL Add Ms 61448 *f* 190 following, Sarah to John, 4th Duke of Bedford, 10 March 1737/8.

6 BL Evelyn Mss, Henrietta Duchess of Newcastle to Lady Evelyn, 'Sept ye 16th 1735'.

7 BL Add Ms 61451 *f* 137 *passim*, Sarah's dialogue.

8 Ibid.

9 Ibid. *f* 124, Sarah's dialogue; Ilchester, Earl of, *Lord Hervey and His Friends*, pp. 229, Hervey to Stephen Fox, 11 September 1735; p. 231, Hervey to Mrs Digby, 6 October 1735.

10 Thomson, op. cit., p. 173. Diana was twenty-five years old when she died, having just entered her twenty-sixth year.

11 Ilchester, op. cit., pp. 230-1; To Mrs Digby, Kensington, 6 October 1735; Ilchester criticises Hervey's 'constant use of antithesis' p. 1. Harris, Frances, *A Passion for Government*, p. 312.

12 Delaney, Mary, *Autobiography and Correspondence*, Series vi, p. 541, The Duchess of Portland to

Mrs Catherine Collingwood, 1 December 1735.

13 Harris, op. cit., p. 312; Thomson, op. cit., p. 178 note 1.

14 BL Add Ms 61447, John Spencer to Sarah, 'Rookley Sep: 30th 1735'.

Epilogue

1. Blakiston, Georgiana, *Woburn and the Russells*, p. 105.

2. Delaney, 2nd series iii p. 167; Harris, *A Passion for Government*, pp. 337–8, Sarah to Johnny Spencer 30 August 1742.

3. Harris, op. cit., p. 278; BL Add Ms 61447, Sarah to Johnny Spencer, December 27 1738. The Bateman sons were John, Viscount Bateman 1722–1802, and the Honourable William Bateman, a Captain in the Royal Navy, 1726–83.

4. Another portrait of Diana wearing an 'antique dress' is catalogued at Woburn, said to be a copy of one at Blenheim, which may be the portrait Mr Whood copied from the one her grandmother had painted for Wimbledon House. See Gladys Scott Thomson, *Letters of a Grandmother*, p. 174; The sedan chair in the Grotto is mentioned in the 1977 Woburn guide, when it was thought to have been used by the 4th Duke in his old age.

Bibliography

MANUSCRIPT SOURCES

British Library: Additional Mss, Althorp papers, Evelyn Mss
Devon Record Office: Seymour of Berry Pomeroy Mss
Westminster Public Libraries: parish registers of St James's Church, Piccadilly

PRINTED SOURCES
(The place of publication is given only when it is not London.)

Bartlett, W. A. *The history and antiquities of the parish of Wimbledon, Surrey*, Simpkin & Marshall, 1865
Battestin, Martin and Ruth *A Life of Henry Fielding*, Routledge, 1989
Battiscombe, Georgina *The Spencers of Althorp*, Constable, 1984
Blakiston, Georgiana *Woburn and the Russells*, Constable, 1980
Bristol, John Lord Hervey, 1st Earl of, *Letter Books* 3 vols., Wells, 1894
Burnett, David *Longleat: the Story of an English country house*, Collins, 1978
Carswell, J. *The South Sea Bubble*, Alan Sutton, 1960
Clayton, Charlotte, Baroness Sundon *Memoirs of Viscountess Sundon*, ed. Katherine Thomson, 1847
Coult, Douglas *A Prospect of Ashridge*, Phillimore, 1980
Curtis, Gilla *Queen Anne*, Weidenfeld and Nicolson Ltd, 1972
Dalton, Charles *George 1st's Army 1714–1727*, 2 vols, Eyre & Spottiswoode, 1910
Davis, Rose Mary *The Good Lord Lyttelton*, Times Publishing Co., Bethlehem Pa., 1939
Dean, Winton *The New Grove Handel*, Macmillan, 1982
Defoe, Daniel *A Tour Through the Whole Island of Great Britain*, Penguin, 1983
Delaney, Mary *Autobiography and Correspondence*, Lady Llandover, ed., 6 vols, Richard Bentley, 1962/3
Delaney, Mary *Mrs Delaney, A Memoir 1700–1788*, ed G. Paston, G. Richards, 1900
Dormandy, Thomas *The White Death, A History of Tuberculosis*, The Hambledon Press, 1999

Erskine, B.C. *Lady Diana Beauclerk. her life and works*, T. Fisher Unwin, 1903

Evelyn, John *The Diary of*, ed. John Bowle, The World's Classics, OUP, 1985

Ewald, Alex Charles *William Congreve*, Ernest Benn Ltd, 1948

Fielding, Henry *Tom Jones*, ed., R.P.C. Mutter, Penguin Books, 1979

Fielding, Henry *A Full Vindication of the Duchess of Marlborough*, 1742

Foreman, Amanda *Georgiana, Duchess of Devonshire*, HarperCollins, 1998

Fraser, Antonia, *The Weaker Vessel*, Mandarin, 1984

Gadd, David *Georgian Summer*, Adams and Dart, 1971

Green, David *Blenheim Palace*, Country Life, 1952

Green David *Gardener to the Queen – Henry Wise [1653–1738]*, OUP, 1956

Green, David *Sarah Duchess of Marlborough*, Collins, 1967

Green, Ruth M. *Costumes and Fashions in Colour*, illus. J. Cassin-Scott, Blandford Press 1975

Greer, Germaine *The Obstacle Race: the fortunes of women painters, and their work*, 1979

Halsband, Robert *The Life of Lady Mary Wortley Montagu*, OUP, 1961

Hamilton, Sir David *Diary*, ed. P. Roberts, OUP, 1975

Hamilton, Olive & Nigel *Royal Greenwich*, The Greenwich Bookshop, 1969

Harris, Frances *A Passion for Government*, Clarendon Press, 1991

Hervey, John, Lord *Memoirs of the Reign of George II*, vol i, Bickers & Son, 1884

Historical Manuscripts Commission, *Buccleuch MSS, Hastings MSS*

Higham, C.C.S. *Wimbledon Manor House under the Cecils*, Longmans, 1962

Holmes, Geoffrey *The Trial of Doctor Sacheverell*, Eyre Methuen, 1973

Hudson, Helen *Cumberland Lodge*, Phillimore & Co. Ltd, 1989

Ilchester, Earl of, ed., *Lord Hervey and His Friends*, John Murray, 1950

Jacobs, Phyllis May *Registers of the Universities, Colleges & Schools of Great Britain & Ireland*, Athlone Press, 1964

Johnson, Joan *The Excellent Cassandra*, Allan Sutton, 1981

Johnson, R. B. *Mrs Delaney at Court and Among the Wits*, Simon Dewes, 1940

Junor, Penny, *Diana, Princess of Wales*, Sidgwick and Jackson, 1982

King, William *Memoirs of Sarah, Duchess of Marlborough*, G. Routledge & Sons, Ltd., 1930

Landon, H.C. Robbins *Handel and His World*, Weidenfeld and Nicolson, 1984

Leigh, Richard Arthur Austen *Eton College*, Spottiswoode, Ballantyne & Co.; Eton, 1927

Lever, Sir Tresham *Godolphin, His Life and Times*, John Murray, 1952

Lynch, Kathleen M. *A Congreve Gallery*, Frank Cass & Co., 1961

Marlborough, Sarah, Duchess of *Letters To Madresfield Court*, John Murray, 1875

Marlow, Joyce: *George I*, Weidenfeld and Nicolson, 1973

Montagu, Lady Mary Wortley *Letters and Works*, 3 vols, ed Robert Halsband, OUP, 1965–7

Montgomery-Massingbird, Hugh *Blenheim Revisited*, The Bodley Head, 1985

Morris, Christopher, ed. *Celia Fiennes Illustrated Journeys*, 1685 – c1712

Nokes, David, *John Gay*, OUP, 1995

Pepys, Samuel *Diary*, ed. Robert Latham and William Matthews, etc., Bell & Sons, 1970

Piper, David *The Companion Guide To London*, William Collins Sons & Co Ltd., 1981

Plum, J.H. *England in the Eighteenth Century (1714–1815)*, Penguin, 1953

Plum, J.H. *The First Four Georges*, Fontana/Collins, 1981

Pope, Alexander *English Works, Vol 6, Minor Poems*, ed. Norman Ault & John Butt, 1954

Rhind, Niel *The Heath*, Bookshop, Blackheath Ltd, 1987

Rowse, A.L. *Windsor Castle*, Weidenfeld and Nicolson, 1974

Russell, John, 4th Duke of Bedford *Correspondence*, 3 Vols, Longman, 1942–6

Sackville-West, V. *Knole and the Sackvilles*, Ernest Benn Ltd., 1984

Sinclair-Stevenson, C, *Inglorious Rebellion*, Panther Books Ltd, 1973

Snyder, Henry L. ed. *Marlborough–Godolphin Correspondence*, Vol 1, Clarendon Press, 1975

Spencer, Charles, *Althorp: The Story of an English House*, Viking, 1988

Sutherland, James, ed., *Restoration Tragedies*, OUP, 1997

Swift, Jonathan *Correspondence*, ed. Harold Williams, 5 vols, OUP, 1963

Swift, Jonathan, *Journal to Stella*, Letters, 2 vols., ed. Harold Williams, Clarendon Press, Oxford, 1948

Thal, Herbert Van *The Prime Ministers*, Vol 1, Allen and Unwin, 1974

Thomson, George Malcolm *The First Churchill*, Secker & Warburg, 1979

Thomson, Gladys Scott *Letters of a Grandmother*, Jonathan Cape, 1942

Thomson, Gladys Scott *The Russells of Bloomsbury 1667–1774*, 1937

Thomson, Gladys Scott, *A Family Background*, Jonathan Cape, 1949

Trevelyan, E.G. *English Social History*, Penguin Books, 1974

Walpole, Horace *Lord Orford's Reminiscences*, John Sharpe, Piccadilly 1818

Waterhouse, Ellis *Dictionary of 18th Century Painters*, Antique Collectors Club, Woodbridge, 1981

Wheatley, Henry Benjamin *Round About Piccadilly and Pall Mall*, 1870

Wiffen, J.H. *Historical Memoirs of the House of Russell* Vol ii, 1833

Wilkins, W. H. *Caroline the Illustrious*, Longmans, Green, & Co. 1904

Williams, Neville *The Life and Times of Elizabeth I*, Weidenfeld & Nicolson, 1972

PAMPHLETS/GUIDES/ARTICLES

Althorp, A Short History of Althorp and the Spencer Family, Raine, Countess Spencer, 1977

Althorp Guide, 1998

Architectural History issue 28, Frances Harris, 'Holywell House St Albans', 1985

Ashridge, A short guide, by Douglas Coult, Ashridge Management College, 1971

The History and Treasures of Beaulieu, Palace House and the Abbey, Lord Montagu, Beaulieu Palace House and Abbey, guide, 1983

Blenheim Park & Gardens, David Green, guide

Catalogue of Pictures, Charles Jervas, 1740, at British Library

Catalogue of Strawberry Hill, 1842, at British Library

Chiswick House and Gardens, Richard Hewlings, English Heritage, guide, 1991

Country Life, Marie Draper, 'When Marlborough's Duchess Built', August 2, 1962

Country Homes, 'Rookley Manor' Kate Faulkner, June, 1987

Divine Poems, Joseph Addison, Printed R. Burleigh

Kimbolton Castle – A Brief Guide, Kimbolton School

Little Gaddesden Parish Church, by Canon Howard Senar, 1973

Rockley – A Wiltshire Village, Mary Roberts (Rockley, Wiltshire u.p.)

Sherborne Castle, Mary March, Sherborne Castle Estates, 1985

The Churches of Shobdon and Their Builders, Leominster Print Service

The Examiner, 1713

The Gentlemans Magazine 1–5

The Perils of False Brethren, Henry Sacheverell, H Clements 1709

The Reading Room, P.R. Harris, The British Library, 1979

The Speech of Henry Sacheverell, D.D. upon his IMPEACHMENT at the House of Lords in Westminster-Hall March 6. 1709/10, at British Library

The Tryal of Dr Henry Sacheverell, J Tonson, London 1710

Vindication of the Duchess Dowager of Marlborough, Henry Fielding, 1742

Index